READING
BETWEEN
TEXTS

LITERARY CURRENTS IN BIBLICAL INTERPRETATION

EDITORS
Danna Nolan Fewell
*Perkins School of Theology,
Southern Methodist University, Dallas TX*
David M. Gunn
Columbia Theological Seminary, Decatur GA

EDITORIAL ADVISORY BOARD
Jack Dean Kingsbury
Union Theological Seminary in Virginia, Richmond VA
Peter D. Miscall
St Thomas Seminary, Denver CO
Gary A. Phillips
College of the Holy Cross, Worcester MA
Regina M. Schwartz
Department of English, Duke University, Durham NC
Mary Ann Tolbert
The Divinity School, Vanderbilt University, Nashville TN

READING BETWEEN TEXTS

intertextuality and the hebrew bible

DANNA NOLAN FEWELL, EDITOR

•

WESTMINSTER/JOHN KNOX PRESS
Louisville, Kentucky

READING BETWEEN TEXTS:
INTERTEXTUALITY AND THE HEBREW BIBLE

© 1992 Danna Nolan Fewell

All rights reserved—no part of this book may be reproduced in any form without permission in writing from the publisher, except for brief quotations in critical articles or reviews. Write to: Permissions, Westminster/John Knox Press, 100 Witherspoon Street, Louisville, KY 40202-1396.

First edition

Published by Westminster/John Knox Press,
Louisville, Kentucky

This book is printed on acid-free paper that meets the American National Standards Institute Z39.48 standard. ∞

PRINTED IN THE UNITED STATES OF AMERICA
2 4 6 8 9 7 5 3 1

Library of Congress Cataloging-in-Publication Data

Reading between texts : intertextuality and the Hebrew Bible / Danna Nolan Fewell, editor. — 1st ed.
    p.   cm. — (Literary currents in biblical interpretation)
Includes bibliographical references and indexes.
ISBN 0-664-25393-8 (alk. paper)

1. Bible. O.T.—Criticism, interpretation, etc. 2. Intertextuality.
3. Bible as literature. I. Fewell, Danna Nolan. II. Series.
BS1171.2.R43 1992
221.6'6—dc20   92-28760

There is no end to the making of texts.
— Ecclesiastes 12:12b

CONTENTS

Series Preface · 9
Preface · 10

Introduction:
Writing, Reading, and Relating · 11
DANNA NOLAN FEWELL

Glossary · 21

PART I
THE BIBLE, INTERTEXTUALITY, AND LITERARY THEORY

1 · Ideology and Intertextuality: Surplus of
Meaning and Controlling the Means of Production · 27
TIMOTHY K. BEAL

2 · Isaiah: New Heavens, New Earth, New Book · 41
PETER D. MISCALL

3 · Intertextuality, Transference,
and the Reader in/of Genesis 12 and 20 · 57
ILONA N. RASHKOW

PART II
BETWEEN GENESIS AND KINGS

4 · Staying the Night:
Intertextuality in Genesis and Judges · 77
DAVID PENCHANSKY

5 · Strange Houseguests: Rahab, Lot,
and the Dynamics of Deliverance · 89
L. DANIEL HAWK

6 · Taking Women in Samuel:
Readers/Responses/Responsibility · 99
TOD LINAFELT

7 · The Importunate Woman of Tekoa
and How She Got Her Way · 115
PATRICIA K. WILLEY

8 · Reading Jeroboam's Intentions:
Intertextuality, Rhetoric, and History in 1 Kings 12 · 133
STUART LASINE

9 · The Fall of the House:
A Carnivalesque Reading of 2 Kings 9 and 10 · 153
FRANCISCO O. GARCÍA-TRETO

10 · Jehoiachin at the King's Table: A Reading
of the Ending of the Second Book of Kings · 173
JAN JAYNES GRANOWSKI

PART III
GENESIS TO KINGS AND BEYOND

11 · A Blessing Cursed: The Prophet's Prayer for
Barren Womb and Dry Breasts in Hosea 9 · 191
DEBORAH KRAUSE

12 · Job and Jacob: The Integrity of Faith · 203
ELLEN F. DAVIS

13 · Samson of Sorrows:
An Isaianic Gloss on Judges 13-16 · 225
DAVID M. GUNN

Bibliography 257
Indexes 273
Contributors 285

SERIES PREFACE

New currents in biblical interpretation are emerging. Questions about origins—authors, intentions, settings—and stages of composition are giving way to questions about the literary qualities of the Bible, the play of its language, the coherence of its final form, and the relations between text and readers.

Such literary criticism is rapidly acquiring sophistication as it learns from major developments in secular critical theory, especially in understanding the instability of language and the key role of readers in the production of meaning. Biblical critics are being called to recognize that a plurality of readings is an inevitable and legitimate consequence of the interpretive process. By the same token, interpreters are being challenged to take responsibility for the theological, social, and ethical implications of their readings.

Biblical interpretation is changing on the practical as well as the theoretical level. More readers, both inside and outside the academic guild, are discovering that the Bible in literary perspective can powerfully engage people's lives. Communities of faith where the Bible is foundational may find that literary criticism can make the Scripture accessible in a way that historical criticism seems unable to do.

Within these changes lie exciting opportunities for all who seek contemporary meaning in the ancient texts. The goal of the series is to encourage such change and such search, to breach the confines of traditional biblical criticism, and to open channels for new currents of interpretation.

—THE EDITORS

PREFACE

In recent years intertextuality, already an important conception in literary theory, has become a lively topic of discussion in biblical studies. Offering new insights into textual relations, intertextuality is changing the way we think about textual production and interpretation.

A few years ago I solicited papers on this topic for the Reading, Rhetoric, and the Hebrew Bible Section of the Society of Biblical Literature. Not only did I receive enough proposals to fill two programs, but I have continued to receive proposals for intertextual readings in subsequent years. The present volume has grown from this ongoing interest. Most of these papers were presented in this section at one time or another. Others have come to my attention through various contacts and conversations.

Three people in particular were instrumental in the production of this volume. Peter Miscall encouraged the enterprise and offered helpful suggestions regarding the shape of the book. David Gunn has been an invaluable sounding-board for the project, serving as a second reader in many instances and assisting in the overall organization. Without the help of Tim Beal, the volume may have never come together at all. He has constructed the glossary, assisted in the copy editing of the various papers, co-ordinated the final versions of the manuscripts, and perhaps most strategically, policed the deadlines for all of us! Above all, his great enthusiasm and dedication has, on more than one occasion, boosted my own commitment to the completion of this project. All three of you have my thanks and my fondest regards.

— Danna Nolan Fewell
July, 1992

INTRODUCTION:
WRITING, READING, AND RELATING

Danna Nolan Fewell

> He sent documents to all the royal provinces, to every province in its own script and to every people in its own language, that every man rule in his own house and speak according to the language of his people.
> — Esther 1:22
>
> "And you may write whatever you please concerning the Jews in the name of the king and seal it with the royal signet, for the writing which is written in the name of the king and sealed with royal signet cannot be rescinded."
> — Esther 8:8

If any book of the Hebrew Bible is concerned with the production and power of texts, if any book exposes the insufficiency of the written word, the book of Esther is most certainly the one. Writing is a major preoccupation within the story world of Esther—writing in response to certain situations and writing in response to yet other writing. No single text is sufficient. There will always be yet another attempt to offer the final word.

Writing is a means of taming both texts and contexts. In Esther, writing vigorously attempts to tame but with limited success. The refusal of a queen to submit to public humiliation gives rise to a royal edict that every man be lord in his own house (Esther 1), an edict that shows merely how fragile male dominance is in the domestic sphere. From an occasion of ethnic (and perhaps personal and professional) tension, there emerges a genocidal dictate to eradicate the Jews (Esther 3). In response, Esther pleads for another text that will undo the first. But, alas, this is not possible. Royal edicts cannot be changed (Esth 8:3-8). Another text might challenge the first, might undermine it, might subvert it, might unseat its authority, but the second cannot merely replace the first. A second text is written (Esth 8:9-14) and its challenge is physically enacted with great violence (Esther 9). The second text "overpowers" the first as the Jews and their friends defeat their enemies. The end of the fighting results in a mass celebration, which is encouraged by Mordecai in another text (a letter) to all the Jews (Esth 9:20-22). Full authorization establishing the date as an annual holiday, however, must seemingly come from Queen Esther. It is her command that fixes the practices of Purim in writing (Esth 9:32). Then, of course, to lend credibility to the story itself, we are told that all these things are officially recorded in the Royal Chronicles of Media and Persia.

Hence we see, in the course of the story, texts claiming authority, granting authority, supporting authority, and wrenching authority away. Texts form the backbone of the status quo (the royal writing that cannot be changed); texts are also the weapon of those (the Mordecais and the Esthers) who seek change. They can function this way because they are all interrelated by virtue of human language. Texts talk to one another; they echo one another; they push one another; they war with one another. They are voices in chorus, in conflict, and in competition.

A lone voice produces a particular sound, and issues a particular communication. To recognize that that voice is not lone after all, but in dialogue with another voice, or host of voices, is what intertextual reading is all about. A dialogue communicates differently than a soliliquy. In a dialogue all voices help to shape meaning. Each single voice is reinterpreted in light of the others. A text declaring that every man must be lord in his own house sounds like an authoritative absolute concerning male responsibility. In dialogue with its surrounding (con)text, however, it becomes part of a very different communication. In light of the circumstances—an excessive and irresponsible king unable to command the unthinking submission of his wife—the document mocks male pretentiousness.

The book of Esther as a whole also has its intertexts, an obvious one being the story of exodus and Passover in the book of Exodus. In both Exodus and Esther, the (human) protagonists are adopted as foreigners in court, and become reluctant redeemers. In both stories, oppressed people are delivered. The deliverance is followed by a religious observance (Passover and Purim) which is established in writing as a tradition to be repeated for all time.

The similarities between the two texts invite conversation. The differences allow each text to be affected by the other.

Divine presence marks a striking difference between the two stories. In the story of Exodus God is a major character, a prime instigator and mover of the plot. In fact, God's concern to establish his sovereignty takes priority over the actual salvation of the people (Gunn 1982:72-96). In Esther, by contrast, God is never mentioned. While issues of pride and sovereignty instigate plot here also, their source is human (Mordecai and Haman) rather than divine. On the one hand, the competition between two ambitious courtiers looks petty when compared with the divine scheme of the exodus. On the other hand, human ambition might also expose divine ambition as somewhat unworthy.

Because of this difference in divine presence, human risks are also in contrast. Moses is assured of success. He is given signs and even an assistant (Aaron). He knows in advance that he will be able, with God's leadership and control, to bring the people out of Egypt. Esther, on the other hand, has no such assurance. Her mediation on behalf of her people puts her life at stake. Rather than being offered signs of strength and success, she is threatened by her cousin Mordecai (Esth 4:13-14).

Without divine guidance and reassurance, Esther faces greater risk than does Moses. The stakes are also higher, as allusion makes clear. In her impassioned speech to the king, Esther declares with effective hyperbole, "We are sold, I and my people, to be destroyed, to be murdered, to be annihilated. If we had been sold merely as slaves, bondsmen and bondswomen, I would have held my peace, for our affliction would not compare to the loss to the king" (7:4).

Esther, like Moses, is able to save her people. The outcome, however, is less grandiose. For Esther and her people there is no "way out" as there is in the story of Exodus. In Exodus the people are allowed to leave the place of their oppression, putting past pain behind them. Esther and her people must stay put, living in uneasy tension with their neighbors, continuing subtle strategies of survival after the immediate threat has passed.

What are these texts saying to each other and what are they claiming for themselves? The exodus and Passover are foundational traditions for Israel, giving them a point of origin and identity, communicating that their God is a caring sovereign who needs the people to maintain his own identity. Esther argues for yet another identity-shaping story, one that obviously cannot replace exodus and Passover, but one that nonetheless decenters them as lone, formative traditions. Within the text, Esther herself issues a symbolic nudge when she declares, on the eve of Passover, a three day fast. The crisis at hand supercedes the traditional feast.

One might also see in "the law that cannot be changed" a veiled reference to Torah. As authoritative scripture, Torah holds pride of place in Jewish tradition. As such its text must be preserved. On the other hand, texts that cannot change are stagnant texts. They become absurd, like those in the story world of Esther, creating massive instability despite their attempt to stabilize. One way to introduce change without changing the text itself is to add another voice to the dialogue. Esther, as it were, elbows its way into the canon of authoritative texts, demanding a hearing and making room for the new holiday of Purim. This text, like rabbinic commentary, keeps the canon from becoming a law that cannot change; it helps to keep the canon alive and talking.

Is the text of Esther saying something radically different from that of Exodus? Despite their similar themes, structures, and the attention to ritual concerns, the two texts do offer very different theological worldviews and very different messages about surviving oppression. In Exodus God is undeniably sovereign. It is God who saves the people, leading them out of Egypt with an outstretched arm. Since Egypt the people have become self-reliant or, at the very least, partners with God. The dialogue between the two texts embodies one, if not the, central theological issue in the Judeo-Christian tradition(s): the relationship between divine will and human freedom.

Another obvious intertext for Esther is the book of Daniel. Both Esther and Daniel 1-6 have been described, and rightly so, as providing a "lifestyle for Diaspora" (Humphreys 1973). Clearly they both are about survival in politically delicate situations.

The character Daniel, like the character Esther, is a foreigner in court, co-opted for service to the oppressor. Daniel, like Esther, undergoes extensive "reprogramming" and training before being introduced to the king. He, like Esther, eventually becomes the king's "favorite." He and his friends are also, on a couple occasions, the victims of conspiracy.

In the midst of these correspondences, however, different gender produces a different story. Daniel and Esther are both chosen for their good looks. Daniel, however, is also chosen for his wisdom. While Daniel masters "the language and literature of the Chaldeans" and receives special God-given interpretive talents, Esther learns the arts of beauty and eroticism. What might be expected of these characters by either monarch or reader? From the king's perspective, Daniel will counsel him in weighty political matters. Esther's task is to make her king feel good. The reader is led to expect that Daniel will survive by his wits and with God's protection, while Esther will have to rely upon the seductiveness of her body.

When Daniel does, on occasion, survive by his wits, we are not surprised. When Esther employs her sagacity, however, many readers are reluctant to give her credit. Her hesitance is seen as a flaw, her caution as timidity. Why can't she just charge in to the king as Daniel does in Daniel 2 and 5? As a man, as a professional sage, Daniel has political and intellectual credibility. As a woman, Esther has neither. Her audience with the king depends upon her physical charm. She knows this. And she also knows that she is not apt to persuade the king with intellectual discussion or moral considerations. Her success depends on pleasing him with her beauty, her deference, her hospitality, and her mystery. Survival, for a woman, is indeed a complicated matter.

Both stories include, of course, "take charge" heroes. Mordecai, Shadrach, Meshach, Abednego, and Daniel (in chaps. 5 and 6) all exemplify "damn the consequences" heroism, openly defying authority and inviting direct conflict. All these characters, however, have someone else they can depend on to deliver them. Mordecai has Queen Esther; Daniel and his friends have God. Esther cannot afford to be so reckless. She only has herself.

While the others heroically risk martyrdom, Esther has no such luxury. Her people's lives depend on her. As Terrence Des Pres (1976:4-5) observes, "When men and women must live against terrible odds, when mere existence becomes miraculous, to die is in no way a triumph."

The absence, or at least the reticence, of God in the book of Esther is one reason she cannot afford to be a brash hero. The book of Daniel, like the stories of exodus and Passover, concentrates on God's sovereignty (Fewell 1991). Human oppression becomes an occasion for the revelation of God's power to deliver and to punish. Suffering, then, is part of God's plan, an opportunity for divine salvation. For Esther the oucome is not so obvious. Consequently, suffering in the book of Esther has no obvious meaning or value.

These varying attitudes vastly affect human motivation. The book of Daniel, for the most part, promotes passivity. The power to deliver from oppression, the power to reshape the future, is solely God's. "Sit tight," urge the apocalyptic chapters in Daniel, "God will take care of things." The book of Esther offers a different prescription: "If you want to change your future, it's up to you to do it." Daniel promises a new world order; Esther suggests you must learn to survive where you are. Daniel declares an end to the oppressive powers that be; Esther reveals that some villains meet their demise (e.g., Haman and sons), but that people's lives will continue to depend upon naive, negligent, and uncaring authorities (e.g., King Ahasuerus). How does one go about changing the future? How much change can be expected? What is the relationship between divine and human responsibility? Neither text offers a final answer.

Esther's intertextual connections are hardly exhausted here. United Methodist women recently chose to read Esther with the book of Ruth for their annual Bible study. Relationships between the Masoretic Esther and the pre-Masoretic text, or the later Greek additions, or later Rabbinic commentary, are often the subject of scholarly discourse. Feminist scholars sometimes compare Esther with other biblical portrayals of women. One might also examine Esther in relation to the cultural (con)text of carnival (cf. García-Treto in this volume) as it is so often played in modern Purim festivities or in relation to the more sobering (con)text of Holocaust (Fox 1991). The possibilities are endless because, indeed, "there is no end to the making of texts" (Eccl 12:12b), or to the making of connections.

* * * * *

I have tried to show through a reading what the term intertextuality suggests, namely, that no text exists in a vacuum. All texts are embedded in a larger web of related texts, bounded only by human culture and language itself. Intertextual reading is inevitable. We cannot, in fact, understand any text without some appeal to other texts. Just as the citizens of Susa were "confounded" when Haman's edict, without explanation or context, first appeared in the streets, so we too would be confounded not knowing the dialogic circumstances of textual production and interpretation.

This book is a forum for intertextual readings. We set out to explore how various texts in the Hebrew Bible are related to one another, and how those relationships affect and effect meaning.

As Tim Beal reminds us in his contribution to this volume, and as it is no doubt obvious in the preceding discussion, discovering intertextual connections is a reader-oriented enterprise. While some texts direct our attention to other texts through explicit allusion, more often it is the reader who perceives textual relations. In the essays that follow, readers see some relations that are surprising and some that may be easily anticipated. Whether offering novel juxtapositions or reexamining long-recognized connections, these readers are seeing and sharing new dimensions of meaning as texts engage one another.

I have not written a great deal about theory here. Due to the facilities of the contributors to this volume, that has proved unnecessary. For matters of theory, I direct your attention particularly to the glossary and to the first three essays. Tim Beal sketches the background of intertextual theory, and offers a program for doing intertextual analysis. Peter Miscall shows us how texts usurp, decenter, and subvert the authority of other texts. Ilona Rashkow explores the reader's relation(s) to texts and intertexts through the psychoanalytic notion of transference.

The second section of the volume is devoted to intertextual readings within the Genesis through Kings corpus. These essays not only raise questions about particular texts, but many of them work together to show how smaller connections might affect one's reading of the larger narrative. David Penchansky and Dan Hawk re-engage (but with rather different lenses) the often-seen connections among stories of hospitality. Both Tod Linafelt and Patricia Willey read 2 Samuel 12 (Nathan's confrontation with David) as a comparative and contrastive key to understanding other characters and episodes in Samuel. Stuart Lasine offers both a diachronic (historical) and synchronic (final form) reading of Jeroboam's character in 1 Kings 12, noting how various intertexts affect one's reading of Jeroboam's intentions. Frank García-Treto reads the story of Jehu's rebellion (2 Kings 9 and 10) against the language and experience of carnival, exposing its subtle subversion of David's story. Jan Granowski, reopening the longstanding debate concerning the significance of the ending of the Deuteronomistic History, explores how intertexts can make sense of 2 Kings 25:27-30.

Part three of the volume brings together texts from different parts of the canon. Deborah Krause and Ellen Davis look to Genesis to enlighten their readings of Hosea and Job, respectively. David Gunn finds, in the suffering servant imagery of Isaiah, an alternative vision of Samson's character.

The methodological and thematic connections among these articles are many. Readers may well find themselves reading intertextually within the volume itself.

Beal's program of analysis involving pre-text, text, and post-text undergirds, with some variation, the readings of Penchansky and Lasine. Krause's argument, too, may be understood to be employing a similar tripartite focus.

Several articles scrutinize character. Linafelt, Willey, Lasine, Davis, and Gunn all use intertexts to assist their reconstructions of various characters in Hebrew narrative. Readers might ask, how crucial are their selected intertexts to their final interpretations? If they had chosen different textual partners, would their characters have looked the same?

Two authors take up the challenge of ambiguous story endings. As Peter Rabinowitz (1987:161) writes, "Endings . . . are not always so neat, and when they are not, the reader is often expected to reinterpret the work so that the ending in fact serves as an appropriate conclusion." Davis finds, in her reading of Job, an appropriate conclusion to the book. Granowski, through her review of strategic intertexts, understands the ending of Genesis-Kings (2 Kgs 25:27-30) to be "intelligible," keeping some hopes alive while closing off others.

As Granowski explores the thin line between captivity and hospitality, some readers may find themselves reconsidering other papers in this volume—more obviously those of Penchansky and Hawk, and in a more nuanced way that of Rashkow. All these pieces show the ambivalence of hospitality: on the one hand it offers asylum; but on the other it confers obligation, and therefore is a means of control. In Genesis 12 and 20, Rashkow sees a triangular schema: male/powerless female/uninvited sex. Such a schema further connects Genesis 12 and 20 to the texts discussed in the articles by Penchansky and Hawk. Both guests and hosts put women at risk.

Might Rashkow's schema also apply to the book of Esther? The king, after all, takes Esther into his palace, offers her hospitality, so to speak. But is she a guest or a captive? How much control does Esther have over her own sexuality? In the end, it is Esther's hospitality which begins to reverse the power relations, allowing her to intercede for her people (cf. Hawk's reading of Rahab).

Gunn and García-Treto reconceptualize their respective texts by deliberately choosing unexpected reading conventions. García-Treto reads a disturbingly violent text, Jehu's slaughter of the House of Ahab, in carnivalesque terms. Gunn, on the other hand, offers a sober reading of Samson, a character more often read as comic, even a buffoon.

As Miscall finds Isaiah troping and trumping Genesis 1, one might imagine Gunn's reading of Samson playing a similar game with Isaiah. Both readings disassemble and reassemble. Miscall's Isaiah turns the simple prose of Genesis into grand poetic rhetoric, while in Gunn's intertextual move the elusive servant infuses complexity into the concrete character called Samson and, by the same token, the concrete figure of Judges constructs particularity in the elusive imagery of Isaiah.

What all these readings have in common is that, in one way or another, they challenge consensual readings. They invite us to read texts differently. They invite us to read different texts together. And they invite us to reflect on why we make the connections that we do.

GLOSSARY

Allusion

Put simply, allusion concerns "the mobilization of unnamed sources and addressees" (Barbara Johnson, "Preface" to Derrida 1981:xvii). Lately, theories of allusion have been brought into closer conversation with poststructuralist theories of intertextuality. Thus, where it has traditionally been defined in terms of implicit, indirect, or hidden reference (i.e., focusing largely on the subtle artistry of the writer), recent discussions (e.g., Ziva Ben-Porat 1976:105-28) focus on allusion as a "text-linking device" which transgresses the boundaries of the text in which it is found (Hebel 1989:8). It is a "device for the simultaneous activation of two texts" (Ben-Porat in Hebel 1989:6). In all this, the emphasis is on how the process of allusion evokes for the reader a larger textual field. As with the determination of an intertext (see below), the question of whether or not the author *intended* to allude need not be raised in detemining what is an allusion and what is not.

Echo

Developed by English scholar John Hollander (1981), the theory of echo has been most fully explored in biblical studies by Richard B. Hays (1989). The figure of echo concerns both the means by which texts relate and a more general theory of textuality. Texts echo other texts, and as such can be understood as "echo chambers." In an echo chamber—that is, in a literary context for echoing—any text being echoed will *sound* differently than it has elsewhere. One value of this theory is that it expresses the intertextual character of all writing while maintaining, in the metaphor at least, a sense of closure (walls) around the text's structure. There can be no echo in a wide open "field" (see "Intertextuality," below).

Inner-biblical Exegesis

This term was developed by Michael Fishbane in his highly influential work on the practice of biblical interpretation in ancient Israel (1985; see also Eslinger 1992). Inner-biblical exegesis is, for Fishbane, the key to understanding biblical growth, showing that "the Hebrew Bible has an exegetical dimension *in its own right*" (1985:14). Not to be confused with tradition-historical criticism, which goes back to the oral sources behind the text, inner-biblical exegesis "starts with the received Scripture and moves forward to the interpretations [also within the Bible] based on it" (1985:7). (See, e.g., Davis, "Job and Jacob," in this volume.)

Fishbane's reading strategy is concerned with "discerning traces of exegesis within Scripture" (1985:10). This involves distinguishing "received Scripture," or "authoritative *traditum*," from subsequent interpretations of it, called *traditio*. His work has been a major influence on discussions of biblical intertextuality, and has opened the door to many other literary-theoretical perspectives as well. (For a comparison of inner-biblical exegesis with poststructuralist theories of intertextuality, see Fishbane 1989.) Fishbane himself, however, leaves less determinate intertextual relations in the Hebrew Bible to others who are more interested in the dynamics of reading "in front of the text" (e.g., the literary topos of the "Matriarch of Israel in Danger," on which see Rashkow in this volume).

Intertextuality

This term was first developed by Julia Kristeva (1980 [Fr. 1969]; 1984 [Fr. 1974]). Not to be confused with notions of literary borrowing or poetic influence, she understood it to describe every discourse, whether written or spoken. Every discourse is intertextual—"a field of transpositions of various signifying systems" (1984:60), "an *intersection of textual surfaces* rather than a *point* (a fixed meaning)" (1980:65; see Beal in this volume). It is for this reason that every text is polyvalent.

For Kristeva, and for others such as Jacques Derrida and Roland Barthes, the basic force of intertextuality is to problematize, even spoil, textual boundaries—those lines of demarcation which allow a reader to talk about *the* meaning, subject, or origin of a writing. Such borders, intertextuality asserts, are never solid or stable. Texts are always spilling over into other texts. Miscall puts it nicely (in this volume): "No text is an island."

Because of its literal expansiveness, intertextuality is frequently regarded as a "covering term" (Miscall) for various approaches to reading texts in relation to other texts.

Intertext

An intertext is a text found in another text (or echoing in another echo chamber). It may be transposed, absorbed, even reversed or transumed (see the essays by Krause and Miscall in this volume). How one determines what legitimately can be called an intertext is a matter of methodological and ideological debate (see Thaïs E. Morgan 1985). For instance, must a reader establish that the author *intended* to draw a particular intertext into her text?

Intratextuality

Developed most fully by George Lindbeck (1984), intratextuality concerns the life (and life-giving force) of a text through a particular stream of confessional tradition. Intratextual analysis begins with a "privileged idiom, text, or text-constituted world" which serves as a "medium of interpretation . . . within which everything is or can be construed." Thus, "in an intratextual religious or theological reading, . . . there is . . . a privileged interpretive direction from whatever counts as holy writ to everything else" (1984:136, n. 5). Accordingly, there is very little room in this theory for the work of the reader, who must make sense of the "world" of the privileged text in the first place. Rather, that textual world/medium acts as a relatively autonomous structure which makes sense of the reader, and which provides that reader with the "grammar" to interpret all subsequent texts. Thus the prefix *intra-* ("within") rather than *inter-* ("between" or "among").

Poetic Influence

Discussions of poetic influence have been, until recently, quite broad, including interests in "anything from religious myths to historical events . . . as they exert pressures on the production or reception of specific literary texts" (Renza 1990:186). One impetus moving discussions of poetic influence closer to theories of intertextuality has been T. S. Eliot's "Tradition and the Individual Talent" (1964 [1919]:3-11), which criticizes the "endeavor to find something that can be isolated in order to be enjoyed." Eliot's focus is on conformity and continuity between the individual poet and precursive tradition (see Penchansky, n. 1, in this volume). Through a process of "depersonalization," according to Eliot, the poet of "full maturity" must deny the pursuit of individual renown and find himself (masc. pronoun intended) within the collective imagination of his poetic tradition. That tradition, while altered slightly by the new poet's work, remains *essentially* the same.

More recently, with the work of Harold Bloom (esp. 1973), discussions of poetic influence have taken on a distinctly psychoanalytic overtone. Here the relation between poet and precursor is understood in terms of an anxiety-ridden father-son dynamic. The son can say nothing new, for the father has said it all and has said it better. The strong poet, however, with a Nietzschean will-to-power, overcomes his father by "misreading" him in ways that make his own work appear more creative and originary. One model for this is the relationship between Satan and God in Milton's *Paradise Lost*. Another might be Christian supersessionism (see Bloom's "'Before Moses Was, I Am': The Original and Belated Testaments" [1984]). For a discussion of Bloom's work in relation to Hebrew Bible studies, see Miscall on "Precursors and Transumption" (in this volume).

Trace

Discussions of trace are frequently bound together with discussions of intertextuality, especially in the work of Jacques Derrida. In every text there are traces of that which has been excluded or repressed (Derrida has called them erasure marks), or even of that which is altogether absent. Indeed, a text's boundaries of meaning are always established through exclusion, repression, and marginalization. But traces remain. When attended to, these traces open beyond the narrow confines of the particular text and into relation with other texts. Traces lead readers to stray into the margins and off the page.

— TIMOTHY K. BEAL

PART I

THE BIBLE, INTERTEXTUALITY, AND LITERARY THEORY

1

IDEOLOGY AND INTERTEXTUALITY: SURPLUS OF MEANING AND CONTROLLING THE MEANS OF PRODUCTION

TIMOTHY K. BEAL

In recent years, discussions of intertextuality in biblical studies have come increasingly into vogue. Yet to anyone entering this new conversation it quickly becomes apparent that the application of this poststructuralist theoretical term is far from uniform; and the lines of influence by which it has been carried into biblical interpretation are nearly impossible to trace. One reason for this seemingly boundless dissemination of "intertextuality" within our discipline is that it has been developed in poststructuralism as a *theoretical* rather than a *methodological* term.[1]

Against hermeneuticist notions of linear tradition-history (traceable lines of influence between authors, texts, and readers) on the one hand, and against structuralist assertions of textual unity and closure on the other, theorists such as Jacques Derrida and Roland Barthes propose intertextuality as that perpetual and indeterminable process of deferral from text to text to text. Intertextuality is, in this sense, that total and limitless fabric of text which constitutes our linguistic universe— Derrida's "general text"—and from which all writings are untraceable quotations, inscriptions, transpositions.[2] Thus Barthes' (1977:146) proclamation:

> We know now that a text is not a line of words releasing a single 'theological' meaning (the 'message' of the Author-God) but a multi-dimensional space in which a variety of writings, none of them original, blend and clash. The text is a tissue of quotations drawn from the innumerable centres of culture.

Similarly, Derrida (1979:84) reflects on

> a "text" that is henceforth no longer a finished corpus of writing, some content enclosed in a book or its margins, but a differential network, a fabric of traces referring endlessly to something other than itself, to other differential traces.

There are, according to this concept, no ostensible lines—either of influence or of boundary—to delimit a text in relation to other texts. Intertextuality is the reason Derrida (1981:63) wrote of texts that, "perpetually and essentially, they run the risk of being definitively lost."

For the practice of intertextual reading, however, as opposed to theories of intertextuality, one must have such lines of delimitation, no matter how arbitrarily they may be set, and no matter how quickly they may be transgressed. That is, no intertextual reading can choose the "general text"—everything, all at once, everywhere—as its object of interpretation. As Jonathan Culler puts it (1976:1384), "it is difficult to make that universe as such the object of attention." And so the practice of intertextual reading must find its place somewhere between the closed structure of a single text (however defined) and the uncontainably surplussive fabric of language (called intertextuality).[3] But what determines which intertextual relationships are legitimate and which are not? And what determines how "rightly" to negotiate those relationships once they are established?

I suggest that the answer to these questions is: the reader's ideology. This essay will explore how intertextuality leads quickly from musings on the Hebrew Bible's *surplus* of meaning to serious talk about biblical interpretation as *production* of meaning. The next step from there is to ask who, or what, controls the means of production. And controlling the means of production is always an ideological activity.[4] Movement from the indeterminate "general text" to particular practices of intertextual reading demands that one ask about the ideological limits, or "strategies of containment" (Fredric Jameson 1981:52-3), that make interpretation possible. It demands, in other words, *an ideological-critical approach to reading readings*.

In order to develop such an approach, I turn to the groundbreaking work of Julia Kristeva (1980; 1984).[5] Kristeva was not only the first to coin the term intertextuality, but she also has engaged Marxian categories of power and production as central concerns for her own theories of language, literature, and subjectivity.[6]

After discussing Kristeva's theory of intertextuality, I will explore how her notion of intertextuality opens new possibilities for ideological criticism in biblical interpretation. Finally, this theoretical discussion will be related to the recent work of Mieke Bal on Judges in order to develop a methodological approach to reading readings which takes advantage of these new insights.

KRISTEVA, BAKHTIN, DIALOGISM

Kristeva first develops the concept of intertextuality in her treatment of the Russian postformalist Mikhail Bakhtin (1984a; 1984b), whose critique of formalism (in which structuralism claims its own roots) runs parallel in many ways with Western poststructuralism.

The starting point for Kristeva's development of the concept of intertextuality is the Bakhtinian notion of *dialogism*. By dialogism, Bakhtin suggests the open-ended, back-and-forth play between the text of the sender (subject), the text of the addressee (object), and the text of culture. In so doing he introduces a dynamic instability which is unallowable in traditional formalisms and structuralisms. Inherent in language itself, this back-and-forth play between and among texts explodes, or *dynamites*, the supposedly closed structure and univocal meaning of any particular text, opening it to further and further reappropriations, reinscriptions, and redescriptions.

Drawing from Bakhtin, Kristeva (1980:66) writes, "Any text is constructed as a mosaic of quotations; any text is the absorption and transformation of another." To read a text with an eye for its intertextual dimension, therefore, is to recognize an inherent transgression of discreet, self-contained textual unity, which renders the quest for "correct" interpretation impossible. The "dialogical space of texts" (Kristeva 1980:66) dynamites the autonomy and univocality of any particular text.

In Kristeva's hands, dialogism comes to play a key role in critiquing both structuralism and philosophical hermeneutics.

Against structuralism, dialogism asserts the centrality of *play* in linguistic discourse (1986b:26), and in so doing denies any counter-assertion of textual closure. A text is always a playful *"intersection of textual surfaces* rather than a *point* (a fixed meaning)" (1980:65). Attempts to close down a text's meaning will always be frustrated, because the text-as-dialogue is always referring beyond itself to other texts and other contexts.[7] The univocality of any piece of linguistic discourse is continually transgressed by its own necessarily many-voiced (*polyvocal*) nature.[8]

Against philosophical hermeneutics, this playfully dialogic notion of intertextuality challenges the notion that interpretation is an intersubjective process (inter*subject*ivity). Texts are not simply equivalent to their subjects (i.e., their writer's intentions).

> Confronted with this dialogism, the notion of a "person-subject of writing" becomes blurred, yielding to that of "ambivalence of writing." (1980:68)

If a text—whether "source" text or its interpretation—is actually an intersection of an indeterminate number of textual surfaces, then to identify its subject is at best highly problematic.[9] More than this, to trace a subject's influences through a particular line of tradition is nothing short of impossible, since a line requires two fixed points. Every piece of discourse is a "field of transpositions of various signifying systems (an inter-textuality)" (Kristeva 1984:60), each of which is in turn an intersection of yet other texts (and so on, and so on).[10]

> Diachrony is transformed into synchrony, and in light of this transformation, *linear* history appears as abstraction. (1980:65)

INTERTEXTUALITY, INTERPRETATION, PRODUCTION

On first impression, Kristeva's theory of intertextuality, via dialogism, delegitimizes any diachronic hermeneutical interpretation of relationships between biblical texts (e.g., in terms of intratextuality [Lindbeck 1984] or inner-biblical exegesis [Fishbane 1985]). And yet, is it not true that, intertextually speaking, *all* interpretations are abstractions? For all interpretations must necessarily delimit a text's possible references in order to come up with a coherent meaning. Every reading must take a particular discursive position within the indeterminate dialogical space of the text in order to "make sense."[11] This is what interpretation is all about. All reading is writing.

This approach, therefore, does not delegitimize a hermeneutical negotiation of relationships between texts any more than it delegitimizes any other sort of reading. It does, however, undermine such a reading's *privileged position* of interpretive authority, placing it on more equal footing with other achronic, synchronic, and even (those academically abominable) typological and allegorical approaches. Intertextuality is, as Peter Miscall puts it (in this volume), a "covering term," under which all varieties of intertextual interpretation are subcategories and, necessarily, "abstractions."

To summarize. Every text—as an intersection of other textual surfaces—suggests an indeterminate *surplus* of meaningful possibilities. Interpretation is always a *production* of meaning from that surplus. The question now comes to the fore: *Who or what controls the means of production?*

In the best of Marxist theory, from Marx himself to contemporary critics like Fredric Jameson, ideology is understood not so much as distortion or false knowledge, but rather in terms of "structural limitation or ideological closure" (Jameson 1981:52; cf. Eagleton 1983:172-3). Thus Jameson describes ideology as a *strategy of containment* (52-3) which imposes meaningful structures on the totality, which is "not available for representation, any more than it is accessible in the form of absolute truth" (55). In this light, ideological criticism is understood as "attention to those . . . containment strategies which seek to endow their objects of representation with formal unity" (54). Moreover, "such strategies of containment . . . can be unmasked only by confrontation with the ideal of totality which they at once imply and repress" (53). Jameson is concerned primarily with unmasking the ways *narrative* imposes ideological closure on the totality of "Real History." Transposing Jameson's work into the present discussion, one may ask how *interpretation* serves as an ideological containment strategy for *intertextuality*, which is taken as a sort of linguistic analogue to Jameson's notion of totality.

It is in this way that intertextuality opens to ideological criticism. If ideology is a strategy of containment, then the interpretive *rules* in biblical studies, which establish closure (i.e., "formal unity") on the general text and legitimize certain intertextual relationships, are certainly ideological. They are, so to speak, modes of production for making sense from a surplus of intertextual possibilities.

READING READINGS:
MIEKE BAL'S COUNTER-COHERENCE IN JUDGES

How might this theoretical discussion be applied to a critique of biblical interpretation? Mieke Bal's recent work (1988b; cf. 1988a) on the book of Judges is suggestive. Judges is one among several books in the Hebrew Bible whose many stories—some wonderfully fantastic, others utterly horrifying—resist neat interrelationships with one another. To make them come together in the form of a single coherent "text" requires rigid control by one containment strategy or another.[12]

Bal argues that the mainstream tradition of biblical interpretation (esp. modern criticism) has produced a coherent reading of Judges based on "the eagerness to narrow history down to a narrative of war and political leadership" (1988b:13). This coherence is due, in large part, to an androcentrism which functions in Judges criticism

> to subordinate the stories about women to the major historiographical project, which is nationalistic and religious, and in relation to which the murder stories are just the unpleasant but unavoidable fulfillment of the divine plan. (1988b:13)

To put her critique in terms of the present discussion, we can say that interpretation history has established a coherence out of Judges' numerous intertextual possibilities which has suppressed issues of gender-based violence and foregrounded the political/religious emergence of Israel. As a strategy of containment, this coherence muffles the voices of the female victims under the clamor of men's battles and the political collaborations of the amphictyony (see also Beal & Gunn 1993). Thus, the dominant coherence in Judges interpretation serves to reinscribe patriarchy from one of Judges' textual surfaces onto the interpretive literature.

And yet the book of Judges is riddled with intertextual tensions which necessarily problematize any attempt to establish unity (1988b:34; cf. 281 n. 4). No coherence can comprehend entirely and absolutely all the voices of such a polyvocal, tension-ridden book.

In Bal's explicitly feminist counter-reading, intertextuality comes to play a key role on at least three levels. First, she reads Judges in relation to its *post-texts*, especially those which have interpreted it in ways that reinscribe patriarchal power relations between men and women.

Second, she reads Judges in relation to its *pretext*, that is, her reconstruction of the society which lies behind it and is inscribed in it. Here Bal reads Judges as playing on a sociohistorical situation of transition between two types of marriage, and concludes by suggesting that "the political violence of wars and conquests is secondary in relation to the institutional violence of the social order. This violence seems to be the inevitable consequence of a social structure that is inherently contradictory" (1988b:281). In this way, Bal's coherence is able to comprehend, on a historical-critical level, the privileged themes of the dominant coherence (war heroes and the rise of Israel as a unified nation) within a more fundamental (to her strategy of containment) category of domestic history.

Third and finally, Bal reads various texts *within* the book of Judges in relation to each other. Focusing on three stories of women killing men and three stories of men killing women, she establishes a counter-coherence which reveals a basic "dissymmetry of power: power over the body, over life, over language" (1988b:32). Here again, in this "spatial" intertextual reading (as opposed to the dominant diachronic/chronological reading), the theme of gender-based violence emerges as fundamental, whereas the violence of wars is comprehended as derivative.

The results of Bal's intertextual counter-coherence are thoroughly transgressive of the "official" patriarchal reading. Univocal coherence is denied, as she introduces intertextual, gender-based *tension* into the book by amplifying the suppressed voices of the victimized women. Moreover, the female murderers are no longer comprehended merely as war heroines; rather, they introduce *maternal anger* into the book (1988b: 197-8). Their violence, like other political violence in Judges, is rooted in the dissymmetry of the gender system, rather than in Israelite nationalism. They kill for the murdered daughters.

The title of this section ("Reading Readings") is at least double. Under such a heading, one could either treat Bal as a model for reading readings ideological-critically, or read Bal's reading from an ideological-critical perspective. The decision about what to do is, of course, itself ideological. I have decided to treat Bal as a model rather than as an object of critique, and in so doing have revealed some of my own ideological investments. For example, I am far more reluctant to take apart a feminist reading of Judges than I am to poke holes in the last 200 years of male-identified, nationalistically motivated critical consensus.[13] Bal's reading is as ideologically vested as any; it is just that her vestments happen to be more like my own, and so more difficult to criticize. Nevertheless, given the theoretical discussion thus far, a few comments ought to be made about Bal's own strategies of containment, according to which her counter-coherence is constructed.

Most obviously, her reading is woman-identified. Within the polyvocal intertextual field of Judges, this is a powerful means to control the production of meaning. Bal is not hindered, moreover, by the fact that Judges devotes far more ink to male heroes and their war exploits than it does to women and gender issues. Drawing from psychoanalysis, Bal gives less attention to the broad surfaces of the text and more to the *traces* of what has been repressed. When attended to, these traces reveal the text's political unconscious of gender-based violence, which is, for Bal, the absent cause of the text's production (its *pretext*). This "hermeneutics of the repressed" (1988b:7) allows Bal to take an ideological position which counters both the mainstream of biblical criticism and what most would consider the mainstream patriarchal force of the book itself.

Another aspect of Bal's containment strategy is its subordination of political history to cultural—especially *domestic*—history. Without excluding them from her counter-coherence altogether, political-historical interests in the text are significantly marginalized. Thus domestic history, which is fundamentally concerned with gender relations (i.e., the household economy), and which has been completely shut out from the dominant coherence, comes to drive, shape, and effectively subsume political history (and political history *writing*).

Implicit in these comments, moreover, is that for Bal, a reading will be either valid or invalid depending on whether or not it can be moored securely within a framework of Israelite history. While her historical claims involve a significant shift from political to domestic history, her reading still relies, to some degree (it is not always clear), on there being a solid, basically ostensible history standing behind and under the text. In so far as Bal's reading continues to depend on a frame of reference in "real" history for its validation, one must wonder whether her strategy of containment inadvertently allows for the theologically driven nationalism so basic to the rise of biblical "Higher Criticism," especially in 19th- and early 20th-century Germany (see Robert A. Oden 1987:1-39).

On the other hand, quite unlike the "official" historical-critical coherence, Bal's historicism does not bracket out critical consideration of the text's *reader*, who is at least partly responsible for producing meaning from Judges in the first place. (She is quite open, for example, about her own interest in making a shift from political to domestic history.) After all, the relation between a biblical text and its reader is intertextual as well. Indeed, interest in this relation has been especially taboo in modern criticism.

MAKING AN APPROACH

In light of these discussions of Kristeva's theory and Bal's practice, I offer the following three methodological questions which may serve as guides for further intertextuality-based, ideological-critical readings of the Bible and biblical interpretation:

1. How does the reader impose limits on the innumerable intertextual possibilities of a particular biblical text? Which possibilities of meaningful relationship are delegitimized in order to produce a definitive, coherent reading?

2. What ideologies—as strategies of containment—does this particular mode of meaning production admit? On this level, questions posed by canon, form, and genre criticism, among others, come into play. But here the interest is not so much in the *intentions* of the interpreters who use these strategies as in how they might *function* to support or undermine certain ideological investments.[14] Which voices are marginalized and which are foregrounded when these critical approaches are put into practice?

3. How might the established boundaries (or "critical consensus") of intertextual relationship—and the strategies of containment which maintain them—be transgressed in order to discover new relationships and prioritize other voices? How can one's recognition of the dialogic, polyvocal dynamics of biblical writing dynamite the established strategies of containment and loosen their control over the processes of production?

Readings of the Bible are not only (and not always) interest*ing*, but always and necessarily interest*ed*; interested either in maintaining the presently legitimate boundaries of meaningful relationship between texts, or in transgressing them. The history of interpretation, as Marx made clear about History in general, is always a history of *struggle*. This is nowhere more obvious than in the history of biblical interpretation. It is therefore of utmost importance that we recognize the basic relations between writing and ideology, and thus between interpretation and power.

NOTES

[1] On the problems of putting the theory into literary-critical practice, see Jonathan Culler (1976:1383-84): Intertextuality is "an extremely difficult concept to work with, as if it were the nature of intertextual space, its codes and conventions, to evade description." Of course, another reason for this dissemination of "intertextuality" in our discipline is that the term has been subjected to the very phenomenon it describes—it will not stay within the bounds of any definition, but continually spills over (see Derrida 1981).

[2] While beyond the concerns of the present discussion, it is noted that the term intertextuality has been appropriated by biblical scholars interested in the relationships of influence between a text and its precursive traditions as well (e.g., poetics of influence). This approach finds roots in T. S. Eliot, among others (1964 [1919]). For a helpful discussion, see Gail R. O'Day (1993).

[3] On the relative ease of using a hermeneutical model for interpreting relations between texts, see David Couzens Hoy (1986: 397-415).

[4] With Jameson, I am following Louis Althusser's general definition of ideology (1971:162) as "the imaginary representation of the subject's relationship to his or her real conditions of existence." Where some Marxists make strong distinctions between scientific objectivism and ideological "distortion," this approach contends that ideology cannot be eluded because scientific objectivism is unattainable; we are always and from the beginning *subjects*—i.e., subjected to ideology. Without denying this reality, the particular concern here is with ideologies that serve to objectify and classify others in terms of gender, race, sexuality and economic class. That is, I am interested in how ideology *functions* in biblical studies as "the link or nexus between discourses and power" (Eagleton 1983:210).

[5] The essay in which Kristeva introduced her notion of intertextuality (1980) was first published in French in 1969. The present discussion will draw primarily from this work. In her dissertation (1984), originally published in 1974, Kristeva transposes this notion into a much broader theory of signifying practice, which involves a tensive relationship between the semiotic (*chora*; which involves the drives and dispositions of the pre-Oedipal, prelinguistic phase) and the symbolic (*thetic*; which involves the positioning of the subject—"I"— within a particular symbolic order). Here, intertextuality comes to play a role in problematizing the symbolic's attempts to present univalent and closed meaning.

[6] While Kristeva pays much attention both to intertextuality and

to language as production, she has not put the two categories into direct conversation concerning the practice of intertextual biblical interpretation. And so, ironically, as I read Kristeva into this discussion, I am instancing her concept of intertextuality: I am creating a field into which various discourses are transposed and placed in dialogue. Within this field of transpositions, moreover, the frontiers of each former discourse will be transgressed and redescribed. Such an approach is in line with Kristeva's own reading strategies. Note, e.g., her response to a criticism of her treatment of Marx at a meeting on psychoanalysis and politics: "I never intended to follow a correct Marxist line, and I hope I am not *correctly* following any other line whatsoever" (1980:1). Cf. her transposition of terms from the "hard sciences," which she calls "'subverted premises' which have little or nothing to do with their status outside semiotics" (1986a:79).

[7] It is important to acknowledge that Kristeva's own discussions of intertextuality are eventually related (1984) to her discussion of the revolutionary *poetic* (i.e., transposing, displacing, absorbing) language of the French 19th-century avant-garde, especially Mallarmé and Lautréamont, which she distinguishes from other discourses (narrative, metalinguistic, and contemplative; 1984:90-106). Here, I take the language of the Hebrew Bible as poetic discourse. In so doing, I may well be transgressing the frontiers of Kristeva's own categories, as she sees poetic language emerging uniquely in the 19th century. See also note 6, above.

[8] Cf. Paul Ricoeur's similar understanding (1975:99) of the tensive dynamic of biblical texts, which he describes in terms of "the transgression of the 'inner' sense to 'outer' reference," a transgression which "explodes the 'closure' of the structure" (101). Unlike Kristeva, however, Ricoeur finally allows this phenomena of rupture to be subsumed under a hermeneutical moment, in which the reader-as-subject fulfills and completes "the world" proposed by the text.

[9] On the disunity and indeterminacy of a text's origins (*qua* subject), see Barthes (1977:146): "Did he wish to *express himself*, he ought at least to know that the inner 'thing' he thinks to 'translate' is itself only a ready-formed dictionary, its words only explainable through other words, and so on indefinitely." Implicit in the discussion here is that what Kristeva writes about the "person-subject of writing" applies equally to the person-subject of *reading*. Neither "source" texts nor their interpretations yield any sort of univalent subject. For this clarification and many others, I am indebted to Jan Tarlin of Emory University. Cf. his engagement of psychoanalytic and poststructuralist theories regarding biblical interpretation (1992).

[10] Because intertextuality has so often been comprehended "in the banal sense of 'study of sources,'" Kristeva has given up the term—which she herself coined—and has replaced (displaced?) it with "transposition" (1984:60).

[11] Cf. Kristeva's discussion (1984:62-3; 143-5) of the symbolic, which is concerned with the positioning of the (heterogeneous) subject within discourse. Its positions are always destabilized, however, by the semiotic, which appears only in traces, or ruptures, within the text. These act as "waves of attack against stases" (1984:28; cf. 1986a). See also note 5, above.

[12] As with any writing, Judges is taken not as a single unified *text* (though nonetheless a book) but as a composite, or mosaic, of many texts—a "field of transpositions" (Kristeva 1984:60). Ironically, such an approach to Judges is more like that of a historical critic than a canonical or literary "final form" critic. This discussion quickly diverges from the dominant historical-critical discourse, however, because it does not presume that any interpretation can get behind and around the "field" sufficiently to comprehend all its voices.

[13] Given the wording here, this may indeed be at least as oedipally vested as it is ideologically so.

[14] For a critique of the patriarchal *functioning* of form criticism in Hos 9:10-17 (Mays and Wolff), see the essay by Deborah Krause in this volume. The narrow boundaries imposed by that form-critical strategy of containment are transgressed by her own intertextual reading of the passage in relation to Gen 49:25.

2

ISAIAH:
NEW HEAVENS, NEW EARTH, NEW BOOK

Peter D. Miscall

INTRODUCTION: INTERTEXTUALITY

Borrowings

How are texts to be related? What are we to make of the obvious and the not so obvious relations that exist between texts? Relations that extend from literal references and quotations to the tenuous ties of common words and letters and to the fact that all texts at least share language as a common basis. One frequent way is to avoid speaking of texts and the connections between them altogether, and to speak instead of meanings, beliefs, philosophies and institutions which are different, and which are therefore expressed differently when people write about them. Other writings, other texts, from a first author are simply there to be used to help express a second author's views and to highlight the differences with the views of the first. In this approach, there is no mention made of texts in tension or in conflict.

This is the realm in which one author borrows from a second and, vice versa, in which the second influences the first. Textual borrowings and influences occur in a relatively undisturbed atmosphere; elements from one text "flow into" (a root meaning of *influence*) the next. The later text takes some elements from the earlier and disregards others. The earlier text can be changed—added to; subtracted from; rearranged—all in the effort to better express and emphasize the different beliefs of the author of the later text.

This has generally been the way of biblical criticism. Borrowing, such as when the early chapters of Genesis borrow from

Mesopotamian literature, is dealt with as fact and as involving specific words, phrases, names, images, themes and structure. The questions probed are focused and factual. From what other literature was this borrowed? When? Why? How has the Hebrew Bible changed the borrowed elements? For what purpose? These questions are answered specifically and confidently. The other texts, whether written or oral, were simply there at the disposal of the biblical author; he could use them or not in whatever way he wanted.

In the discussion of borrowing, there are varying amounts of scholarly detail on particular words and phrases, on the specific text(s) borrowed from, and on the conjectured date(s) of such borrowing. Differences between the earlier and the later texts are ascribed to differences in the beliefs, cultures and literary styles of the respective authors. There is little or no talk of textual authority and power, especially as they are affected by influences and borrowings.

In regard to Genesis 1:1-2:4a, Ephraim Speiser (1964:9) is confident that the "biblical authors were indebted to Mesopotamian models for these early chapters not only in matters of arrangement but also in some subject matter." The indebtedness "is borne out of actual facts." The points of contact are with the *Enuma Elish*, the Babylonian creation story; the correspondences include both details and structure, the order of events. Speiser draws some conclusions.

First, there is a close relation between "the biblical approach to creation as reflected in" the Genesis text and "traditional Mesopotamian beliefs." Speiser relates biblical approach and Mesopotamian beliefs, not Israelite and Babylonian texts. Second, since the Babylonians are earlier, they "did not take over these views from the Hebrews . . . [the] opening account [of Genesis] goes back to Babylonian prototypes, and it is immaterial whether the transmission was accomplished directly or through some intermediate channel" (10). Again, there is no mention of texts and textual relations, and this is a process of transmission, of untroubled movement through a channel.

Third, "the date of the take-over cannot be determined within any practical limits . . . The creation account could have entered the stream of biblical tradition sometime in the latter half of the second millennium." To influence is to enter the stream or channel, to flow into. Fourth, "derivation from Mesopotamia in this instance means no more and no less than that, on the subject of creation, biblical tradition aligned itself with the traditional tenets of Babylonian 'science'" (10-11). There are no troubles in the borrowing. We have indebtedness, transmission, take-over, entering the stream and the congruence of approaches, traditions, beliefs and even science.

However, fifth, "since the religion of the Hebrews diverged sharply from Mesopotamian norms, we should expect a corresponding departure in regard to beliefs about creation . . . the biblical account of creation displays at one and the same time a recognition of pertinent Babylonian sources as well as a critical position toward them" (11). Speiser's discussion of these differences and this critical position is devoted to an exposition of the unique aspects and tenets of Israelite monotheism which can be forcefully expressed by being contrasted against the Mesopotamian beliefs. The religious beliefs are different, and therefore the stories of creation are told differently, and the differences are manifest in the manipulations of the details and structure of the Babylonian story by the Hebrew story.

Texts and Intertexts

But there is another way to relate texts. There is something else to be made of the relations between one text and another. Much contemporary criticism is concerned with textuality and intertextuality. Texts are thought of and read first as texts, as material and specific words on the page arranged in a specific order. These texts refer to other texts and exist in a world of texts; anything "written" is a text. Textual reading starts, and to a great extent remains, with texts and with words and does not totally and finally put them aside in favor of some meaning or belief—authorial or historical—that is presumed to be what the texts and the words are about. Attention is paid to the words and to what they say and don't say whether or not this attention, this close reading, results in a clear meaning. Reading may lead into an ambiguous and undecidable situation.

This attention also revolves around questions of textual status and authority and not just around the status and authority of disembodied (detextualized) institutions, systems of belief, philosophies and such. For example, why borrow anything from another text? If there is borrowing, what is the effect on the borrower and the borrowee? Does a text gain or lose stature by borrowing or by being borrowed from? Why borrow from one text and not from another?

"Intertextuality" is a covering term for all the possible relations that can be established between texts. The relations can be based on anything from quotes and direct references to indirect allusions to common words and even letters to dependence on language itself. The effect of the relations can extend from support and agreement to one text's rejection and attempted destruction of the other. Writers who use the term and concept of intertextuality generally imply trouble and disturbance in textual relations. Relations between texts are never paradisiacal; texts can only exist in a fallen world. The major writers I have in mind are Julia Kristeva (who first introduced the term intertextuality into critical parlance), Roland Barthes, Jacques Derrida, Barbara Johnson, Paul de Man and Harold Bloom. Nietzsche and Freud can be included in this list as well, since they are texts to which these more contemporary writers frequently refer. To even speak of "(inter)textualists" is to enter the realm of texts.

The relationship between two texts is equivocal. It includes, at the same time, both acceptance and rejection, recognition and denial, understanding and misunderstanding, and supporting and undermining. To recognize that a text is related to another text is both to affirm and to deny the earlier text. It is affirmed as a type of model and source, while it is denied by being made secondary to the later text, precisely by being regarded as a model and a source that has been superseded. The later text displaces its model.

For example, a commentator on a text—here Speiser on Gen 1:1-2:4a—accepts and supports the text's authority by asserting that it is worthy of commentary and by explicating its meanings and implications. At the same time, the commentator modifies and even undermines the original text's authority by declaring that it needs commentary (i.e., it is not clear enough on its own), and that this commentary is what the original text really means (i.e., the original text does not mean what it says). Speiser is aware of both aspects. After eight pages of telling us, in his words, the exact meaning of Gen 1:1-2:4a, he closes with the comment, "At all events, the text should be allowed to speak for itself" (13). For a commentator or for any critic, including myself, anything but this is allowed.

Displacement, decentering, dispersal and dissemination are four terms that, combined, provide another perspective on intertextuality. Instead of borrowing and influence, instead of a stream of tradition that flows on and into texts, we have texts that displace and decenter one another—we do not have to follow historical priority here—by dispersing and disseminating each other's parts or elements: letters, words, sentences, themes, images, characters and plot.

From the perspective of intertextuality, textual authority and status are always in question since texts are interdependent and use each other. No text is an island. Displacement and decentering, rather than replacement and chaos, are two terms and concepts that attempt to express the questioning of authority and status and not the complete loss of either. The text is not undone and replaced. It is displaced and shifted from its former position of authority. It may have moved elsewhere but it is still somewhere. It does not disappear. To destroy a text's center is to reduce it to chaos; to decenter it is to move the center elsewhere, an elsewhere that is no longer an absolutely controlling and dominating site. Textual authority and status are in question because the original text no longer has the necessary site and center to exercise its previous authority. But the authority and status are "in question" and are not totally removed or denied.

Precursors and Transumption

This is an opening for Harold Bloom's theory (and practice) of reading and writing, a theory that speaks not of easy borrowings and smooth influences but of the anxiety of influence, of the burdensome feeling of belatedness (of coming too late on the scene) and of the conflict with a precursor. He has combined insights and materials from groups as diverse as Jewish Gnostics, classical rhetoricians and Sigmund Freud to produce what is both a theory of literary writing and a "practical guide" to reading.

For Bloom, writing and reading, which are two sides of the same coin, are dominated not by establishing meaning and truth but by confrontation with another. In the confrontation power and possession are sought; desire and a Nietzschean will to power are the driving forces. The writer seeks to establish himself over against and in place of the other text. Given belatedness—the feeling that a previous text or texts are too powerful and great to allow one to write something new—the response to this confrontation must be aggressive and must involve desire and violent self-assertion. The new text can be written only by dispossessing and displacing the former, the precursor.

One of the main figures or rhetorical devices employed by the belated writer in this conflict and attempt at displacement is *transumption* or *metalepsis*.[1] This refers to troping on a trope, by which one figure of speech leads to another and then on to others so that a series of figures of speech is formed. "The reader is led from one scene to another allusive second scene, to a third, and so on" (Fletcher 1964:241). Any aspect of the text, including sound, can be played off in the construction of the series. This is a specific mode of dispersing any part or element of a text, particularly any figure or trope. John Hollander (1981:133) calls it "interpretive allusion" which is marked by an "ellipsis . . . of further figuration" (115), that is, the latest or the belated text wants to end the series with itself: it has performed the last trope!

For Bloom a major feature of the figure is its attempt to make the early late and the late early—to project the belated writer back before the precursor. By entering into the series of tropes and by claiming to close it off, the late writer makes it look as though he started it all, as though he were the first ever to use the trope. For Hollander this temporal sequence involves "taking the consequent for the precedent" (1981:134). Bloom offers a powerful biblical example (1984:3-14). John's Jesus says "Before Abraham was, I am" (John 8:56-58). Thus he tropes upon the verb "to be" as in Exod 3:14, where the LORD says "I am who I am" (*'ehyeh 'asher 'ehyeh*) to Moses, playing upon his divine name Yahweh. By putting it this way, therefore, John's Jesus casts (tropes) himself back before Abraham and before Moses.

The book of Isaiah is my focus. I read it as one book and not as the combination of three or more separate works. A Bloomian model could be applied to the relations between Isaiah and other Ancient Near Eastern (ANE) literature such as Egyptian and Babylonian sun hymns, creation myths, royal inscriptions, legal collections and wisdom books. The Canaanite myths, particularly that of Baal and Anat, are also precursors. And the conflicts and striving to replace another in these myths accord well with Bloom's agonistic model.

However, I want to examine the relations between Isaiah and another part of the Hebrew Bible, Genesis, specifically Gen 1:1-2:4a. Bloom provides the main parameters for the reading but not the controlling model or metaphor. Given the responses of many feminist critics, I do not feel bound to Bloom's extreme emphasis on conflict, aggression and will to power. All of that exists but there is also sisterhood and belonging to a tradition and will to community (see Kolodny 1985:46-62; Gilbert and Gubar 1984). Both aspects need attention and both receive it in Isaiah.

I read Isaiah and Genesis as intertexts without deciding or arguing for a particular historical priority. This is a literary or poetic reading and not an argument for a specific chronology of historical authorship. I want to read Isaiah in light of Genesis, and to assess the impact of some of the associations between them. From this stance, I read Isaiah clashing with and attempting to displace Genesis. The associations are such that Genesis, particularly 1:1-2:4a, is dispersed into Isaiah in a variety of ways; *transumption* or *metalepsis* is a major mode.

ISAIAH AND GENESIS

In the beginning God created the heavens and the earth.
Hear, O heavens! Give ear, O earth! For the LORD speaks.

Genesis opens majestically: "In the beginning." Isaiah calls to the same heavens and earth, but the opening is prosaic: "The vision of Isaiah, son of Amoz, which he envisioned concerning Judah and Jerusalem in the days of Uzziah, Jotham, Ahaz, Hezekiah, kings of Judah." Although something is to be made in Isaiah of the opening chapter of Genesis, it will not be simple repetition. The close of Isaiah provides a clue: "O look! I am creating new heavens and a new earth; and the former things are not to be remembered or come into the heart" (65:17). And "the new heavens and the new earth which I am making are standing before me" (66:22).

Isaiah tropes on Genesis 1 at the start of his book and by the close has made clear his purpose: a new heavens, a new earth and a new book.[2] "Remember not the beginning things ... I am making something new" (43:18) intones the prophet quoting the LORD. Among "the beginning things" (*ri'shonot*) not to be remembered is the report "In the beginning" (*bere'shit*) which, in the Hebrew Bible, is also the title of the book of Genesis. The letters, words and themes of Genesis 1 are dispersed throughout Isaiah; this is a new creation, a new book, and not just a translation of Genesis 1.

In mapping the relations between Genesis 1 and Isaiah, I take two approaches, both of which employ the figure of speech *transumption* in which one figure, word or image leads to another and then to another and so on. A *transumptive* style results in a "crowding of the imagination" (Fletcher 1964: 240-41) as images, themes and words pile up on each other. First I examine words and phrases from Genesis 1 that are scattered through Isaiah; second, I explore how Isaiah, in turning upon Genesis 1, goes beyond it into Genesis 1-3, the rest of Genesis, into Exodus and into other ANE texts. The result of the mapping is not a new interpretation of Isaiah, in the sense of a new specification of "what it means." Rather, the result is a new reading, in the sense of offering a different way of talking about Isaiah and about its relations with another Biblical text.

Words

Darkness and light are central in the opening verses of Genesis. Isaiah begins with his address to the heavens and the earth and then, in the remainder of chapter 1, swerves from creation to the sins of Israel. After the vision of exalted Jerusalem in Isa 2:2-4, a voice exhorts, "O house of Jacob! Come! Let us walk in the light of the LORD!" Light, the particular word (*'or*) and the image, runs throughout Isaiah and is employed with a variety of meanings. The brilliant light that Jacob is to walk in extends from chapter 2 to the vision of restored and gleaming Jerusalem in chapters 60-62. "Arise! Shine! Your light has come!" The passage includes light's opposite as well. "The darkness covers earth and gloom, peoples" (60:1-2).

This light is glorious, life-giving and saving. It is the light of the sun, the light of day, which vivifies the world and provides sight. It dispels the darkness of night. "The people walking in darkness see a great light" (9:1). The servant is "a light to the nations" (42:6; 49:6) providing life, sight, justice, salvation and release from the darkness of the dungeon (42:7). This is the light of Genesis: "God saw the light, that it was good."

This is not always the case. "The Light of Israel will be a fire ... it will burn and consume his thorns and briers" (10:17). This fire burns and destroys (47:14); it is the blazing sun and its heat (4:6). This light desiccates and blinds. With it the darkness of a shadow is protective and saving (4:6; 32:2; 49:2).[3]

Light (fire) and darkness (shadow) disperse into the text of Isaiah, and in the process they are redone and transformed. We are working with tropes of *transumption* (*metalepsis*), not of translation (metaphor). The same dispersal is encountered with other words and phrases from Genesis 1. They occur throughout Isaiah, not just in one part. Genesis 1 is not transported into Isaiah 1. It is not repeated verbatim and in the same order.

"The earth was without form [*tohu*] and void [*bohu*]." Isaiah 34 tropes on Genesis and envisions a demonic creation of violence, blood, fire and fiendish creatures. This creation was anticipated in Isaiah 24-26 which presents a horrific vision of falling, withering and blood. Adam and Eve, as a sign of life, cover themselves with fig leaves (*'aleh te'enah*; Gen 3:7), but now, as a sign of death, "leaves [*'aleh*] wither [or, fall] from the vine as they wither [or, fall] from the fig tree [*te'enah*]" (Isa 34:4).[4] Over this demonic earth, the LORD stretches "a line without form [*tohu*] and a plummet of void [*bohu*]" (34:11). And "the city of chaos [*qiryat tohu*] is shattered" (Isa 24:10). These passages return us to the never-never time just after or before creation as the LORD'S creation in Genesis is undone or transformed. Indeed, in 40:17, 23; 41:29; and 44:9 the LORD regards parts of his creation as nothing (*tohu*).

The transformation, the undoing, can be done even more powerfully; the darkness and formlessness of Genesis 1 can be cast out and negated. The creator God of Genesis 1, *'elohim*, is displaced by the LORD, Yahweh, who is just that creator God.

> Thus says the LORD, the creator of the heavens—He is The God! [*hu' ha'elohim*]—the fashioner of the earth and its maker: he established it; not formless [*lo' tohu*] did he create it . . . "I am the LORD . . . I do not speak in secret, in a hiding place in a dark land [*'erets*]. I do not say . . . 'Seek me in chaos [*tohu*].'" (45:18-19)

"The spirit [*ruah*] of God brooded upon the face of the waters." *Ruah*—spirit, wind and breath—suffuses Isaiah: the burning spirit of judgement (4:4; 28:6); the wind, blowing and desiccating (7:2; 57:13); the LORD'S spirit (11:2; 42:1; 59:21); the LORD'S breath and wind which can desiccate or vivify (11:15; 40:7; 57:16); and, finally, human breath and spirit (11:4; 38:16; 66:2).[5]

The spirit brooded (*merahepet*). "Brood" (*rahap*) does not occur in Isaiah but other possible combinations of the root consonants—r/h/p—do. First, there is *parah*, to blossom and a blossom: blossoms dry (5:24); the wilderness blooms (34:1-2; see 17:11; 18:5; 27:6); and the people's "bones blossom like grass" (66:14). Second, there is *hapar*, to blush and be ashamed: used of the people (1:29; 54:4); of the sun and the moon (24:23); and of Lebanon (33:9). And third, we find *harap*, to defy, challenge and disgrace: used of seven women (4:1); of God's people (25:8; 51:7; 54:4); of Assyria (37:1-24); and of Babylon (47:3). "The poet goes from one word to another that sounds like it, to yet another, thus developing a chain of auditory associations getting the poem from one image to another more remote image" (Fletcher 1964:241); in this case, from brood to blossom to shame.

"Upon the face of the waters . . ." Water, waters, sea, river and streams are ubiquitous in Isaiah and present the same dual meaning that light does. Water can be life-giving and refreshing, as it is in chapters 35, 41 and 43, or it can be a death dealing flood and torrent, as in 8:5-8, 10:22 and 28:1-22. With water Isaiah accords with Genesis 1 where water is a source of life and where it is also the water of chaos that must be held in the deeps or above the firmament.[6]

These are a few selected examples; others could be developed from Genesis 1 and followed through Isaiah more thoroughly and with more attention to context in Isaiah. In Isaiah, the words and letters are not scattered aimlessly and separately; they do come together at different points and in different combinations. Genesis 1 is disassembled and then reassembled although now decentered and dispersed.

Beyond Genesis 1

Both Genesis 1 and Isaiah trope, in their own distinctive ways, upon other ANE texts, especially myths. Genesis does it predominately by elision; gone are the threats, conflicts and struggles of many ANE creation myths. Some of the divine characters of ANE pantheons, such as sea and sun, have become created objects shorn of any personality. Although Isaiah reintroduces the conflict and struggles and alludes to many of the themes and characters of the myths, he tropes upon them by turning them into poetic images and themes (Frye 1982:92). He incorporates the myths into his allusive, multi-level style in which a passage can at once refer to the power of the physical sea, the Mediterranean; to God's creation in Genesis 1; to the event at the Red Sea; to Baal's victory over Yamm; to a god's victory over Rahab; and to the exiles' return from Babylon.

> Awake, awake, put on strength, O Arm of the LORD!
> Awake, as in days of old, generations of long ago!
> Are you not the hewer of Rahab, the piercer of the Dragon?
> Are you not the one who dries up [*harab*] sea, the waters of the great deep?
> Who makes a way in the depths of the sea for the crossing over of the redeemed?
> The ransomed of the LORD return; they come to Zion with song. (51:9-11)

The passage is instructive because of the violent and catastrophic creation and because it tropes on ANE myth, on Genesis 1 and on Exodus through talk of redemption, the LORD'S outstretched arm and the crossing over. The sea is split and dried for the people to cross over. This is an excellent example of a transumptive style that leads us from one text to another and then to still others.

In Isaiah 4, Isaiah combines creation and exodus and trumps them. The survivors, the remnant, will be washed —implying water—and cleansed by "a spirit of judgement" and by "a spirit of burning." Over the entire site of Mount Zion (see Exod 15:17), "the LORD will create a cloud for day, and smoke and the brilliance of a flaming fire for night." Over all there will be a canopy and pavilion which will serve for shade, refuge and shelter (Isa 4:2-6). The passage tropes upon creation—this is the first use of *bara'*, to create (Gen 1:1), in Isaiah—and upon the column of smoke by day and of fire by night which light the way for Israel (Exod 13:21-22; 14:19-24). The passage also tropes on the cloud that marks the presence of the LORD at Sinai and of his glory in the tabernacle (Exod 19:9-16; 24:15-18; 33:9-10; 34:5; 40:34-38). Whereas the column is an image of movement towards a goal, the cloud is an image of stasis and permanence.

In Isaiah the goal has been reached and the permanence attained. God creates a new heavens and a new earth which, by interpretive allusion within Isaiah, are equated with Zion and Jerusalem, the LORD'S holy mountain—they are the goal of the new exodus. And the new heavens and the new earth stand like a column before the LORD, "and the word of our God stands forever" (40:8).

Acts and Words

Genesis 1 is a narration of God's creative acts and words. "And God said, 'Let there be light.'" In Isaiah, the LORD's first words refer to a type of creation and then swerve to rebellion, that is, Genesis 3, rather than the good creation that God saw. "Sons I rear and raise, and they rebel against me."[7]

In the first week God's creation is perfect. It is all good, very good (Gen 1:31), not marred by evil or by any negative; there is nary a no, a not or a nor in Genesis 1. This is all changed in Isaiah, where there is rebellion, sin and iniquity. The people "don't know" and "don't understand." They must "cease to do evil, learn to do good" (Isa 1:16-17). This alludes to the tree of the knowledge of good and evil. The good of creation is not yet or no longer present with this people. The LORD, their God (Isa 1:10), does not see or look for, but rather hides his eyes (1:15). Yet the people can "eat the good of the earth," if they are willing and obedient (1:19). The events in Eden, especially the association of eating and obedience, remain close at hand.

However, the evil, the dross, can be removed and the rulers restored "as in the beginning" (*bari'shonah*; Isa 1:26). We are far from that other "in the beginning." But not so far.

> [The sinful people] are ashamed of [*bosh*] the oaks which you value [*hamad*], and you blush [*hapar*] because of the gardens that you have chosen. But you are like an oak with withered (or, fallen) leaf, and like a garden that has no water in it. (Isa 1:29-30)

We know of another garden that "the LORD God did not rain upon" and that was watered by a spring, and we know of other trees, those of creation and those of life and the knowledge of good and evil. The latter leads to shame (*bosh*; Gen 2:25) when Eve finds the tree valuable (*hamad*) for wisdom.[8]

We also know of another garden, a demonic place, "that has no water in it," but only blood, brimstone and burning pitch (Isaiah 34). Here the hosts of heaven wither or fall "as leaves fall from the vine, like those falling from the fig" (34:4). Above I noted the allusion to the clothing made from fig leaves (Gen 3:7); one image leads to another and to yet another as

Isaiah's allusive style crowds our imagination.

Within Isaiah "they are ashamed" (*yeboshu*, Isa 1:29) tropes upon "to be dry" (*yabesh*, e.g., Isa 15:6; 40:7-8, 24; 42:15; 44:27; 56:3). The associated noun is *yabbashah*, dry land. "The poet goes from one word to another that sounds like it ... getting the poem from one image to another," in this case, from shame to dryness. Movements from shame to dry to dry land occur throughout Isaiah; we are dealing with *transumption*, not translation. Amongst the scatterings we encounter this passage:

> But now listen, O Jacob my servant, O Israel whom I have chosen! Thus says the LORD, your maker [*'oseh*], your fashioner [*yotser*] in the womb who helps you: "Fear not, O my servant Jacob, O Jeshurun whom I have chosen! For I pour water on the thirsty ground and streams [*nozelim*] on the dry ground; I pour my spirit on your seed and my blessing on your offspring. They spring up among grass, like willows by streams of water." (Isa 44:1-4)

God proposes to make (*'asah*) humanity, the Adam (Gen 1:26), and fashions (*yatsar*) the human being, the Adam, from the dust of the earth. The maker and fashioner of the world and of humanity in Genesis 1 is the maker and fashioner of Israel in the womb. God creates the Adam: "God created humanity in his own image, in the image of God he created it; male and female he created them" (Gen 1:27). Now the image of male and female is returned to God the maker (male) and the fashioner in the womb (female).[9]

> And God said, "Let the waters under the heavens gather into one place so that the dry ground [*yabbashah*] can appear." And it was so. God called the dry ground earth [*'erets*]. (Gen 1:9-10)

In Isaiah, water and streams are poured out upon the dry ground which had been gathered and separated from the waters. The spirit of God which "brooded over the face of the waters" (Gen 1:2) is now poured out upon Israel's descendants, his seed (*zera'*), and is poured out like water and like the LORD's blessing which was once given to humanity (Gen 1:28).

They are to eat plants bearing seed (Gen 1:29; *zera'*). All this pouring out results in new growth and bounty, a new Eden.

The short passage in Isaiah 44 plays upon Genesis 1-3 and beyond into Genesis and Exodus through the mention of Jacob and Israel; Jacob is the patriarch in Genesis whose name is changed to Israel; his descendants become the nation Israel in Exodus. Water, dry land and spirit (*ruah*) combine creation (both in Genesis and in ANE myth) and exodus.

> The LORD drove the sea with a strong east wind [*ruah*] all night and made the sea dry land [*horabah*] . . . and the Israelites went in the middle of the sea on dry land [*yabbashah*]. (Exod 14:21-22)

> The deeps cover them [the Egyptians] . . . with the breath [*ruah*] of your nostrils, waters pile up, streams [*nozelim*] stand as a heap, the deeps freeze in the heart of the sea . . . you blow your breath [*ruah*]; sea covers them . . . You stretch out your right arm [*yamin*], earth swallows them. (Exod 15:5-12)

Isaiah's allusive, transumptive style sets in motion a series reaching back into ANE myths, Genesis and Exodus—a series that Isaiah seeks to close by precluding further figuration. This is a new book and a new vision of the new heavens and the new earth which the LORD is creating; the things of the past, whether acts, words or books, are to be forgotten. Read Isaiah and not these other books! The new heavens and the new earth—the new Jerusalem, the LORD'S holy mountain—stand before him. The word of our God stands forever! Does also "the word which Isaiah son of Amoz saw concerning Judah and Jerusalem"?

NOTES

[1] The trope of *transumption* or *metalepsis* was introduced into contemporary criticism by Angus Fletcher in a lengthy footnote discussing Samuel Johnson's comments on Milton's style. He refers to Quintillian's definition of the trope (1964:241). John Hollander's entire book is an analysis of metalepsis/transumption as a mode of allusion which he, in his own transumptive manner, calls "echo." He deals

with the trope most explicitly in his last chapter, "Echo Metaleptic" (1981:113-32), and in an appendix, "The Trope of Transumption" (133-49). He discusses the classical forebears at some length. Bloom (1982; 1984), in his turn, looks back to both Fletcher and Hollander.

[2] I use the name Isaiah to refer both to the whole book and to the presumed author of the book; I am not referring to the 8th-century prophet who appears in Isaiah 6-8 and 36-39. Also, I use Genesis 1 as a shorthand for Gen 1:1-2:4a.

[3] See Miscall (1991) for a wider ranging treatment of light and fire imagery in Isaiah.

[4] In Hebrew "wither" (*nabal*) and "fall" (*napal*) are very close in pronunciation. In Isaiah they are also close in meaning, especially in this passage, since withering of leaves implies their falling; therefore, the passage employs the preposition "from," which is the reason for my double translation. Isa 24:7 anticipates the withering of the vine.

[5] There are still other Isaianic references for the wind (17:13; 27:8; 32:2; 64:5); the LORD'S spirit (30:1; 40:13; 44:3); the LORD'S breath (27:8; 40:24; 59:19); and human breath (26:9; 29:24; 31:3; 54:6; 57:15).

[6] In Gen 7:11 (and 8:2) and Isa 24:18, the destructive flood comes because the "windows of heaven open."

[7] In Isa 24:5, the earth is polluted because its inhabitants have broken "the everlasting covenant" (*berit 'olam*); and in Isa 26:21 the LORD punishes the guilt and the bloodshed of the earth's inhabitants. These recall Cain's shedding Abel's blood (Gen 4:1-16), the rule against shedding blood (Gen 9:1-7), and the following "everlasting covenant" (vss. 8-17)..

[8] In Isa 60:19-61:11, restored Jerusalem is described as a garden, a new Eden. This is forecast in 37:35. The LORD will protect (*gannoti*) Jerusalem. The verb to protect, *ginnen*, can be related to garden, *gan*, as a denominative. The LORD'S protection of Jerusalem then is realized in this transformation of her into a garden.

[9] In Isa 27:11, however, the people's maker and fashioner will no longer have compassion or mercy on them. See Trible (1978:12-23 and 75-80) for a related discussion of the Genesis 1 passage.

3

INTERTEXTUALITY, TRANSFERENCE, AND THE READER IN/OF GENESIS 12 AND 20

ILONA N. RASHKOW

Since the techniques of post-structuralist literary critics have been appropriated by our discipline, sequential narrative episodes which reflect upon each other are now described as "intertextual." Intertextuality exists on both micro- and macro-levels. On the smallest linguistic level (individual words and phrases), the relationship is easily recognizable. Repetitions and shifts represent the basis for a wealth of scholarly material. The study of lexical similarities and differences is, in fact, one of the mainstays of biblical criticism. Adele Berlin, among others, explores how "lexical cohesion" (the ways in which words are linguistically connected within a sequence) plays a role in interpretation, and how awareness of this relationship can lead to better readings (1989). In a very different kind of criticism, Harold Bloom (1976) examines "poetic crossings," the ways in which a text can destroy its own integrity if examined within the framework of lexical similarities and differences.

Biblical scholars have studied intertextuality on a larger level as well. "Type-scenes" are intertextual in that they relate narrative events using fixed modes or sequences of action. However, type-scenes are most often discussed in terms of the biblical *writer's* ability to shape the text, rather than the *reader's* role in interpreting it. James G. Williams (1980), for example, suggests that Genesis 12, 20, and 26 exemplify variations on the formulaic convention "the wife/sister scene," and explores the way in which each *author* uniquely employs the basic pattern, emphasizing that elusive "authorial intention." Similarly, Robert Culley (1976) outlines the patterns of content found in each account of the wife-sister tale, contrasts and compares them, and provides a review of scholarship on oral narrative, again focusing on the *authorship* of folkloric material.

"Typology" is also intertextual, since characters and scenes symbolically prefigure later events (most often, the "Old Testament" is read as a prefiguration of the events of the "New"). Of course, the Hebrew Bible also has several self-contained examples of typology. Joel Rosenberg (1984:51) points out the following: "The parting of the waters of Creation anticipates the parting of the Reed (or "Red") Sea for Israel. The escape of Noah in an ark (*tevah*) anticipates the escape of the infant Moses in a cradle (*tevah*) on the Nile. The descent of Abraham to Egypt in time of famine and his exit from Egypt with great wealth anticipate the events of the Exodus story. The building of the desert tabernacle anticipates the building of the Temple in the days of Solomon. . . ." Thus, intertextuality exists on several levels, not only in narratives which seem repetitive.

The focus of this paper is the literary topos dealing with the "Matriarch of Israel in Danger."[1] In three places in Genesis, *different* combinations of patriarchs, matriarchs, foreign kings, and social settings are recorded, but the scenario and key terms basically coincide. All three passages give essentially the same story: a patriarch and his wife visit a foreign land. Fearing that the woman's beauty might become a source of danger to himself as the husband, the man resorts to subterfuge by claiming that his wife is his sister. In Genesis 12, the encounter involves Abraham and Sarah with the ruler of Egypt. The incident is repeated twice: in Genesis 20 the same couple confronts Abimelech of Gerar; and in Genesis 26 Abimelech is similarly embarrassed by Isaac and Rebekah. Although there are three patriarch/wife/other occurrences in Genesis, for the sake of brevity, this paper focuses only on the Abraham/Sarah cycle (Genesis 12 and 20).

Read as type-scenes, these wife-as-sister tales have been important not only for proponents of the documentary hypothesis, but other scholars as well. Anthropologists have studied them for information about tribal culture;[2] comparatists note contemporaneous epics which provide parallels to the motif of the abduction of the hero's beautiful wife;[3] and theologians argue that Genesis 20 is a moral revision of the core tradition in Genesis 12, the earlier narrative reflecting the sensuality and immorality of pagan nations, while the later emphasizes God's direct, protective intervention.[4] Clearly, scholars of many disciplines eagerly acknowledge the intertextuality of Genesis 12 and 20.

Recently, however, another interest of post-structuralist literary critics, the *reader* of the text, has been appropriated by our discipline, shifting focus to the *process* by which individual readers confer meaning and perceive this intertextuality. One explanation is transference, a phenomenon long-recognized in the psychoanalytic process, a process quite similar to that of reading. The relationship of the reader and the text replicates that of analyst and analysand, interpreter and code. However, the roles of analyst and analysand in reading are not as clearly defined as in the psychoanalytic process, because the status of that which is analyzed, the text, is not that of a patient: the text has authority, the very type of authority by which Jacques Lacan (1977) defines the role of the *analyst* in the structure of transference. Just as the analysand views the analyst as "a subject presumed to know," the reader approaches the text as the very place where meaning, and *knowledge* of meaning, reside. Thus, the reader simultaneously occupies the place of analyst *and* the place of analysand.

According to the psychoanalytic account of transference, the structures of the unconscious are revealed by the analyst's encounters with the analysand's discourse. The analyst, in effect, repeats the experience described by the analysand. Just as transference is a repetition linking the analyst to the analysand, reading is a repetition of the text it seeks to analyze. Prior readings, particularly those which have narrative similarity, are not errors to be discarded, but revealing recurrences of textual structures. It is through transference that the analysand coaxes the analyst to play out the scene he or she has in mind, a scene based upon intertextuality. As a result, this self-reflexiveness does not produce or induce a closure in which the text is the thing it describes, but rather leads to a multiplicity of representations, a plurality of meanings. And plurality, here, does not mean *several* meanings, but rather that the text cannot be reduced to *a* meaning.

Intertextuality allows that all texts are reflections of all other texts. That is, they all contribute to the production of meaning because they have already been read (or as Julia Kristeva writes, "every text is the absorption and transformation of other texts" [1971:146]). The reader *of* the text exists since a work can be read only in connection with or against other texts. The method by which this occurs is transference: the reader is caught up in and reenacts the drama he or she thought was being analyzed from the outside (hence the reader *in* the text). Intertextuality and transference work effectively to divide the text against itself, creating both a need for response and a response to the need. Meaning is simultaneously within the text and outside it, hence the reader *in/of* the text.

The relationship between intertextuality and transference, the "reader-*of*-the-text" and the "reader-*in*-the-text," lies in the dynamic interaction between text and reader, free-ranging play of mind and organizing response. Like analysis, reading is a two-part process consisting of disorganization and reorganization, taking the text apart and putting it back together again. Janus-faced, the reader looks back in the text for clues to explain ambiguities while simultaneously looking toward future possibilities and larger patterns, based on individual response (intertextuality and transference). Textual duplications lead outward to larger motifs, and tentative explorations in different directions condense into one focused moment, not to provide the *authoritative* interpretation, but rather to afford new perspectives, find new relationships, change emphases. The reader re-creates the text, combining intertextual episodes with his or her own characteristic processes of mind (transference). By focusing on evasions, ambivalences and points of intensity in the narrative, words which do not get spoken, words which are spoken with unusual frequency, doublings, etc., the reader in/of the text finds the "sub-text" which the work both conceals and reveals. The reader focuses simultaneously on the text itself (common rhetorical or stylistic features, its intertextuality) and the response to the text (transference).

Reading, as analysis, thus relies on two simple strategies: on one hand, paying attention to everything, and on the other, mistrusting seemingly obvious implications, being open to the sudden switches and rearrangements that reveal alternate messages and expose the dynamic play of meaning behind what may seem to be a simple statement. For the reader in/of the text, interpretation does not proceed from partial to definitive meaning and then come to rest, but instead is an ongoing process. Elements of narrative cohesion constantly shift, blurring the distinctions between provisional and "fulfilled" meanings, between shadows and truth. Reading, like analysis, becomes an activity of repressing and reconstructing, of forgetting and remembering, and that activity, by its very nature, resists completion. The reader confers meaning retrospectively; earlier narrative elements retain a provisional status until the reader reaches another meaning based upon subsequent episodes. Intertextuality and transference, notions usually attached to contradicting visions, become interdependent, for the very notion of fulfillment suggests that things must be fulfilled, and are not yet.[5]

It may sound as if I am invoking Freud to justify the kind of free associational play in biblical scholarship that recently has become familiar in literary studies. Indeed, when Freud came to America in 1908, with his strange discoveries about the way the mind works, he warned, "I bring you the plague." Certainly, current literary criticism has plagues of its own, whether caught from Freud or not. And, of course, there is a certain irony in the application of literary theory to biblical texts.[6] On the one hand, literary critics view texts as disunified, deconstructed, or in the Lacanian model, a hodgepodge of disconnected symbols. Yet, at the same time, they paradoxically welcome the acceptance of the biblical text as a "quasi-unified whole" in order to "rescue" the Bible from source critics.[7] The problem seems to be polar thinking: either texts make meaning and readers are superfluous, or readers make meaning and texts are superfluous. But neither makes meaning alone. It is not texts *or* readers; it is texts *and* readers, the relationship of intertextuality (reader -*of*-the-text) and transference (reader-*in*-the-text). The reader is no more autonomous than the text; rather, the reader and the text are interdependent. Hence the reader in/of the biblical text.

Since this self-reflexivity also occurs in subsequent readings of the same narrative, obvious intertextual episodes trigger transference to larger motifs, and as a result, individual narratives are read within the context of the larger biblical story, rather than as discrete tales or moral historiographies. One narrative episode can be read only in connection *with* or *against* another. The plot develops and events become sequential rather than redundant, providing a grid through which antecedent scenes are re-examined, not to enhance an initial impression, but to qualify and complicate it.

Reading within this larger text, the patriarch/wife/other motif goes beyond these obviously related tales to resound a larger pattern: patriarch/wife/other becomes male/powerless female/ uninvited sex. A male is willing to sacrifice a female who is *ostensibly* important to him; the sacrifice of the powerless female usually involves sex; and the male becomes more powerful as a result of this forced prostitution.[8] In these Genesis narratives, one can oxymoronically hear echoes of female voicelessness and its attendant sexual danger or violence, echoes of Lot's two daughters,[9] Hagar,[10] and the unnamed concubine of Judges.[11] As in analysis, the relationship of intertextuality and transference in Genesis 12 and 20 becomes most apparent when examining the discourse in both episodes. In the process, textual speech-acts and the narrator's comments extend the narrow wife-sister tale to this broader motif.

It is difficult to distinguish the strictly rhetorical elements of discourse from other dimensions of the text since hidden wishes or conflicts are always part of the latent content.[12] Of course, while the reader cannot overlook the importance of sheer communication embedded within the text—that between characters or a character's internal thoughts, as in the psychoanalytic use of transference—it is equally dangerous to ignore the exchange between speaker and listener, between text and reader. Discourse analysis belongs to many fields, but it seems particularly appropriate to psychoanalytic literary study, for words can mean more than they seem to mean and do more than they seem to do. The significance of words may even lie in the simple fact that they are utterances, regardless of content or presentation.[13]

Examining discourse extends the discussion in linguistic circles about the relationship between gender, language, and social structure. There is a curiosity about and compelling concern with the question of who speaks in given situations: discourse can be understood as a form of domination, with speech use as an index of social values and the distribution of power. In Genesis 12 and 20, it is through Abraham's discourse that he reverses his less propitious circumstances to a higher level of success and social elevation.ABraham's marginality and insecurity are replaced by wealth and a more stable status at the cost of sacrificing his wife.

The converse of speech—silencing—is also an important consideration[14] since the character who is denied discourse often experiences narrative suppression as well. Both Genesis 12 and 20 are told from the male point of view. Except for the indirect quotation of 20:5, Sarah neither speaks nor takes any action. Even the very discourse of the other characters negates her individuality: not one of them refers to Sarah by name, only by personal pronoun or as Abraham's property. Pharaoh's identification of Sarah is "she," "your wife," "her." Abimelech identifies Sarah as "she" or "she herself." Abraham tells Abimelech "she" is "my sister" and even objectifies Sarah by using "this" (zo't) instead of "she" or "Sarah" when predicting the Egyptians' reaction to their marital relationship ("This is his wife"). Even God views Sarah from this perspective when speaking to Abimelech: in his dream, Abimelech is told that he is a dead man for having taken a $b^{e'}ûlat\ ba'al$, usually translated as "a man's wife" but meaning literally the "possession of a possessor."[15] Textual repetition transfers the recognition of Sarah as powerless to the reader, linking the analyst and analysand (interpreter and code), and causing them to change roles: the reader *of* the text becomes the reader *in* the text when Sarah is silenced.

Abraham's first discourse in Genesis 12 contains both his proposal to Sarah and his rationale:

> I know that you are a beautiful woman, and when the Egyptians see you, they will say, "This is his wife." They will slay me, but they will let you live. Please say you are my sister, that it may go well with me because of you, and that my life may be spared on your account. (Gen 12:11-13)

Abraham's initial argument is narrow and truncated. He claims to fear that the Egyptians will kill him because Sarah is beautiful. It seems strange, however, that Abraham would entertain these fears since, according to what we are told later, Sarah was only ten years younger than Abraham, that is, sixty-five years old. Nor is it evident what Abraham hopes to gain by presenting Sarah as his sister. C. F. Keil and F. Delitzsch (1971) claim that Abraham will stand in a better position to protect Sarah as her brother than as her husband, but Abraham says nothing about her protection. John Skinner (1925) argues that the Egyptians will see a beautiful woman and murder her husband so that one of them can have her, but this assumes that in ancient Egypt murder is preferable to committing adultery.

In any event, Abraham's discourse does not include a discussion about any presumed Egyptian immorality. Abraham's expressed concern is for himself, despite the "logical" argument he presents. While his rationale is that the Egyptians will kill him and let Sarah live, he says nothing about the predicament Sarah could be in by masquerading as his sister (see Miscall 1983:32). Abraham's discourse seems to explain that residence in a foreign place with his wife will result in his murder. For Abraham, beauty, desire, and murder are connected: the first two necessarily and inevitably lead to the third. But the murder that Abraham explicitly states he fears is averted by his deception, at the cost of Sarah being taken as Pharaoh's wife. And there seems to be little doubt that sexual intercourse occurred, since Pharaoh states directly "I took her to me as a wife," the same phrase used in reference to Hagar and Abraham which resulted in the birth of Ishmael.

Since discourse often reflects hidden desires, perhaps Abraham's real motive is a hope to receive gifts from the Egyptians, and his words "that it may go well with me because of you" are a euphemistic way of saying that by abandoning his wife to the lust of a foreign potentate, he might derive material advantage. Certainly Abraham shows no regard for Sarah's welfare, as his language demonstrates ("so that it may go well with me . . . that *my* soul may live . . ."). Perhaps Abraham sees Sarah as expendable because she has no child, and wants to be rid of her as a wife. Or perhaps Abraham is not concerned about Sarah because he views Lot as his descendant.[16] Significantly he uses the verb *harag*, best translated as "slay" and connoting ruthless brutality,[17] to draw attention to his exaggerated fears and to convince Sarah and the reader to participate in his subterfuge. Abraham devises the plan so that all will be to his advantage, ignoring Sarah's potential danger.

Although many commentators argue that Sarah is an accomplice in Abraham's plan,[18] discourse analysis allows that her role is due more to her powerlessness than to her willing agreement. Sarah does not speak in this episode, and the narrator offers no comments on her feelings, her response, or on what she says to Pharaoh. Her silence is not an indication of complicity, but helplessness. Sarah is not a co-conspirator, but rather a silent object, a pawn, and is effectively suppressed as Pharaoh's discourse with Abraham shows. When Pharaoh discovers the deception, he cites what *Abraham*, and Abraham alone, has said to him. Abraham, the protagonist, chosen by God, is contrasted with Pharaoh who, from the beginning of the scene, is depicted as just. It is Pharaoh, not Abraham, who is concerned about the consequences of adultery. It is Pharaoh, not Abraham, who discerns that the plagues were sent because of Sarah's exploitation. Even when Pharaoh remonstrates against Abraham, he does not mention the hardship of the plagues but rather stresses the wrong of Abraham's action. By placing the condemnation against Abraham in the mouth of Pharaoh, the contrast between Abraham and the foreigner who seems better acquainted with the demands of this deity is overwhelming.[19]

The foreign ruler's speech to Abraham is impassioned, and transference forces the reader to react similarly. Pharaoh speaks quickly, in a series of accusatory statements that leave Abraham no time to respond. Indeed Abraham, whose artful discourse convinces Sarah to pose as his sister, can only remain silent as he faces two accusers, Pharaoh and the reader, who are completely correct in their accusations. "What is this you have done to me? Why did you not tell me that she is your wife? Why did you say, 'She is my sister,' so that I took her to me as a wife? And now, behold your wife, take and go!" In these two verses Pharaoh stresses Sarah's relationship to Abraham, a relationship Abraham is content to abrogate. Sarah is Abraham's wife, and Pharaoh, like the reader, is shocked that Abraham would sexually exploit her. Pharaoh's repulsion over Abraham's actions is revealed in the very words of his demand that Abraham leave: "take" (*laqah*) normally requires an object or a prepositional phrase; by omitting it Pharaoh's utterances are even more impassioned.[20]

Intertextuality and transference allow the reader in/of the text to confer meaning to the second part of Gen 12:16 ("And he had sheep, oxen . . ."). It is a retroactive explanation, in detail, of the first part of that same verse, "and Abraham was well treated." That is, these gifts are the foundation of Abraham's wealth. Abraham benefits materially by prostituting his wife,[21] and his ruse is so successful, in fact, that once more he has Sarah pose as his sister, this time in Gerar. Now his actions are even more appalling because of the narrative context. In Genesis 12, there is little or no chance that Sarah would become pregnant even if Pharaoh did have sexual relations with her. By chapter 20, however, the reader knows that Sarah will have a child in less than a year.[22] God promised Abraham twice, and Sarah learned of the promise when she overheard the divine conversation with Abraham. In fact, the very next scene tells of Sarah's pregnancy and the birth of Isaac. Abraham is fully culpable in placing Sarah in the position of being violated by another man. Indeed, if she *had* stayed with Abimelech, even the paternity of her child would have been in doubt, and any adulterous relationship would have had serious consequences because of her imminent pregnancy: Sarah found in the harem of Abimelech to be pregnant with another man's child would have meant certain death.

Abraham's exploitation of Sarah this second time is unfathomable. Unlike the earlier episode, when famine compels the couple to travel, there is no explanation for their sojourn in Gerar. Further, Abraham does not claim to fear being killed because of Sarah's beauty as he did when he approached Egypt, which casts doubts upon his later rationale to Abimelech.

Abimelech's discourse is as significant as Pharaoh's. Like Pharaoh, he chooses his words well when speaking both to God and to Abraham. He appeals to God's sense of justice and professes his innocence. He proves to the deity and, through transference to the reader, that Abraham lied to him, and he employs a solemn oath, the formulaic phrase "in the integrity of my heart," to reiterate his innocence.[23] In a series of pointed questions, he berates Abraham four times, without even pausing to hear his reply. Only in the last question does he leave time for Abraham to answer, demanding, "What did you see that you did this thing?"

Abraham responds with weak excuses. What is striking in a narrative filled with moral discourse between Abimelech and God is the absence of a similar position in Abraham. While Abimelech accuses Abraham of bringing a great sin upon him and upon his kingdom, and of "doing things which should not be done," Abraham does not respond to Abimelech's actual questions, and neither God[24] nor the narrator comment on Abraham's reprehensible actions.

Abraham claims he perpetrated the deception because there was "no fear of God in this place." However, there seemed to be *substantial* "fear of God" on the part of both Abimelech and his servants. In fact, Abraham's discourse contradicts even *this* excuse when he claims that he had asked Sarah "*at every place* . . . say of me, 'He is my brother.'" Abraham's words are suspect. He claims that Sarah is actually his half-sister, but this is not confirmed by the narrator nor by any other dialogue or genealogical source either before or after this scene.[25] Indeed, throughout this episode, Abraham gives inaccurate information, even when he states that "God caused me to wander" (20:13), although, if read from a Freudian perspective, perhaps Abraham's word choice *was* appropriate since the verb he uses, *hit'û*, not only means "cause to wander" but also "mislead".[26] And Abraham has indeed "misled"—misled Pharaoh, Abimelech, Sarah, and the reader. It is impossible to miss the irony in Abraham's remark that he asked Sarah to describe him as her brother because of her *hesed*, a word usually translated as "loyalty."

Intertextuality and transference highlight Abraham's lack of concern for Sarah, his willingness to sacrifice her for his own material gain. Abimelech, like Pharaoh, increases Abraham's wealth and social standing. The irony is that Pharaoh, Abimelech, and the reader all understand the immorality of adultery, and the crime of female sexual sacrifice more readily than Abraham.

Samuel Sandmel (1961) suggests that the tales exemplify inner-biblical aggadah, that is, one version "corrects" and explains another. And for the reader in/of the text, the tales *do* exemplify inner-biblical aggadah; the tales *do* explain one another. The reason for Abraham's deception is buried rhetorically deep within the resolution of the larger biblical tale, a part of the dénouement rather than the opening motivation. When Abraham offers the excuse that Sarah is indeed his half-sister and that they have made public only one side of their family relationship as a precaution throughout their travels, Abraham does not perceive his actions as anything more than a minor deception.

But here intertextuality and transference affect something more fundamental than the characters' experiences or the plot alone: they affect the reader as well. The reader in/of the text has become wary of that infamous "referential fallacy"[27] with a heightened sensitivity to all the ways in which conventional, literal-minded expectations about meaning are defeated. The most scandalous thing about Abraham's ignominious actions is that we are forced to participate; the reader's innocence cannot remain intact since there is no such thing as an innocent reader of this text. The scandal is not simply in the text, but resides in the reader's relation to the text. What is outrageous is not simply that of which the text is speaking, but that which makes it speak to the reader.

NOTES

[1] Michael Fishbane (1985:11-12) calls this literary device a "scenic-compound."

[2] Joel Rosenberg (1986:78), e.g., claims that the "wife-as-sister" motif is important because it is one of several kinds of episodes which illustrate Abraham's contact with foreigners, and one in which the question of foreignness, as such, is most at issue. From this point on, "spouse=kin; foreigner=non-spouse." Susan Niditch (1987) concurs, and views these narratives as an expression of deep concern about Israelite identity, marriage inside and outside the group, the fear of incest, and the fear of foreigners.

Other anthropological approaches have used the wife-as-sister theme to explain that the Hurrian society marriage bonds were strongest and most solemn when the wife had simultaneously the juridical status of a sister, regardless of actual blood ties. According to E. A. Speiser (1964:91), a man would sometimes marry a girl and at the same time adopt her as his sister. Violations of such sistership arrangements were punished more severely than breaches of marriage contracts, the practice apparently a reflection of the underlying fratriarchal system which gave the adoptive brother greater authority than was granted the husband. By the same token, the adopted sister would enjoy correspondingly greater protection and higher social status. Recent research in the Nuzi archives, as quoted by Nahum Sarna (1989:102-3), sheds some interesting perspectives. One document reads that "Akkulenni son of Akiya . . . sold his sister Beltakkadummi as sister to Hurazzi of Ennaya," and another document records a marriage-contract of "Akkulenni son of Akiya, contracted with Hurazzi son of Ennaya" in which "Akkulenni shall give his sister Beltakkadummi as wife to Hurazzi." In other words, Beltakkadummi enjoyed the dual status of wife-sistership which endowed her with superior privileges and protection, over and above those of an ordinary wife. Accordingly, Sarna argues that Sarah and Rebekah were both holders of this wife-sister privilege, peculiar to the society from which they came and in which the legal aspects of their marriage were negotiated.

[3] For example, there is a Canaanite narrative of King Kertet who lost his "lovely spouse Hurrai," through whom he was supposed to be destined to carry on his line, and had to mount a military campaign to recover her. In Greek literature, there is Helen of Troy, who was twice kidnapped, once in her youth by Theseus and again after she married Menelaus. In fact, it was her abduction to Troy by Paris which caused the Trojan War. Another strikingly similar incident is the Egyptian "Tale of Two Brothers," in which Bata's beautiful second wife "mira-

culously" comes to the attention of Pharaoh, who has her hunted down and brought to his palace. There he makes love to her, even though he knows she is married. Comparatists note that it is reasonable to assume that similar sagas circulated about the matriarchs of Israel, and were collected and incorporated into the patriarchal narratives. Presumably, the uncommon beauty of the progenitrix of the people of Israel was a matter of national pride, as were also the comings and goings of the patriarchs at the courts of kings.

[4] Robert Polzin (1975), e.g., finds recurring messages in the three versions concerning adultery, wealth, progeny, and *God's blessing*. Samuel Sandmel (1961:110-111) and Klaus Koch (1969:123-5), bothered by the lacunae in Genesis 12 regarding Abraham's motivations, the purity of Sarah, *the role of God*, and the responsibility of the foreign king, claim that the authors of Gen 20:1-18 and 26:1-17 reinterpreted the original narrative and transformed it in the light of their particular interests. Similarly, Baruch Halpern (1983:62) claims that the variations in the three narratives represent deliberate distortions of puzzling or unacceptable texts. According to Halpern, Genesis 20 is an E variant of J picaresque episodes in Gen 12:10-20 and 26:6-11. In Gen 20:1-18 God is acquitted of savaging Abraham's innocent dupe (20:4-6; cf. 12:17). But more important, Abraham is defended (by appeal to literal, or what we might call technical grounds [20:12]) against the charge that he lied. Since the moral justification offered in all three versions (12:11-13; 20:11; 26:7) is regarded as insufficient to bear the weight of Abraham's lie, Halpern suggests that the author of Genesis 20 has consciously reworked his materials to expunge the potential blot from Abraham's character. In this instance, as has long been observed, a hagiographic bent determines the manner in which the author supplements his source.

[5] Rabbinic exegesis here offers a model, as suggested by the term *midrash* itself, taken from the root *d-r-sh*, "to study, to seek." The relation of rabbinic commentary to contemporary critical thinking has received much attention. See, e.g., Geoffrey Hartman and Sanford Budick (1986), and Susan Handelman (1982).

[6] Lynn Poland (1990), among others, discusses some of the difficulties involved in applying literary criticism to biblical texts (and the tensions which have developed in the academy as a result), particularly with regard to a unified "intention" on the part of the biblical writers.

[7] See, e.g., James Kugel's polemical reproach that literary methods ignore the Bible's religious character (1981:217-36); see also the reply by Adele Berlin (1982:323-327) and Kugel's response (1982: 328-332).

[8] Robert Polzin's seminal article (1975) discusses the primary relationship(s) of males and females as reflected in the patriarch/wife/foreign king stories in Genesis. Peter Miscall (1979) argues

for an extension of Polzin's study to include the Abigail/David and David/Bathsheba stories (1 Samuel 25 and 2 Samuel 11-12, respectively) on the basis of a more general view of the characters involved, and develops a series of five narratives which take the form of a moral treatise. In the cases which Miscall cites, however, sex is not necessarily uninvited by the woman, or at least not overtly resisted.

[9] Lot, e.g., offers to have his daughters raped by all the men of the city in order to spare the divine messengers, who are clearly capable of defending themselves. The vast majority of (male) commentators judge Lot as a righteous character while they dismiss the threatened sexual abuse of his daughters as "oriental hospitality." However, there are no indications from the Hebrew Bible that sexual abuse or other violence is condoned if done in the service of "hospitality" (see the introductory discussion of hospitality by Bruce J. Maline [1985: 408-9]).

[10] See Sharon Jeansonne's discussion of Hagar as a powerless woman (1990:43-52).

[11] See Phyllis Trible (1984:9-35) for a particularly lucid, yet disturbing reading of Judges 19-21.

[12] Paul Ricoeur (1970:573) calls this aspect of discourse analysis the wish for "recognition." Geoffrey Hartman (1975:37) refers to it as the wish for "presence," for a relationship.

[13] Recently the literary implications of narrative discourse have been developed. While earlier scholars talked about the meaning of particular symbols, now scholars are beginning to focus on the social and dialectical aspects of the symbol, as well as the implications of using a symbolic medium at all. (See, e.g., Anthony Wilden's comments [1975:230].)

[14] Ruth Bottigheimer (1987:52) discusses speech and silencing on four levels in a literary text: narrative, textual, lexical, and editorial. The character who is condemned or cursed to a period of silence experiences narrative silencing in the plot; the distribution of direct and indirect or reported speech offers the potential for silencing a character at the textual level; silencing may also grow out of verbs used to introduce direct or indirect speech (certain verbs validate the speech that follows, while other introductory verbs mark subsequent speech as illicit); and the author or editor may comment on the text within the text.

[15] The more usual word for "wife" is 'ishah. The expression $b^{e'}ulat\ ba'al$ is used rarely and when it is used, it is in negative situations. Deut 22:22, e.g., states that "if a man is found lying with a woman who is a $b^{e'}ulat\ ba'al$, they will die, the two of them." Similarly, Isa 54:1 states that "more are the sons of the desolate than of the $b^{e'}ûlah$." Here "sons-of-the-desolate," the chiasmas to the $b^{e'}ûlah$, is negative since the verb sh-m-m is often applied to land that is plundered, raped, and destroyed (see, e.g., Isa 49:8; Ezek 33:28), or when

used in the adjectival form in relation to people, connotes being destroyed by the enemy (in the "rape of Tamar" episode of 2 Samuel 13, Tamar remains *shomemah* in the house of her brother Absolam). Isa 62:4 also sets the *be'ûlah* in opposition to the "desolate."

[16] David Clines (1990:70) provides an interesting analysis of this situation. According to Clines, since Lot appears to be the only possible candidate for the fulfillment of the promise of progeny to Abraham, Sarah is disposable: "nothing hangs upon her continued survival."

[17] See, e.g., *harag* used to describe Cain's slaying of Abel (Gen 4:8), Esau's plan to murder his brother (Gen 27:41), and the mass slaying of the men of Shechem by Simeon and Levi (Gen 34:25-26).

[18] Susan Niditch (1987:57), e.g., contends that "the language of the account suggests that Abram relates to Sarai lovingly and implies that they *undertake the trick together*" (italics mine).

[19] The antagonist's scolding of the protagonist, "Why did you not tell me that she is your wife?" (Gen 12:18) expresses a clear attitude of opposition to sexual exploitation, an assumption that all people are subject to this ethical precept, even kings. Perhaps, however, only foreign kings are held to this level of morality, if the women-stealing tendencies of kings in 1 Samuel 8 and, more specifically, of David and Bathsheba are any indication. Certainly, in Genesis 12, a foreign monarch is shown to be more fastidious than the Judean patriarch.

[20] See also Gen 24:51, where Laban expresses similar exasperation when he tells the servant that Rebekah may go after his attempts to keep her have failed.

[21] Peter Miscall (1983:42) comments on Abraham's wealth and concludes that it was acquired improperly since it is not accompanied by the birth of a child and is therefore not a sign of blessing.

[22] One of the first scholars to make this observation was Peter Miscall (1983:32). See, in particular, the discussions by J. P. Fokkelman (1987:48) and David Clines (1990:75-77).

[23] This oath is also found in 1 Kgs 9:4; Ps 78:72; and 101:2.

[24] God's actions in these narratives are certainly difficult to reconcile. He punishes Pharaoh, Abimelech, and their houses, but not Abraham. In fact, immediately after the encounter with Abimelech, the LORD visits Sarah, and she bears Isaac (Gen 21:1-5). Perhaps the text is questioning the very notion of causality (see Paul de Man [1979] for a general discussion of the issue of causation as motive and intention).

[25] E. A. Speiser (1964:93) holds that Abraham's account that Sarah is his half-sister is part of Sarah's legitimate genealogical information. He concludes that "the ultimate purpose of biblical genealogies was to establish the superior strain of the line through which the biblical way of life was transmitted." Other scholars claim that Abraham is using the term "sister" as one of endearment, and note that such usage is common in early Eastern cultures (Songs 5:1, 2). Accord-

ing to Adin Steinsaltz (1984:22), the appellation "my sister" refers to the "chief-wife" as opposed to other, secondary wives. While it is true that Sarah comes from the same ancestral land as Abraham, no other information about her background is given by the narrator or any of the characters. Abraham's story that she is his half-sister is never verified and is, at the very least, suspect. It has often been noted that the remark presupposes a matrilineal system, for a man marrying the daughter of his father would avoid incest only on the assumption that the blood-line passes through the mother. See, e.g., Edwin Good (1981:95).

[26] See, e.g., Isa 3:12; 9:15; and Hos 4:11.

[27] Michael Riffaterre's term (1978).

PART II

BETWEEN GENESIS AND KINGS

4

STAYING THE NIGHT: INTERTEXTUALITY IN GENESIS AND JUDGES

DAVID PENCHANSKY

INTRODUCTION: DEFINITIONS OF INTERTEXTUALITY

Before beginning, I must define that elusive (and allusive) term, "intertextuality." Critics have isolated three distinct definitions, all concerning the exchange of information between separate and seemingly independent texts. This osmosis between discreet textual blocks occurs without regard to chronology; that is, exchanged information moves backwards and forwards in time.[1] It also occurs without regard to genesis; for example, the text credited as the source of others can and often is transformed through its contact with other, more derivative texts.

Derrida defines intertextuality as "the interweaving of different texts (literally 'webs') in an act of criticism that refuses to think of 'influence' or 'interrelationship' as simple historical phenomena" (Spivak 1976:lxxxiv).

The following three definitions, then, have to do with how widely one desires to define "text."

First Definition—The Literary Text

"Text" might be defined narrowly, as written and preserved material. "Intertextuality" would then be the relationship between juxtaposed literary texts. This relationship might find its source in the process by which the texts were formed. *More likely*, it originates in the mind of the interpreter who juxtaposes two or more disparate texts in a creative fashion.

Unfortunately, this form of intertextuality has limited many applications of the concept. In its least creative form this approach becomes a kind of cross-referencing, an elaborate index of repeated words, concepts and theological motifs.[2]

Second Definition—The Social Text

The definition of text, however, may be widened to include "the text of culture." The environment in which a literary text is produced provides a social "text" which is "read" by the author, and which interacts significantly with that author's work. Texts are shaped by the ideological climate, and in turn contribute to and shape that climate.[3] This too is intertextuality.

Third Definition—The Interpretive Text

Finally, the interpreter (in this case myself) and the audience (you and anyone else who might read this) interact with the text in new and creative ways. New insights and relationships spring up continually. This too is a significant and fruitful area for intertextual exploration.

The juxtaposition of other previously existing texts creates a *new product*. These three definitions taken together (there is much overlap in actual demonstrations) indicate that the object of examination is that textual production. This new text is a conflation of the others, and must be read, processed, and transformed into a story that includes elements of the various texts, but is in fact a new and fertile field for the interpretive process.[4]

FIRST DEFINITION: INTERTEXTUALITY OF THE LITERARY TEXTS

I have chosen three texts: Genesis 19, which speaks of Lot and the strangers in Sodom; Genesis 24, in which Abraham's servant travels to Haran, seeking a wife for his master's son; and Judges 19, which follows the travesty of the Levite and the unnamed woman identified as his concubine.[5] All three stories concern hospitality, a festive reception provided for the guest. All three deal with women who are powerless to order and direct their own lives.

All three, moreover, are marked by the repetitive use of the term *l-y-n*, "spend the night."[6] There is symbolic resonance in this word that makes it an appropriate key to the three passages. It is the sought-after social link between people, symbolized by the act of "staying the night." As a request, it is plaintive and pathetic; as a fact, it is a resolute sealing of fate between two distinct social worlds. Within this three-text complex, it is possible to isolate two distinct stories. The first is found in Genesis 19 and the second episode of Judges 19; and the second is found in Genesis 24 and the first episode of Judges 19. Judges 19 links the two stories into a single coherent narrative. One might even say that the story of the Levite and the unnamed woman is a conflation of the other two.[7]

The first story, in its nearly generic form, I will call "The Threatened Guest."[8] A man comes under the protection of a household in a foreign land. The host is also a newcomer. Citizens from the community want to rape the guest. The host refuses, and offers his virgin daughter or daughters to the crowd instead, which has no effect. The guest intervenes, taking the initiative, and protects both his own personal integrity and that of his host. The nature of that intervention will be crucial in all expressions of the story.

In the second story, which I will call "The Delayed Guest," a suitor arrives at the house of the proposed bride and makes arrangements to take away the woman to the house of the bridegroom.[9] The suitor is favorably received. The host continues to importune the guest to stay, although the guest has communicated his desire to depart. The results vary and are the key to the intertextual link. In Judges the Levite remains with disastrous results; in Genesis 24 the servant of Abraham leaves and things go well for his mission.

Of course, what interests us are not the points of commonality between the two stories, or the uses of each story, but rather how the subtle and not-so-subtle variations indicate the tension or ideological struggle that occurs at the junctures of the juxtaposition.

"The Threatened Guest" appears in a similar fashion in Genesis 24 and the second episode of Judges 19, but differs in the following ways:

1. Whereas the two strangers or angels remain aloof from Lot and seem reluctant to accept his hospitality, the Levite and the old man from Ephraim participate in a sincere, deep-hearted mutual exchange of obligation. Phyllis Trible (1984:72) even suggests that the Levite gives the unnamed woman as a gift to his host.

2. The attempts of neither host to sacrifice his daughter was accepted. The two angels in Genesis 19, however, protected the women and the host by blinding the crowd. The Levite, by contrast, protected the host by offering the unnamed woman to the crowds.

3. Both cities (Sodom and Gibeah) are destroyed; but in Genesis, Lot and his daughters escape, while in Judges the unnamed woman dies.

"The Delayed Guest" also contains significant variations in its two expressions in Genesis 24 and the first episode of Judges 19:

1. In Genesis, Rebekah is consulted about the time of departure; the unnamed woman in Judges is not consulted.

2. In Genesis, Abraham's servant refuses the extended offer of celebration, whereas the Levite feasts for five days.

3. In the Genesis account, all parties prosper, and Abraham's son is granted a prudent wife. In Judges, however, the delay results in brutal gang rape and mutilation of the unnamed woman, the near destruction of an entire tribe in internecine warfare, and kidnap and forced mass marriage.

A pattern emerges when I examine these three texts in juxtaposition. The protagonists fare poorly in the Judges tale when compared to the dramatic deliverance in both Genesis stories. Whether through the Levite's lack of persistence to continue on his important mission, or through God's disinclination to save, the main characters in the Judges account do not do well. The disastrously negative outcome of the Judges narrative points to an important societal critique. It says, "We are not as good as our ancestors." A retelling of the same story ("The Threatened Guest") results in dissimilar outcomes, because the Israelite societal structure has broken down. The time of the Judges is inferior to that of the ancestors and, by extension, the time of the writing of this tale is inferior to some golden age in Israel's distant past.[10]

SECOND DEFINITION: INTERTEXTUALITY AND THE SOCIAL TEXT

The second intertextual interpretation occurs when the three juxtaposed texts are in turn juxtaposed with this "text" of Israelite society. It is difficult to demonstrate conclusively the exact nature of Israelite society at the time or times when these accounts were written. Our primary source for information about this society is the texts under examination.

The three texts taken together comment on Israelite societal attitudes towards gender roles; they reflect female victimization by males, and males bonding in friendship to other males. The structure of the story of "The Threatened Guest" (Genesis 19 and the second episode of Judges 19) places women at the margins of Israelite society—they are objects of barter, means by which the male (important) members of society can remain secure and proud.[11] Genesis 19 breaks this pattern in that the two angels intervene to preserve the integrity and perhaps the lives of Lot's daughters. In contrast, the Levite and his host in Judges engage in an elaborate friendship ritual, each trying to achieve a greater sacrifice than the other:[12] "Take my daughter."[13] "On the contrary, my friend, take my woman, I insist." In this ritualized relationship, women are seen as cultic objects, the means of exchange.[14]

When the Levite condemns the unnamed woman, he only heightens the sense of chivalry and generosity on the men's part. The Levite "wins" the ritual conflict of hospitality. The unnamed woman is tortured and subsequently dies. There were no "angels" to strike the crowd with blindness. Even more, we are horrified by the command of the Levite to her broken body: "Get up. Let's go." This is more horrible even than her subsequent dismemberment.

In life the women are parcelled out, bartered and sold.[15] In death, the unnamed woman (called concubine, defined only in relationship to her husband) is cut up like Saul's oxen. This suggests different avenues of intertextuality. She is cut up as a sign of ritual offense against the honor of the Levite.

"The Threatened Guest" in Genesis 19 raises the same issues of male bonding. Lot assumes a bond of hospitality between his house and the two visitors. He would sacrifice everything, probably his life if necessary, to fulfill the obligation to his guests. He is enmeshed in a cultic web that proscribes his every choice and behavior. He would oppose the whole town, in which he too was a *ger*. He would offer his virgin daughters. The women here too are objects, neither consulted nor protected.[16]

Lot's attempt to assume the ritualized patterns of male friendship and hospitality are less successful. The angels reject Lot's offer of ritualistic male bonding, instead opting for more humanistic and individual valuation. They intervene and preserve the lives of the women, albeit as members of society who possess inferior social status.

"The Delayed Guest" in Genesis 24 and the first episode of Judges 19 works similarly. Here, as in the Lot story, the male bonding is rejected, first by the refusal to "stay the night," and second because Rebekah is consulted.[17] As a result, the mission is successful and all concerned prosper.

What takes place in Judges 19, however, is not a model of hospitality, as many insist,[18] but rather a parody of ideal home-welcoming and treatment of strangers. The father-in-law, for purposes unknown, uses the formula of hospitality to manipulate the Levite, to prey upon his weakness and his lack of resolve. This contrasts dramatically to the determined resistance to the *same* manipulation in Genesis 24, and this time the one resisting is merely a servant, a representative of another's interests. The consequences of giving in to such manipulation are severe, and they follow inevitably in a string of divine causality.[19]

Although the male participants in the Judges narrative act inhumanely in their relations with women, the narrative tone of the story constitutes an attack on male social structure. The text generates a sympathetic reaction to the death of the unnamed woman.[20] What must these texts have assumed regarding the underlying social codes, texts, and previously constituted restraints? How were they heard? What audience did they reach, and what reactions did they generate?[21]

Who spoke thus? What is the ideological conflict that would have produced these texts, texts that castigate Israelite men for their treatment of women, and disparage the ancient and sacred rites of male bonding and hospitality? There are several possibilities.

First, one might see a deliberately feminist impulse in these texts, an attempt to show the mistreatment of women in a bad light, for purposes of societal change or liberation.

On the other hand, one might see these texts as antifeminist, reflecting a general misogynistic polemic. The Levite is a sympathetic figure, and the wrongs inflicted upon the women are accepted by the readers in its ancient context.

Finally, one might see the entire feminine issue as irrelevant to the text. Ultimately, it is immaterial that it was a woman who died; the text was really about the tribal conflict, and the Levite's behavior was never questioned. This too seems to be a misogynistic sentiment. Attention is drawn to the woman, and especially to the political aspects of her social existence as a woman, rendering it doubtful that any other part of the story can draw us away from that. To read the text without regard to the theme of female oppression is necessarily a misogynistic response to the story. Silence in the face of abuse, even literary abuse, is a kind of complicity.

The validity of a feminist reading will be explored, examining the idea of a social critique of male bonding over the female sacrificial victim. It would seem that scholarship has not yet made an adequate accounting of the presence of some radically feminist perspectives within the Hebrew Bible. We have noticed them, appreciated them, but have failed to generate an account of what sort of groups might have produced them.[22] One must engage in speculative and imaginative effort to reconstruct what might have been the social "text" that is suggested by these juxtaposed stories. For instance:

Once there was a woman secretly harboring sympathies for the goddess, perhaps Asherah. She is of a literary bent, being from the group in Israel, teachers probably, who educated their women. At school she became acquainted with Asherah's cult, although many of her classmates disapproved, believing that Yahweh needed no appropriate consort, being complete in himself.

She wrote for a wider audience, the wealthy nobility in Jerusalem, and the guilds of priests and Levites who travelled the country. She created her works intuitively, but necessarily in outward conformity with the official Yahwistic cultus in Jerusalem.

Her work pictured powerless women in a sympathetic light, and highlighted clever ones who could overcome their social role through wit and resourcefulness. What she wrote struck a sympathetic chord in her audience, gaining for herself an anonymous notoriety in literate Israel. Her work was incorporated by the priests, reluctantly perhaps, into their official collections of sacred writings.

Or we might construe these texts as the literature of a feminist intelligentsia. This was their literature. These were their texts, their stories, in which patterns were mixed with legends of the matriarchy, Miriam, Sarah, Rebekah, Leah, Hagar. These stories gave them the courage to live marginally, in a fashion resembling the witches in New England. A literature that would reflect a society that worships the goddess would have innate respect for the female characters, but societal constraints would require a formal assent to the structures of orthodox patriarchal Yahwism. Although the texts do contain an attack on misogynistic practices, they function rhetorically to provide a sympathetic point of view from the perspective of the female character.

Here is another possibility: only men wrote literature at that time. They were the only official and literate storytellers too; what the women spoke about and passed along among themselves will forever remain in obscurity, depending as it did on marginal and therefore unpreserved media.

The author of these stories, from this view, wrote in an attempt to render characters that lived. In aspiration he markedly resembled a modern author in this way. This led him to a sympathetic portrayal of women, and he offered a silent protest against societal inequities. His desire for verisimilitude (which requires empathy) led to sympathy for women and sensitivity to their plight. These stories of human sympathies were preserved.

But I must confess that none of these answers seem satisfactory. They all have serious flaws and lack any strong textual or artifactual support.

THIRD DEFINITION: THE INTERPRETIVE TEXT

The third understanding of intertextuality requires us to take into account our own participation in the act of interpretation, as we produce a new text every time we process old information. This form of intertextual reading is most difficult—like trying to see your eyes without a mirror.

It is odd that these readings reflect many of the current ideological concerns of our guild. Perhaps the nature of these texts is totally unavailable to us, and all that we have are our own ideological concerns. Perhaps I take every text and compel it to reflect my politics by highlighting certain characters and scenes. We might then say, "thus are all texts to all interpreters, and we necessarily work within that reality." Or this process might contain a negative connotation—a dishonest imposition on alien material, the interpretive work of an oppressive ideology, that is, mine.

These observations cause us to doubt that our readings are more than just reflections of our ideological biases. One is led to doubt the whole process of interpretation as a result. Must we reconcile ourselves to an inevitable mystery, that we will never know exactly what it is we look at? Or is this a challenge to more serious and focused exploration?

I affirm the feminist critique, but question giving it a warrant in the juxtaposed texts, as if I were describing something that exists outside of myself and my own concerns. And yet I fight for this reading.[23]

I don't know. The intertextual discourse has disarmed me, and undercut my confidence in my ability to read a text, or by extension, to change society. That we in the guild continue to do both is a tribute to our tenacity, or our stupidity, or both.

NOTES

[1] T. S. Eliot (1964 [1919]:5) writes, "what happens when a new work of art is created is something that happens simultaneously to all the works of art which preceded it. The existing monuments form an ideal order among themselves, which is modified by the introduction of the new . . . work of art among them. The existing order is complete before the new work arrives; for order to persist after the supervention of novelty, the *whole* existing order must be, if ever so slightly, altered."

[2] Culler (1981:108) notes of this definition: "Intertextuality is the family archive—when one explores it, one stays wholly within the traditional canon of major poets."

[3] Culler (1981:103, 108) notes how intertextuality may "designate . . . its participation in the discursive space of a culture." He quotes Kristeva, "Every text is from the outset under the jurisdiction of other discourses which impose a universe upon it."

[4] Although at times I seem to be discussing the texts individually in what follows, without regard for the others, in fact I am dealing with a conflated story that irregularly moves among the others, lighting first in this one, then another.

[5] I appreciate Phyllis Trible's effort (1984) to identify the woman using terms not related to her obligation to the Levite. I will not refer to her as "the concubine," but rather as the unnamed woman.

[6] In Genesis 19, Lot asks the strangers to spend the night. They refuse, saying, "we will spend the night on the street" (two occurrences of *l-y-n*). In Genesis 24, Abraham and his servant spend the night with Laban (one occurrence). In Judges 19, the father asks the Levite "be pleased to spend the night." On the fifth day, the Levite refuses to spend the night (two occurrences). In the second part of Judges 19, the Levite and the concubine spend the night in Gibeah. No man took them into his house to spend the night. The old man entreats them not

to spend the night in the square (three occurrences).

⁷ For the debate concerning the temporal priority of one or the other of the stories, see Niditch (1982) and Lasine (1984).

⁸ By generic, I mean a form of the story that combines, as much as possible, the features of the other two.

⁹ There is a similar motif in Book V of the Odyssey. Calypso wishes to keep Odysseus from leaving her on her island. The Goddess Athena intervenes at the very beginning of Book V, and says the following to Zeus: "He is pent up in an island now, overwhelmed with misery, he is in the domain of the nymph Calypso, who is keeping him with her there perforce and thwarting his return to his own country." Only after Hermes is sent to Calypso by Zeus does she relent and allow Odysseus to build himself a raft. It is his journey on this raft that starts Odysseus off on the adventures for which the book is famous. Odysseus is detained in several other spots as well—the whole journey homeward requires him to extricate himself from the snares set by various hosts. He himself then must punish the guests at his own home who have abused him as their absent host when he finally returns. (I am grateful to Dr. Michael Jordan, English Department, University of St. Thomas, for pointing out this analogy.) See also Tobit 8:19-10:12.

¹⁰ History-like texts (and perhaps all texts) contain a societal comment, a perspective on the time they were written.

¹¹ I assume here that Judges 19 reflects the truer pattern of "The Threatened Guest." The opposite might be true, but I doubt it. Judges 19 breaks rather than affirms social bonds, which makes it less conventional. This is not to say that Matthews (1991; 1992) is incorrect in noting the social violations in the Judges 19 story. Rather, the surface scrupulosity in Judges masks a totally compromised and corrupt procedure at its heart. This is exactly the point.

¹² Note Trible's allusions (1984) to the unnamed woman as a sacrificial victim who dies for the sins of others.

¹³ The old man from Ephraim also offers the unnamed woman, either because she is also his possession at this point (Trible) or because in the explosive tension of that moment, he felt he must secure the safety of the Levite at any cost, and so presumed to sacrifice the Levite's "property" as well.

¹⁴ These friendship rituals (aside from having a practical value) keep the chaos at bay, and as such qualify as a ritualistic/cultic act. The objects of exchange between friends (that is, the women) therefore become cultic objects.

¹⁵ By "women," I refer to the unnamed woman, the daughter of the old man, and Lot's daughters, all unnamed.

¹⁶ The preservation of the daughters is an afterthought; the narrative emphasis rests more fully on the strangers' miraculous powers and not female salvation.

¹⁷ Rebekah is consulted not by the guest but rather by the

family. In this passage, obligation to females is acknowledged by all male parties. In the Judges passage, neither the father nor the Levite think to consult the unnamed woman.

[18] E.g., Niditch (1982), Matthews (1991; 1992).

[19] What is the reason for this attempt at delay? Perhaps the father/brother extends the welcome because of his love and emotional attachment to his daughter. This is unlikely; it is easy to imagine Rebekah's brother or the unnamed woman's father sacrificing either of them to a hungry crowd, as did the old man and the Levite. Or perhaps the attempted delay is an attempt to get something from the guest—a final bribe of some sort. There also remains the possibility that the host tries to keep the visitor because of friendliness and a general desire to share the bountiful blessings of Yahweh. Or perhaps his effort is an attempt to gain time to evaluate the suitor and see if he is still good enough for his daughter/sister. If so, the unnamed woman's father is a dreadful judge of character. One last reason for the delay might allow for an oddity of bedouin hospitality, which regards as awkward any attempt to take your leave of the host's compound (see Zeid 1965:245-59). But traditions of hospitality are meant to grease social contacts and not to increase friction. It is likely that the ancient reader would feel some discomfort at the cloying refusal to let go on the part of the two hosts in "The Delayed Guest." It is interesting to compare this with our delight at Abraham's persistence with Yahweh in an effort to save Sodom.

[20] Violent death does not intrinsically produce a sympathetic reaction towards the victim. Witness the graphic description of the death of King Eglon of Moab, a decidedly unsympathetic figure.

[21] The texts portray social customs in scrupulous detail. Did the acts of the male protagonist seem appropriate to the original reader? Would a host commonly insist on a longer stay? Was it a social gaffe for a guest to insist on an early departure? Would the original audience be horrified at the offer of one's virgin daughter to a violent crowd? Would the guest be expected to make a counter offer? Much depends on whether or not we assume the original audience reacted with horror to these events (as we would).

[22] Carol Meyers (1988) has endeavored to show that women in the ancient world (particularly Israel) possessed avenues of power that are not readily apparent in an examination of the normal social power structures. Harold Bloom, in a highly speculative monograph (1990), suggests that a woman was largely responsible for the Yahwist material. He fails, however, to account for how such a woman would have gained the skills, support, and audience for such a work.

[23] How it would come out in other texts is a subject for further study.

5

STRANGE HOUSEGUESTS: RAHAB, LOT, AND THE DYNAMICS OF DELIVERANCE

L. DANIEL HAWK

The stories of Lot (Gen 19:1-29) and Rahab (Josh 2:1-24; 6:22-25) both relate escapes from doomed cities. The first story tells how Lot, the nephew of Abraham, escapes from the city of Sodom before the city is destroyed by the fire of Yahweh. The second relates the story of Rahab, a Canaanite who exacts an oath from two Israelite spies and thus escapes the slaughter visited upon the inhabitants of Jericho. On the surface, the two stories seem to have little else in common. Lot's story is set against the backdrop of judgment on wicked cities, administered by two divinely-appointed messengers. Rahab's story is connected to the account of an Israelite military campaign and employs a motif common in folktales; a resourceful woman saves her family through cunning and opportunism.[1]

A careful comparison, however, indicates a striking concurrence in vocabulary between these stories, a feature first noted by F. Langlamet (1971) in the course of a compositional analysis. In each of these texts, for example, there are references to the men of the city, to knowing and not knowing, and to the demonstration of mercy. There are also parallel imperatives: a demand to "bring out the men" who have come to the city and a command to flee to the hills (Langlamet 1971:180-83).[2] A large percentage of the lexical parallels occur at relatively the same points within each of the stories—an indication of correspondence in structure and theme as well.

The stories also employ a common plot sequence, which comprises five episodes. The common story line begins when two men enter a city doomed to destruction and take shelter in the house of a citizen of the city (Gen 19:1-3; Josh 2:1). The second scene in both stories occurs later in the evening, when men of the city come to the house and demand that the strangers be brought out (Gen 19:4-11; Josh 2:2-7). The crisis is averted when the men are effectively repulsed. The common story then moves to dialogue as the characters discuss the imminent destruction of the city and make arrangements for the salvation of the host and his or her family (Gen 19:13-14; Josh 2:8-14). Another section of dialogue follows and is set within the context of an escape from the city (Gen 19:15-22; Josh 2:15-23). In this case, the dialogue involves a protest against the initial arrangements and a successful attempt to modify them. The final scene reports the destruction of the city, as well as the deliverance of the host and family at the hands of the two men (Gen 2:22-29; Josh 6:15-25).

The lexical parallels and common story line are not necessarily indications that each story represents a divergence from a single source. Rather, Joshua *appropriates* elements of the story of Lot to tell the story of Rahab; the story of Rahab's deliverance from Jericho is rendered after the pattern of Lot's rescue from Sodom. In the process, a significant transformation takes place. Although the *roles* of the characters in both stories coincide—the two Israelite spies correspond to the two angels of Genesis 19, while Rahab corresponds to Lot—the *traits* of the characters are reversed. The characters in Joshua thereby take on surprising and unconventional attributes. The spies exhibit Lot's traits—passivity, fluctuation, and impotence—while Rahab takes on the characteristics of the angels—initiative, urgency, and command.

The transformation is evident from the beginning. In the Genesis story, two angels meet Lot at the gate of the city, express their intention to spend the night in the town plaza (*rahob*), but then accept Lot's hospitality. The Joshua story begins with the report that two spies are sent by Joshua to reconnoiter Jericho and go to the house of a woman, a prostitute named Rahab (*rahab*). In both cases, the two visitors are seemingly diverted from their initial course of action. While this diversion will lead to a happy outcome in Genesis—the deliverance of Lot and his family—the diversion in Joshua foreshadows trouble. Rahab represents the temptations of Canaan; the Law of Moses repeatedly warns of the seductive power of the women of Canaan, who "prostitute themselves to their gods and will make your sons also prostitute themselves to their gods" (Exod 34:16b; cf. Deut 7:3-4; 31:16-18). The narrator's report that the spies "come to" (*bo'*) Rahab's house and "lie there" (*shakab*) suggests seduction; both terms are common signifiers for sexual intercourse.[3] The matter-of-fact report of Joshua's narrator therefore effectively injects a note of impropriety at the very beginning of the story.[4]

The sexual overtones become more pronounced as the stories move into the second scene. In Genesis, the men of the city surround the house and shout a demand to Lot (vs. 5).

> They called to Lot and said to him, "Where are the men who came to you tonight? Bring them to us that we may know them."

A similar demand is made by the king's men in Joshua 2, who come to Rahab's house by night seeking the Israelites (vs. 3b).

> Bring out the men who have come to you, who have come to your house, because they have come to spy out the entire country.

Lot's response to the Sodomites is feeble and fearful. He pleads with the lawless mob to refrain from harming those who have taken shelter under his roof and attempts to mollify the men by offering them his daughters, "who have not known a man" (Gen 19:18). Rahab, in the presence of the representatives of the law, offers a more confident response. She has hidden her guests on top of her roof and also speaks of "not knowing" (vss. 4b-5a).

> Yes, the men came to me, but I did not know where they came from. When the gate was shut for the night, they left. I do not know where the men went.

The declarations are meant to deceive, but they are also ironic. Rahab does, after all, "know" men. Yet her claim of "not knowing" accomplishes what the "not knowing" of Lot's daughters cannot. Lot's offer of his daughters seems only to enrage the crowd of men surrounding his house. He must finally be saved by his guests, who strike the mob with blindness. Rahab, however, can take care of herself. With a string of imperatives, she exhorts the king's men to pursue the spies before it is too late. The men quickly leave on a search as futile as that of the Sodomites, who blindly grope for the door (vs. 7; cf. Gen 19:11). The door slams shut on the men of Sodom; the gate slams shut on the king's men.

The third scene consists primarily of dialogue, as deliverance from the imminent cataclysm is negotiated. The angels speak to Lot with a sense of urgency, exhorting him to gather his family and informing him that they are about to destroy the city. Lot does as he is told but is not able to gather his entire family together; his sons-in-law do not take him seriously (Gen 19:14).

The corresponding scene in Jericho represents a significant reversal. Here Rahab, not the two spies, speaks with urgency and dictates the course of action and conversation. The spies mirror the passivity of Lot; after the king's men depart, they once again prepare to "lie down" (vs. 8a). Rahab, however, realizes that the spies are in a predicament and recognizes her opportunity to gain deliverance. She, not the spies, speaks of approaching doom, couching her declarations in the language of praise to Israel's God (vss. 9b-11).[5]

> I know that Yahweh has given you the land and that your terror has fallen on us; all the inhabitants of the land have despaired because of you. We have heard how Yahweh dried up the waters of the Red Sea before you when you came out of Egypt and what you did to the two kings of the Amorite on the other side of the Jordan—Sihon and Og, whom you put under the ban. We heard and our hearts melted, and everyone lost their nerve because of you, for Yahweh your god is God in the sky above and the earth below.

One might have expected such words from the spies, who are familiar with Yahweh's promises to dispossess the inhabitants of Canaan. From the mouth of an accursed and "terror-stricken" Canaanite, however, the words are strange and discordant.

The words of acclamation are a prologue. Shifting from declaratives to imperatives, Rahab presses her advantage. Reminding the spies that she has just delivered them, she demands a response in kind (vss. 12-13).

> And now, swear to me by Yahweh, because I have shown mercy to you, that you will show mercy to the house of my father, that you will give me a sign of truth, that you will spare my father, my mother, my brother, my sister, and all those with them, and that you will deliver us from death.

The spies are quick to catch the implications of Rahab's words; her "mercy" may quickly vanish if her demands are not met. They immediately agree to the arrangement (vs. 14).

> The men said to her, "Our lives in place of yours to the death! If you do not divulge this situation, then, when Yahweh gives us the land, we will be loyal and faithful to you."

Unlike Rahab, the spies utter no acclamations of praise or faith. They seem concerned only about saving their lives.

The contrast against Lot and the angels is striking. Here the *visitors* require deliverance. They must depend on the graciousness of their hostess and passively accept the terms offered. The hostess effectively dispels the threat to the spies, making possible their escape from the city, and subsequently dictates the terms of her own salvation.

In the process of escaping the city, another dialogue takes place. This time the conversation involves an attempt to modify the program of deliverance. Lot, having been unsuccessful in gathering his entire family, is warned to leave the city immediately. He is so hesitant, however, that he must virtually be dragged from Sodom, along with his wife and two daughters. The narration moves at a compelling pace. The angels issue a series of four imperatives, directing Lot and his family to flee to the hills with all haste (Gen 19:17b).

> Flee for your life! Do not look behind you. Do not stop anywhere in this region. Flee to the hills so that you will not be consumed!

These commands meet with more resistance. Instead of heeding the directives, Lot pleads with the angels to allow him to stay in the plain and requests that he be permitted to flee to one of the surrounding villages. The angels comply with his request and reiterate the command to flee.

The Israelite spies in Joshua also attempt to modify the conditions of deliverance and seem to do so in the process of escaping the city. The escape is facilitated by Rahab, who lowers the spies out her window and down the city wall. As her guests dangle from a rope, Rahab directs them to flee to the hills (vss. 15-16).

> She lowered them through the window with a rope, because her house was in the city wall and she lived in the wall. She said to them, "Go to the hill country so those who are pursuing you won't overtake you. Hide there for three days until those who are looking for you return. After that, you can go on your way."

Like Lot the spies protest and attempt to revise the terms of deliverance, placing additional restrictions on the oath they have made: a scarlet cord must be tied to the window and all family members must stay within the house (vss. 17-20).[6]

> The men said to her, "We are innocent of this, your oath, which you made us swear! Look, we are coming into the land. Tie this scarlet thread in the window from which you lowered us. Gather your father, mother, brother, and all the house of your father to yourself in the house. Anyone who goes out from the doors of your house, their blood will be on their head. We will not be obligated. Also, if you divulge this business of ours we will not be obligated to your oath which you made us swear."

Lot's protest is a manifestation of fear, reluctance, and doubt. For some reason he is unwilling to trust the angels' assurance that he will be safer in the hills than in one of the villages on the plain (Gen 19:18-20). The protest made by the Israelite spies is of a different nature. Now outside the city, they evidently realize that the agreement they have made with Rahab represents a serious infraction of the divine directives for dealing with the inhabitants of Canaan; the Law of Moses permits no exemptions from the ban where the Canaanites are concerned (Deut 7:1-6; Exod 34:15). The added provisions sharpen the terms of the agreement so that it will be more difficult to honor, while the protests are a disavowal of responsibility for the oath. Three times the spies declare their innocence (*naqi*; vss. 17, 19, 20). The agreement is, they assert, "your oath which you made us swear" (vss. 17, 20), as if the oath could be nullified by the claim that is was made under duress. "This was not our fault," they seem to say. "This is *Rahab's* oath, and she made us swear to it."

Both stories conclude with a description of the destruction of the city and a final reference to those who have escaped. The destruction of Sodom is related from two perspectives. First, on the plain, Lot's wife turns back to view the rain of sulfur and fire and turns to salt. Second, from a distance, Abraham sees the smoke of the cities ascend to heaven. The reference to Abraham is significant. Lot's relationship to Abraham is what has saved him: "God remembered Abraham and sent Lot out of the midst of the catastrophe" (vs. 29).

The end of Rahab's story is delayed by three chapters of intervening material and is not related until Joshua 6. Jericho, too, is utterly destroyed (although in this case the Israelites do the killing). But before the city is put to the torch, Joshua reminds the two spies of the oath made to Rahab. He directs them to fetch her and her family and "lead them to rest" (*yannihum*) outside the Israelite camp (vs. 23), just as Lot and his family are "led to rest" (*yannihuhu*; Gen 19:16) outside the city. Unlike Lot, however, Rahab escapes with her household intact; her entire family leaves the city with her.

As with Lot, Rahab's story concludes with an explanation for her deliverance. She is spared because "she hid the messengers [*mal'akim!*] that Joshua had sent to reconnoiter Jericho" (vs. 25). Only here are the spies denoted by the term *mal'akim*, the same term used to denote the two visitors to Sodom (Gen 19:1). Perhaps this is the narrator's last nod to the story of Lot.[7]

The story of Lot's rescue from Sodom overlays Rahab's story, thereby placing the latter against a dark and threatening backdrop. By evoking the story of Lot at every point in the story of Rahab, the narrator elicits the mood of wickedness and impropriety that characterizes the former episode. The Israelite spies are "seduced" by a Canaanite prostitute and commit a serious violation of Yahweh's commandments—hardly an auspicious beginning for a campaign of conquest. The allusions to Lot's story increase the sense that something very wrong is happening at Jericho, despite Israel's subsequent success.[8]

On the other hand, the bringing together of the two stories also elicits a significant challenge to exclusivistic notions of salvation. By transforming key elements of Lot's story, the narrator transforms the common theme of deliverance. Like Lot, the Israelite spies are passive and powerless. Unlike Lot, Rahab aggressively negotiates her own salvation by saving others, and thereby effectively rescues her family. Who is more worthy of salvation, these Israelite spies whose memory of things Yahwistic is short, or this prostitute who acclaims the works of Yahweh and attains salvation for herself and her family? Who is more worthy of salvation, the passive and reluctant Lot, who is spared because of his genetic relationship to Abraham, or this Canaanite woman who seizes her opportunity to survive and claims her place in the promised land? What determines deliverance or doom?

NOTES

[1] See particularly Zakovitch's reading (1990), which sees a combination of two kinds of stories in Josh 2: a "spy story" and the story-type of "the woman who rescues the man."

[2] Langlamet provides a catalogue of seventeen lexical correspondences between Genesis 19 and Joshua 2, and fourteen correspondences between Joshua 2 and Joshua 6. He concludes that the lexical parallels demonstrate that the texts are the work of the same author, the Yahwist.

[3] For other instances of *bo'* see Gen 6:4; 16:2; 30:3; 38:8-9; Deut 22:13; 1 Sam 12:24; 16:21; Ezek 23:44; Prov 6:29. For *shakab* see

Gen 34:7; 39:7,10,12; Exod 22:16; Num 5:13; Deut 22:23; 28:30; 2 Sam 12:11.

[4] The act of sending the spies is itself rather ominous. A previous mission of spies into the land resulted in disaster (Num 14:1-25; Deut 1:19-40). Furthermore, the spies are sent from Shittim, the place where Israelite men "prostituted themselves" with the women of Moab and worshiped the Baal of Peor (Num 25:1-5).

[5] Rahab, remarkably, articulates the words of Moses. Her opening words allude to a relevant section of the "Song of Moses" (Exod 15:1-18).

> Your terror has fallen on us and all the inhabitants of the land have despaired because of you. (Josh 2:9)

> All the inhabitants of Canaan will despair.
> Upon them will fall your terror and dread. (Exod 15:15b-16a)

Her closing acclamation, moreover, recalls an exhortation of Moses.

> For Yahweh your god is God in the sky above and the earth below. (Josh 2:11b)

> Acknowledge today and take to your heart that Yahweh is God in the sky above and the earth below. There is no other. (Deut 4:39)

[6] The significance of the scarlet cord has occasioned much discussion. And yet, it may signify nothing more than a coded signal to the spies. The cord (*tiqwat*) is a sign of Rahab's waiting or hope (*tiqwat*). And it is scarlet (*shani*) because it is a signal to the two (*shney*) men who have made the oath.

[7] It is worth noting that the stories of Rahab and Lot both conclude with etiological remarks. The story of Rahab ends with the note that Rahab "lives among the Israelites to this day" (Josh 6:25). The story of Lot ends with a final episode in which "Moab" and "Ammon" are begotten from incestous relations with his daughters. The narrator's concluding remarks here correspond to those of the narrator in Joshua: Moab "is the father of Moab to this day" (Gen 19:37) and Ben-ammi "is the father of the Ammonites to this day" (Gen 19:38). Thus both stories conclude with references to the continuing existence of the descendants of the "host character."

[8] This text has received a positive reading by virtually all commentators. The readings generally ignore or downplay the transgression that the oath represents and focus instead on the faith of Rahab or her acclamations of praise to Yahweh. Thus the story is often regarded as a text that introduces the affirmations of holy war. See particularly the discussions in Butler (1983:25-35), McCarthy (1971: 165-75), and Tucker (1972:66-86).

6

TAKING WOMEN IN SAMUEL: READERS/RESPONSES/RESPONSIBILITY

TOD LINAFELT

It is now a commonplace observation that interpreters are giving less attention to the practices of historical criticism, and more to literary (and even deconstructive) reading strategies.[1] Following the insights of literary theorists such as Wolfgang Iser (1980:50), who writes that "the convergence of text and reader brings the literary work into existence," biblical scholars have begun to see the important role played by the reader in the production of meaning. With meaning no longer perceived as an objective entity to be extracted from the text, biblical interpreters must now engage in more self-critical and ethically responsible readings.

It is this state of affairs that prompts Elisabeth Schüssler Fiorenza (1988:3-17) to call for an "ethics of accountability" in biblical interpretation. Schüssler Fiorenza argues for a critical stance that "engages biblical scholarship in a hermeneutic-evaluative discursive practice exploring the power/knowledge relations inscribed in contemporary biblical discourse and in the texts themselves." While this call has been answered by a number of scholars on a theoretical level (e.g., Beardslee 1990; Fowl 1990), there remains a dearth of biblical readings that take seriously this ethics of accountability.[2]

This study of the Samuel narrative (with a special focus on 2 Samuel 12) is in part a response to Schüssler Fiorenza's trenchant analysis of the state of biblical studies. By examining an often-ignored theme, the taking of women as a sign of male power, I hope to unmask the pervasive androcentric ideological commitment in the texts themselves. Then, by critically evaluating some of the dominant readings of this narrative, particularly with regard to the character of YHWH, I hope to unmask the androcentric ideological investment of contemporary biblical discourse.

As some feminist interpreters have observed, however, the Bible often "makes provision for its own critique" (Fewell 1990:300).[3] And so I will attempt to move beyond simply deconstructing other voices. By taking an intertextual approach to the narrative, I will offer alternative ways of theological counter-reading that I hope are more ideologically aware and ethically responsible.

TAKING WOMEN IN THE EXTENDED SAMUEL NARRATIVE

Throughout the larger narrative of the books of Samuel, David is presented as a man who "takes" in order to establish his power. Often it is women, presented as the possessions of other men, who are taken in this rise to power. We may see this by tracing the theme throughout the larger Samuel narrative, with special attention to the Hebrew word *laqah*, or "take," as it occurs in relation to women.

In 1 Samuel 25 we find the story of Abigail. When Nabal, Abigail's husband, refuses to give David the supplies he demands, David determines to kill Nabal and take what he wants. He is stopped by Abigail, who brings a large peace offering and convinces David not to kill Nabal, thereby saving David from bloodguilt. Here our key word shows up, as David "takes" (*laqah*) from Abigail's hand what she has brought him (25:35). As both Gunn (1980:100-101) and Miscall (1986:152) have noted, what Abigail brings for David to "take" is an offer of her hand in marriage. There is no cause, moreover, to read into this offer any great love for David on Abigail's part. Her shrewd address to David indicates that she knows how power works in an androcentric world. Like it or not, she will be taken, and she might as well prepare as best she can for survival. The story ends with an approving YHWH smiting Nabal on behalf of David, and David sending messengers to "take" (*laqah*) Abigail as his wife.

1 Samuel 25:43 reports that, in addition to Abigail, David also "took" (*laqah*) Ahinoam of Jezreel, and that "both of them

became his wives." David's power is indeed growing. He has been able to take two women as wives in the space of 1 chapter, effectively connecting himself to both northern and southern power bases. But David's power is not yet absolute. For as the narrator reminds us in the last verse (44), "Saul had given Michal his daughter, David's wife, to Palti the son of Laish." We begin to see the complex role that women play in this power struggle between Saul and David. David is growing stronger, as evidenced by his "taking" of Abigail and Ahinoam. Yet Saul still sits on the throne for now, as evidenced by his power to "give" Michal, David's wife, to another.

The mention of Michal calls to mind 1 Samuel 18, where the control of women is integral to the struggle between Saul and David. In verses 7 and 8 we learn that Saul has become angry because "the women" have sung the refrain "Saul has slain his thousands, and David his ten thousands." Later in the chapter, as David becomes more and more popular, Saul attempts to gain the upper hand by promising his elder daughter Merab to David, only to give her to another. Saul then uses Michal to lure David into a trap. He sets a bride price of a hundred Philistine foreskins, thinking that David will surely fall by the sword of his enemy. The plan fails, and David's rising power is evident once more as he essentially *takes* Michal from Saul.[4]

David's power is challenged, however briefly, in 1 Samuel 30, when the Amalekites make a raid on his village. As we read the list of all that has been taken (vss. 1-5), the narrator builds to the most important and potentially devastating fact: "David's two wives had also been taken captive." Once again, we find the fundamental connection between power and the taking of women. Indeed, effects seem immediate, for in the next line we read, "David was greatly distressed; for the people spoke of stoning him" (30:6). The only hope, it seems, is for David to take back his wives.

The challenge to David's power is only momentary, though, for David pursues the Amalekites and is able to recover "all that the Amalekites had taken [*laqah*]," and most importantly, "David rescued his two wives" (30:18). We have good reason to suspect that it is not for their sake that David rescues them, but for his own. For the narrative knows that a king who cannot keep his own wives from being "taken" is no king at all!

We find this connection between male power (specifically male *royal* power) and the possession of women even more explicit in 2 Samuel 3. Here again we find David growing "stronger and stronger," while "the house of Saul became weaker and weaker" (3:1). The evidence given by the narrator in support of this statement is, on the one hand, a list of David's six sons, each born to a different wife. On the other hand, we learn that in the house of Saul, Abner is "making himself strong" by having sex with Saul's concubines. Ishbosheth, the son of Saul, tries to confront Abner, but is unable, because "he feared him" (3:11). The implicit message communicated by the narrator is that once the royal concubines have been taken, the power of the king is seriously compromised.

The point is reinforced in 3:12-15, as David finally regains possession of Michal (after having fled in 1 Samuel 19), the last advantage that the house of Saul holds over him. In a move that is obviously politically motivated, David sends messengers to Ishbosheth with the demand that Michal be returned to him. "And Ishbosheth sent and took [*laqah*] her from her husband Paltiel the son of Laish" (3:15). While Ishbosheth is able to exercise power over Paltiel, the house of Saul is virtually impotent in the face of David's virility.

The pinnacle of David's rise to power is recounted in 2 Samuel 5. After perceiving that YHWH has established him as king over Israel (5:12), "David took [*laqah*] more concubines and wives from Jerusalem" (5:13). David no longer struggles with any individuals for power. His political power in Israel is now absolute, as demonstrated by his ability to take women from throughout Jerusalem at will. David's power, then, is unequivocably established, and his taking of women will go unchecked--until, that is, the encounter with Nathan in 2 Samuel 12:1-15a.

TAKING WOMEN IN 2 SAMUEL 12:1-15

2 Samuel 12:1-15a is a strategic scene in the larger story of David, Bathsheba, and Uriah (2 Samuel 11-12).[5] The scene is

clearly bounded by the coming and going of Nathan the prophet. Between Nathan's entrance and exit we have the famous indictment of David. Note the symmetrical construction:

> Nathan comes (*bo'*) to David. (1a)
>   *Movement 1*
>   Nathan's parable. (1b-4)
>   David's response. (5-6)
>   Nathan's verdict. (7a)
>   *Movement 2*
>   YHWH's speech. (7b-12)
>   David's response. (13a)
>   Nathan's verdict. (13b-14)
> Nathan leaves (*halak*) David. (15a)

In contrast with his monopoly on the narrative up until this point, David has only two lines in the pericope, and both function in a self-condemning manner. In his first line (vss. 5-6) he condemns himself unknowingly. His response is couched in righteous indignation and royal outrage. In his second line (13a), the indignation and outrage are gone. David knowingly condemns himself as the one who has sinned. These two self-condemnations are particularly ironic in light of the effort thus far in Samuel to convince the reader of David's perpetual innocence.[6] One might hear echoes of David's rhetorical questions in 1 Samuel 26:18. "For what have I done? What guilt is upon my hands?"

The bulk of the scene is taken up by Nathan's parable in movement 1 and YHWH's speech in movement 2. Both of these function as scathing indictments against David. As with David's self-condemnations, the first (1b-4) is couched in terms not yet brought to light. Nathan speaks in a parable, so that David is unable to see the truth fully. Yet David is the only one who is unable to see the truth, for the reader has just learned that "the thing which David had done was evil in the eyes of YHWH" (11:27). For the reader there is no doubt to whom the parable refers.

Indeed, any doubt that David might have is dispelled in Nathan's first response, "You are the man" (7a). This terse, but devastating reply shatters the myth that David is beyond reproach. The Hebrew phrase, *'attah ha'ish*, wonderfully emphasizes that, in the final analysis, David is simply a man. David is not addressed as "king," or "lord," or even "prince," but simply as *ha'ish*, the man.

The second condemnation of David (7b-12), as is so often the case when YHWH finally speaks, holds nothing back. Like David's own second self-condemnation, this condemnation is unambiguous. As David's anger burned against the rich man of the parable, so now does YHWH'S anger burn against David, whose particular sins are named with a vengeance.

As many scholars have noted (e.g., Brueggemann 1985:55; Gunn 1989:139), this text is pivotal to the larger story of 1 and 2 Samuel. It is, no doubt, a turning point in the narrative. Here, we have for the first time a pronouncement of evil upon David (12:9). It is also the first time that David's power is challenged and, following this point in the narrative, David's power is never as sure as it once was. It signals the beginning of serious trouble for the house of David, trouble that is not averted as easily as Nathan's declaration of forgiveness in verse 13 would have David believe.

Gunn (1989:141) has observed that this story comes just as David is at the point of securing his house and kingdom. David's victories have been sweeping, and the war against the Ammonites seems to be in the final phase (11:1). David has "taken" just about anything that he could want. But then comes the confrontation with Nathan. The word "take" (*laqah*) is prominent in this story. It occurs five times in 12:1-15a (twice in vs.4, and vss. 9, 10, and 11). Each time it refers (either directly or metaphorically, as in Nathan's parable) to the taking of women. As noted above, it is this recurring theme and its implications that have most informed my own reading of this passage.[7] It is also this theme that constitutes much of what Brueggemann (1985:41) has called "the painful truth of the man." As we look at movement 1 (12:1-7a) we see this painful truth of the man David. As we look at this theme in movement 2 (12:7b-15a), however, we see what I have chosen to call "the painful truth of YHWH."

Movement 1: The Painful Truth of David (12:1-7a)

We have seen that Nathan's indictment, while couched in the form of a parable, is a powerful condemnation of David. Central to this condemnation is the idea of "taking." The rich man, who has many sheep and cattle, is contrasted with the poor man who has only one ewe-lamb. The relative importance of the single ewe-lamb to the poor man is emphasized by its lengthy description, in contrast to the minimal description of the rich man's sheep and cattle. The description turns into a veritable tear-jerker, as the reader prepares for the despicable actions of the rich man. Predictably, in verse 4 the rich man, unwilling to take (*laqah*) from his own vast flocks to feed a guest, took (*laqah*) the single beloved ewe-lamb of the poor man.

Yet in this story, we discover for the first time (along with David) that there is a limit to his taking. His taking (*laqah*) of Bathsheba (ironically set against Joab's taking of Rabbah from the Ammonites, 12:27-28), has prompted Nathan's parable about the rich man who does not hesitate to take from the poor man. With the phrase, "you are the man," the painful truth of David has been revealed. It is the painful truth of a man who thought his power was unbounded, and who would go to any length to cover up his indiscretion; even to the point of killing the loyal and innocent Uriah.

While the truth of the man is revealed, however, the even more painful truth of the relentlessly androcentric system goes unaddressed. For it is not really David's taking of women that is condemned, but rather this particular taking of a woman from this particular man Uriah. Notice that the point of the parable is not that any wrong has been done against the ewe-lamb, but that the man from whom it was taken has been wronged. We find no condemnation here of the idea that women are property to be taken in order to reinforce male power. The condemnation rests on the fact that Uriah represented no threat to David, and indeed was an asset to him, so that the taking of *his* wife was wrong.

Is there no escape, then, from the controlling ideology in which women are valued only as means to the political ends of men? The reader may recall Hannah's song from 1 Samuel 2:

> YHWH is a God of knowledge,
> and by him actions are weighed.
> The bows of the mighty are broken,
> but the feeble gird on strength.

YHWH, as evoked by this poem, is the one who exalts the poor and needy; YHWH is the God of the powerless and marginal. So the reader anxiously moves on to movement 2 of our scene, knowing that here YHWH finally speaks; expecting that finally things will be set right, and women will no longer be seen as sheep to be taken and given as men please.

Movement 2: The Painful Truth of YHWH (12:7b-15)

As the second movement opens, the reader may indeed have hope that YHWH will take the side of those in the narrative who have no voice. The movement begins in a promising way. Lore Segal (1987:119) observes:

> The God of the Second Book of Samuel is not the manifest pillar of cloud by day and fire by night that led the community of Israel through the wilderness and who talked to Moses mouth to mouth, seeing wickedness present and to come . . . The Lord has grown civilized, no longer offering to wipe us off the earth or to disinherit Israel, but promising David's descendants appropriate paternal chastisement with simultaneous paternal love.

Yet here we find an exception to the rule. For, to borrow Segal's own phrase, "the Lord [comes] thundering down on the page." The voice of YHWH bellows forth in a narrative where it has been strangely lacking, and David's unlimited power is jeopardized.

But readers hoping for justice will find their hopes dashed. For here the truth of YHWH is only the truth of David writ large. Certainly, YHWH condemns David, and harshly. We have seen that in verse 9 the actions of David are for the first time named "evil." In addition, David's taking (*laqah*) of Bathsheba is twice condemned; in verse 9, and again in verse 10. Also condemned is the sordid way in which David has used Uriah's loyalty to betray him (emphasized by the mentioning of his name twice; a

6 · Tod Linafelt: Taking Women in Samuel

name that the narrative will not forget; cf. 2 Samuel 23:39). To be sure, the reader feels some justice in this.

But what about the treatment of women as sheep? What about women being played as pawns in the power games of men? We are devastated to find in scene 2 that YHWH is complicit in such activity:

> I anointed you king over Israel,
> I delivered you from the hand of Saul,
> I gave you your master's house,
> *I gave you your master's women.*

YHWH admits—perhaps even brags—that it was not David who took the women from those he bested in the Samuel narrative. Rather, it was YHWH who "gave" (*nathan*) the women to David.

If power is defined as the ability to take women from another, then YHWH is indeed the most powerful, for only YHWH can take David's women, as promised in verse 11:

> I will take [*laqah*] your women before your eyes, and give [*nathan*] them to your neighbor, and he shall lie with your women in the sight of this sun.

The narrative would have us know, furthermore, that YHWH does not make idle threats. This verse is fulfilled in 2 Samuel 16:22: "So they pitched a tent for Absalom upon the roof; and Absalom went in to his father's concubines in the sight of all Israel." In case we should think that it is a coincidental chance of events, the narrator reminds us in 16:23 that the counsel given by Ahithophel (the one who advised Absalom to take his father's concubines), "was as if one consulted the word of God." If YHWH's speech is reliable, then YHWH has used the concubines to punish David. Once again, no thought is given to the women themselves, just as no thought was given to the women that David's enemies were required to forfeit to David as he increased his power and solidified his position as king.

Even after YHWH enters the narrative, women remain as sheep, possessions to be taken by and given to whichever man has the most power. When David's power goes to his head, YHWH steps in and takes his wives as a reminder that YHWH is the final power. Unlike the song of Hannah, this text is finally less concerned with YHWH's justice, than with YHWH's power. Yet as Emil Fackenheim (1990:80) reminds us, "even *in extremis* the supreme display of divine 'Power' is fragmentary unless it turns into a display of 'Justice' also."

AN INTERTEXTUAL REREADING OF THE CHARACTER OF YHWH

As the decidedly androcentric history of interpretation might have warned us, commentators have typically ignored the injustice against women in this narrative.[8] In particular they seem reticent to deal with the implications for the character of YHWH. McCarter (1984:305) effectively protects YHWH by saying that "trouble arises out of [David's] house." The narrative, however, makes clear that trouble is not passively "arising," but that YHWH is actively raising it. This is made explicit by the intensive use of the Hebrew *wa'ani*, "and *I*," in verse 12. There is little question that YHWH is presented as the acting subject.

Another interpreter (Hertzberg 1964:314) goes so far as to affirm the taking of David's wives as "a fitting punishment," with no consideration of how fitting it is for the women who are taken as punishment for the actions of men. Mauchline (1971: 254), too, writes that "the open shame which is to befall David's wives is fit penalty for the secret act of shame which he committed against Bathsheba." How can one blindly affirm that the raping of women is "fit penalty" for a man's sin? It seems that in so doing, Mauchline believes he has preserved a sense of YHWH's justice. But is this kind of justice worth preserving? Hertzberg (1964:314) goes on to write that in this passage, "God's justice is not suspended even for the mightiest." Unfortunately, justice *is* suspended for those without might.

The interpretations generated by this narrative are all too similar, especially in the apparent ease with which they settle the ethical questions raised. For the reader who wishes to maintain an ethics of accountability, however, meaning is not so easily settled. Escaping the androcentric ideology which attempts to justify YHWH'S actions requires an intentional act of counter-reading, or "reading against the grain."[9] It is with this task in mind that we will find an intertextual reading strategy helpful.

One way of counter-reading this narrative (and its interpretations) is to read the character of YHWH in an ironic light. The Hebrew Bible in general, and 1 and 2 Samuel in particular, are often construed as masterfully ironic. But interpreters have been noticeably reticent to acknowledge the character of YHWH as either the instrument or the subject of the narrator's irony. Meir Sternberg, for example, goes to great lengths to demonstrate the ubiquity of irony in the Bathsheba/David/Uriah story. He writes (1985:207-9) of "irony," "counter-irony," "ironic purposes," and an "ironic framework," all in the space of three pages! Yet even so sophisticated an interpreter as Sternberg refuses (ironically, we might venture) to entertain the idea that the character of YHWH may be subject to the same ironic treatment:

> ... he [sic] escapes the sharper ironies directed against all other subjects. Far from the butt of such irony, he is its beneficiary, ultimately its engineer. (1985:155)

But is YHWH indeed immune to ironic interpretation?[10] An ironic view of YHWH may help us settle the narrative tensions in a more ethically responsible way than a simple consolatory theism, which assumes *a priori* that YHWH'S actions are just.[11]

Such an ironic counter-reading may be achieved by reading 1 Samuel 8 as an intertext of 2 Samuel 12. In 1 Samuel 8, when the people ask Samuel for a king to govern them, Samuel replies by saying that a king is necessarily one who takes. He takes sons for the army and daughters for perfumers; he takes the best of the land, its produce, and the animals that graze upon it (1 Sam 8:11-17). In its immediate context, the phrase "he will take your daughters" (vs. 13) seems like a simple statement of the king's need for many servants. But in light of the rampant taking of women in the Samuel narrative, it begins to take on more ominous tones. By the time the reader discovers in 2 Samuel 12 that YHWH too is actively taking women to show *his* (masculine pronoun intentional) power, the intertextual relationship with the earlier phrase "he will take your daughters" becomes freighted with subversive irony for the character of YHWH.

When construed as an intertext for the taking which is condemned in 1 Samuel 8, YHWH's speech in 2 Samuel 12 is anything *but* an example of justice. Rather, it is an ironic indictment of the corruptions of kingship and "earthly power that invites, seduces, and destroys" (Brueggemann 1991:266). As Hamlet's feigned madness leads to real madness, so YHWH's decision to move through the world of human politics leads to a vested interest in that world. By showing that even YHWH is not immune to the seductions of politics, the skillful narrator uses a sort of hyperbole to subvert the unlimited power of the king.[12] The reader may even imagine, retrospectively, that the seduction began in 1 Samuel 8; YHWH, seeing the willingness of the people to give over such power, leans over to Samuel and whispers "Hearken to their voice, and make them a king."

The reader might, however, be justifiably skeptical about finding such an ideological counter-stream running through the text. But as David Penchansky (1991:20) observes:

> Even in cases where the author sets out to support the ideological constraints of society, the act of writing highlights the flaws in societal assumptions, and leads to the deconstruction of those assumptions.

The underlying dissonance in society is reflected in the dissonance of the text, and the struggle of competing ideologies is re-enacted with every reading. Indeed, as Italo Calvino (1986:102) puts it, "it is from their very irreconcilability that the drama comes into being."[13] No matter the effort put forth by a society to banish subversive ideologies, they inevitably show up in the text. The ideologically aware reader may legitimately counter-read the narrative, as we have done above, in order to unmask and claim the subversive (and in this case liberative) strand.

In the end, of course, some readers may decide that the text is irredeemably androcentric. No matter how much energy is expended "reading against the grain," the dominant ideology cannot be subverted. For readers who have no theological stake in the text, this may not present a problem. They can simply dismiss it wholesale, along with the God it portrays. But for those of us for whom this text is canon, and cannot but deal with the God portrayed, there remains an option to "consolatory theism." We may engage in the quintessential Jewish activity of contending with God.

Elie Wiesel (1978:6) has written that "the Jew knows that he [sic] may oppose God as long as it is in defense of God's creation."[14] We may oppose the YHWH of the narrative in defense of the women who are taken (and continue to be "taken" in one way or another) in the power games of men. Here too we are aided by an intertextual approach to the narrative. By reading intertextually we may "cite God against God" (Fackenheim 1990:42). We may defiantly recite the Song of Hannah back to the YHWH of 2 Samuel 12. We may demand a hearing, for "we were there at Sinai when [God] taught us the law by which we judge him [sic]" (Segal 1987:123). To justify the actions of YHWH as interpreters have typically done, is tantamount to renouncing this law. Such an interpretive stance would mean disregarding the Song of Hannah and its subversive role in this literature. In order to remain faithful to the YHWH who struggles against the ideological rules of the narrative, we may render judgment on the YHWH who is bound by those rules.

So we wrestle with this text, and in so doing we may find that we wrestle with God. Like Jacob, we may go away limping, not sure exactly what it was with which we wrestled. But like Abraham, we must press the question, "Shall not the judge of the earth do justice?" (Gen 18:25)

NOTES

[1] For an overview of recent developments see Gunn (1987a).

[2] Both Beardslee and Fowl address directly the issues raised by Schüssler Fiorenza. Of the two, Beardslee's treatment is by far the more compelling. Contrary to Fowl's representation of her argument, Schüssler Fiorenza presupposes neither a "supercommunity" that transcends the pluralistic interests of interpreters, nor an "ahistorical trans-cultural" understanding of justice (Fowl 1990:392-5). Consider, for example, Schüssler Fiorenza's statement (1988:14): "Not value-neutrality but an explicit articulation of one's rhetorical strategies,

interested perspectives, ethical criteria, theoretical frameworks, religious presuppositions, and sociopolitical locations for critical public discussion are appropriate in such a rhetorical paradigm of biblical scholarship."

3 For a more detailed discussion of this dynamic, see Tolbert (1983) and Weems (1991).

4 See Exum (1990) for an analysis of how Michal's story is co-opted by the narrative to serve its "phallogocentric ideology."

5 Brueggemann (1985:65) offers a treatment of why chapters 11 and 12 should be considered together. See also Bal (1987:24) for the dangers of considering only a section of the narrative.

6 See for example the three stories in 1 Samuel 24/25/26. All three stories go to great lengths to show how David refrains from violence. Note in particular the concern in chapter 25 that David remain free from "bloodguilt." David's innocence is also asserted in 2 Samuel 21-25.

7 My reading is akin to Randall C. Bailey's, who writes that this is "a story of political intrigue in which sex becomes a tool of politics" (1990:88). Bailey offers a detailed and fascinating study of the political undercurrent of 2 Samuel 10-12, but the scope of his study does not allow for sustained reflection on the character of YHWH.

8 One notable exception is Alice Laffey (1988:121) who writes, "David's punishment is not understood to be against his concubines who become sexual objects for another man. They are given no consideration. They are possessions of David who must be surrendered to another man, in payment for his having seized the possession of Uriah." Given the introductory nature of the book, however, Laffey does not not engage in a detailed consideration of the theme.

9 Gerald Graff (1990:171) describes "reading against the grain" as "a method which does not take the texts' apparent contexts and intentions at face value, but looks at the doubts they repress or leave unsaid and how this repressed or 'absent' element can undermine or undo what the text says."

10 My understanding of irony is similar to that described by D. C. Muecke (1982:31) as "saying something in a way that activates not one but an endless series of subversive interpretations."

11 Umberto Eco (1983:67) has written that "the postmodern reply to the modern consists of recognizing that the past, since it cannot really be destroyed, because its destruction leads to silence, must be revisited: but with irony, not innocently." It is in this way that we may "revisit" the character of YHWH in this narrative, fully aware that our use of irony is a strategic alternative to relegating YHWH to silence.

12 This line of interpretation is lent support by socio-political readings that identify an "ideological ambivalence" (Rosenberg 1987:142) in the narrative's treatment of kingship in general. Since the

story deals with a period of liminality in Israel's history, that is the shift from decentralized power to monarchy, the reader may expect to find mixed evaluations of royal power. I am grateful to Deborah Krause of Eden Theological Seminary for helping me to see this connection.

[13] See also Boris Uspensky (1973:9), who writes of "several ideological viewpoints which together form a fairly complex network of relationships."

[14] Wiesel has said in an interview, "I rarely speak about God. To God, yes. I protest against Him. I shout at Him. But to open a discourse about the qualities of God, about the problems that God imposes, theodicy, no. And yet He is there, in silence, in filigree" (Plimpton 1988:250).

7

THE IMPORTUNATE WOMAN OF TEKOA AND HOW SHE GOT HER WAY

PATRICIA K. WILLEY

Second Samuel 11-14, four primary chapters of the court history of King David, tell one sequence of events in two mirror halves. The episodes are doubled: Chapter 11 relates a sexual crime resulting in murder—David violates Bathsheba and then arranges for the slaying of her husband Uriah. Two chapters later, history repeats itself: sexual crime results in murder again, when David's oldest son Amnon rapes his half-sister Tamar. For this he is killed by Absalom her brother, who subsequently flees the country. Following each of these episodes, in chapters 12 and 14, one of the king's two most important advisors tries to change the king's understanding of the previous event. In chapter 12 Nathan confronts David with his crimes against Bathsheba and Uriah. In chapter 14, David's general Joab sends an unnamed woman from the town of Tekoa to persuade the king to bring his son home. In neither story does the messenger state his or her purpose outright. Each uses deceit, telling David a fiction to elicit his royal judgment, only afterwards revealing that the tale is about the king himself. David hears, acts accordingly, and that is the end of the matter.

Or so it seems. These two judgment episodes, presented back to back, prompt readers to notice first their striking similarities. Since typescenes in biblical narratives often share intents, story lines, and outcomes, it is no surprise that these two episodes have been interpreted as parallel accounts. A vast majority of readers have cheered the Tekoite woman's success just as they have Nathan's.[1]

But as Robert Alter (1981:47-62) and David Damrosch (1987:250-60) have pointed out, repeated typescenes like these rely for their effect not only on their adherence to convention, but also on their deviations from the expected story. As I hope to show, the desire to read the story of the Tekoite woman as an episode running parallel to the Nathan story in its intent and outcome has required interpreters to discount textual difficulties, ignore syntactic and structural problems, overlook logical fallacies, and rationalize glaring non sequiturs. A more critical appraisal reveals that this story is very different from its counterpart in chapter 12. In fact, its outcome is almost the direct opposite of that of the Nathan story, gaining much of its effect from its clever parody of the contours of the previous story.

Nathan's judgment scene had presented a picture that was painfully clear. Starting with the flat authorial statement that the thing David had done to Bathsheba and Uriah was evil in God's eyes, the scene progressed simply and smoothly through Nathan's story about the poor man and his ewe lamb and the rich man who killed her. David's vehement judgment against the rich man missed not a beat, nor did Nathan's stinging reply, "you are the man!" Nathan's judgment speech as well was unmistakably clear, as was David's confession, "I have sinned against Yahweh."

But the scene opening two chapters later is a study in ambiguity and chaos. To begin with, each character's motives are shrouded in mystery. First there is Absalom, who has killed his brother in the absence of the king's justice—the brother who also happens to be his greatest rival to the throne.[2]

Then there is David. Immediately after the murder and flight, we read that the king "mourned over his son day after day," but it is not clear which son is being mourned. Three years pass. The next sentence about the king contains an unresolvable textual problem and several highly ambiguous words. Every major modern translation reads something like this: "The king longed to go out to Absalom, because he was comforted over Amnon, since he was dead." But Fokkelman (1981:126), noting the textual problems, claims that this sentence has been misread, and suggests, "David longed intensely to march out against Absalom, for he was grieved about Amnon, that he was dead." I think he is half-right. It can be read either way. In fact, several words in this verse are so multivalent that there is more than one way to derive either reading. Though the English cannot show it, the king's ambivalence is being portrayed for us by unresolvable ambiguity on the textual level.[3] We do not know what the king thinks; perhaps, the narrative suggests, even he is not sure.

Next to be considered are the motives of Joab, king David's general and longtime companion. Joab the treacherous, the dominant of the three brave, brash, and loyal sons of Zeruiah, who murders for the king's own good whether he likes it or not (2 Sam 3:17-39), is the only person entrusted with David's guilty secret concerning Uriah. It is Joab, in fact, who orchestrated Uriah's battlefield death. What makes Joab so formidable is that what he lacks in moral scruples, he more than makes up for in pragmatic enlightenment, political clarity, and devotion to David's rule. But here, like the other characters, this normally transparent general acts in a puzzling and ambiguous manner. Why Joab wants Absalom home we can only guess. In fact, this time his political instincts could not be more mistaken.

The woman Joab sends to speak to David is not named, but only described by the phrase *'ishah hakamah*. This phrase has been almost invariably translated, "wise woman." Fokkelman (1981:141) goes so far as to call less glorifying descriptions "inane, gravely depressing, and sexist." However, the same adjective was just used in even more superlative form in 13:3 (*'ish hakam m'od*) to describe Amnon's friend Jonadab, the one who helped him entrap Tamar. Nobody ever calls Jonadab wise, but rather crafty or shrewd. We cannot simply assume that the same adjective in the very next chapter is meant as a compliment. The story itself will tell us whether or in what sense the woman of Tekoa is wise.

What motivates the Tekoite woman to take the risk of confronting the king of Israel while Joab waits safely in the wings, we are not told. Perhaps she is so sympathetic to his view, and so confident of her success, that she steps willingly into this dangerous role, but I find it unlikely. It has been suggested that she was somehow coerced into the job by General Joab.[4] Like Tamar (2 Sam 13:12-13), like the woman of Abel

Beth-ma'acah (2 Sam 20:18-19), and like Bathsheba herself (1 Kgs 1:17-21)—that is, like every other speaking woman in this narrative—she could be a potential victim forced to negotiate shrewdly for her safety. But the narrator does not tell us her motives either, and we are left only to speculate.

The story opens with hazy motivations and progresses to puzzling dialogue. Coached by Joab, the woman comes in a disguise that places her parallel to the king: just as he *yit'abel*, "mourned," so Joab instructs her, *hit'abli*, "mourn." Just as he mourned "day after day," so she is to appear to have mourned "many days." Just as his mourning seems to be divided between the dead and the living, so her mourning is for the dead son while her concern is for the living one.

"Help, O King," she begins.

> Truly I am a widow, my husband is dead. And your servant had two sons, and the two of them quarreled in the field, and there was no one to tear them apart, and the one struck the other and killed him. Now all the family has risen up against your servant, and they have said, "Give up the one who struck his brother, so we may kill him for the life of his brother, whom he murdered. Yes, let us annihilate the heir." They will quench the coal I have left, so as to remove my husband's name and remnant from the ground.

Her case finds its strength in extenuating circumstances: her widowhood and looming bereftness, the nearly accidental killing, the greed of her relatives, and her potential loss of patrimony. Because her case differs substantially from the king's own, her story arouses no significant suspicions.

Though her suit seems just, the king demurs. "Go home," he says, "and I myself will give orders concerning you." Other than "begone," he has not said anything at all. In fact, when Pharaoh "gave orders concerning Abraham" in Genesis 12 it meant he was kicking him out of the land. Perhaps the king wishes to consult his advisors before making a decision. Or perhaps he is, as Absalom will later suggest (2 Sam 15:3-4), not interested in playing judge.[5]

So far things have not gone well. The woman has told her whole story and has failed to elicit the spontaneous outpouring of sympathy that Nathan's story evoked. Now she must beg. "Upon me, my lord the king, be the sin, and on the house of my father! May the king and his throne be guiltless."[6]

The king is hardly moved: "The one who is speaking to you, bring him to me, and he will not continue to touch you." He has not guaranteed the life of her son, nor promised to take any particular action. In fact, he has put the burden on this woman to drag her powerful adversary to the palace before he will consider her suit. Whether she can do this before her son is killed is, evidently, her problem.

So she begs once more, this time invoking God. She gets her result. In the same verse, as if pressing to end the conversation, the king swears by Yahweh: "Not a hair of your son shall fall to the ground." For once he gives more than she bids.

Now her most dangerous task remains: she must make this royal judgment stick to the king himself. But unlike Nathan, she has not gained the persuasive strength to discard the deception and expose the king in four syllables. Cautiously she asks permission to speak further.

The next speech is a garbled mixture of strong words and deferential phrasing. Suddenly and ever so briefly discarding her guise, she makes a six-word frontal attack, using a second-person finite verb for the first and only time: *lamah hashavtah kazo't 'al 'am 'elohim*—"Why did you think thus about the people of God?" Though she has not yet accused the king of anything except thinking, she seems poised on the brink of a grave accusation. But from here on her speech dissolves into infinitives, incomplete sentences, garbled grammar—and nearly subliminal impressions.

No translation is adequate for what comes next, but approximately she says: "From the king's saying this thing, as being guilty in order for the king not to bring back his outcast one . . ." This is not a sentence: there are no finite verbs at all, but only three infinitives governed by prepositions. Only the two more innocuous of these (*mdaber and lbilti hashiv*) are in any way connected with the king, and the more judgmental (*k'ashem*, "as being guilty") is left to dangle by itself.

Interestingly, English translators generally doctor this sentence with finite verbs to yield a smooth reading. The NRSV says, for instance, "For in giving this decision *the king convicts himself*, inasmuch as the *king does not bring* his banished one home again." The RSV, NEB, RNEB, JB, NJB, TANAKH, NIV, NAB, NASB, and TEV likewise all revamp the grammar on the rather large assumption that the author meant to write a sentence. These translations inappropriately alter the woman's speech from massive confusion into the sort of blatant accusation that interpreters expect to find.[7]

Taken as it stands, the woman's garbled speech functions like a Rorschach test for both the king and the reader. After expressing her strong disapproval of some indeterminate thought the king has (and we can think of many), she has brought up a loosely connected list of proposed topics: the people of God, "this thing," sin/guilt, and the return of the outcast one. The only definite referent, the outcast one, is still rather vague when we remember that there is no indication in the story that Absalom was banished. In fact, the narrator made it clear three times (13:34, 38, and 39) that Absalom fled.

When too much attention has been given, even indirectly, to the actions of the king, the woman retreats into aphorisms and God-talk. "For surely we will die, and like water which is poured out on the earth which will not be gathered . . . God will not take a life—he will devise means to not cast out from him an outcast one." Still incoherent, yet still sprinkled with subtle reminders: the inevitability of death, the universality of schemes and, again, the outcast one. Then she retreats even further, returning step by step to the disguise in which she came, saying,

> And now which I have come to say this thing to the king my lord, that the people have frightened me . . . And your servant said, "Let me speak to the king—perhaps the king will do the word of his handmaid. For the king will heed to save his handmaid from the hand of the man to destroy me and my son together from the inheritance of God."

Thus, after a momentary hint of her real message, in three highly ambiguous sentences she moves back to the pretense that she has come about her son. Along the way she again strings together a vast array of topics—"this thing," the people, fear, and a proposal that the king act—and refers indefinitely to either the king's situation, or hers, or both. "And your servant said, 'May the word of my lord the king be a resting place, for like an angel of God, so is my lord the king, judging good and evil.' May Yahweh your God be with you." With this flattery-bedangled request and blessing she ends her speech.

Why is the woman's speech so strange and garbled? It is not a property of the book's dialogues in general; Nathan's speech was not only grammatical, but full-fraught with structure. Nor does this incoherence plague other women's speeches. While the other three women in the court history do, like this woman, employ a more sophisticated vocabulary than both the narrator and the male characters, the only other time when sentences break down is with Tamar. Not before the rape—there she is relentlessly logical and rhetorically masterful. But after the rape, her words are urgent, marginally grammatical, condensed, just as we might expect from a person in her situation.

Rather the narrator is, I submit, thinking more deviously than we are, and using language more subtly than most readers and translators have suspected. This garbled and ungrammatical form of speech protects the woman from accusations of slander. She may be operating here as shrewd politicians or timid employees do, suggesting by innuendo things they would never be foolhardy enough to come out and say. It is the speech of the fearful, who know how thin the ice is beneath them.

At this point, according to Nathan's precedent, it is time for the king to be smitten to the heart and repent. Time to acknowledge his self-judgment and to accept the consequences. But he does no such thing. Instead he fires one fatal shot into her story: "Is the hand of Joab with you in all this?"

Unabashed, she answers with brazen flattery, ostentatious frankness, and merciless scapegoating. "As your soul lives, my lord the king, no man may turn to the right or the left from all that my lord the king has said![8] For your servant Joab, he commanded me, and he put all these words into the mouth of your servant."

And now, finally, she seems poised to reveal a motive. She

presents Joab's reason for this scheme: *lb'avur sabev 'et-pney hadavar*, "in order to turn the face of the thing," another hopeless mass of ambiguity. Translators have rendered it variously: "in order to change the course of affairs" (NRSV); "to come at the issue in a roundabout way" (NAB); "to conceal the real purpose of the matter" (TANAKH). Perhaps the NEB is most faithful to the ambiguities here: "to give a new turn to this affair." Once again, we are teased with a suggestion that tells us nothing definite.

All is lost now. The woman has failed to secure a commitment from the king, she has been unmasked, and Joab has been implicated. Joab stands to be chastised, and the woman stands guilty between the two most powerful men in the land, the king whom she has attempted to deceive and the general whom she has failed to help.

But then, inscrutably, the king grants Joab's wish. Though he has not noted any connection between his sons and hers; though he ignores her hints of his guilt; though he knows Joab's duplicity; though—as it turns out—he could not make a worse mistake, the king tells Joab, "I have done this thing. Go and bring back the lad Absalom." Then, complying with the letter but not the spirit of Joab's request, the king refuses to see his son. No reconciliation results even when they do meet; rather, civil war breaks out and Absalom dies.

The Tekoite woman has failed in her purpose; she has succeeded; she has finally failed—the reversals keep us guessing. Where did things go awry?

We had come to this story knowing that a similar strategy succeeded magnificently just two chapters ago. But this story's striking similarities to the previous one should not blind us to the vast differences—differences that undermine Joab's chances for success.

The first difference is simply the position of the two characters in relation to the king. Nathan was an advisor who had the king's ear; in fact, he was represented as God's mouthpiece. But this woman is a stranger with no claim on the king, sent probably because Joab knows the king does not trust him. Joab has gambled away the advantages of familiarity and authority.

7 · Patricia K. Willey: The Importunate Woman of Tekoa

The next set of differences lies in the nature of the tales they tell the king. Problems abound here, but the two most crucial are:

First, Nathan's is an open-and-shut case that even a child can legislate: the rich man did what was wrong both legally and morally. But Joab's case is complex and ambiguous, requiring subtle knowledge of the laws about murder, revenge, and inheritance, and calling for verification of the woman's claims concerning the spontaneity of the murder and the malicious intent of her family. Further, while Nathan is asking David to uphold both law and morality, Joab is asking the king to weigh one morality against another. This, as David seems to realize, is beyond his ability to judge on the spot.

Second, once Nathan secured David's judgment, he was sure to convict the king, both because his case resembled David's case in deep structure (the rich thoughtlessly taking the poor's precious one) and because the rich man's crime was morally and legally less heinous than David's—so that, logically, if the rich man who killed a lamb was guilty, then David who killed his officer was more guilty. But even if the woman does finally tease a favorable judgment from the king (after three tries), establishing a damning relationship between her case and his is problematic. Her scenario consists of too many extenuating circumstances, weakening the connections. Additionally, the injustice she fears (the murder by greedy relatives of her only remaining son, who did not premeditate the murder) is far more heinous than the king's refusal to restore Absalom to his presence, making the king *less* guilty. It is even more heinous than any plans the king might have to bring Absalom to justice for his long and coldly premeditated murder. So even a strong and willing judgment on her case does not transfer organically to David's.[9]

Because of these infelicities, things begin to go awry. Unlike Nathan, the woman has to coax a balky customer. From that point on her position is quite tenuous.

In both scenes, a judgment speech follows the completed fiction. As I have noted, glaring grammatical differences between Nathan's speech and the woman's also highlight the certainty and clarity of his point, as well as the diffuseness of hers.

Nathan's sentences are clear and direct. Twenty-one independent clauses can be counted, using twenty finite verbs and one nominal sentence. Only four dependent clauses are used. Of the three infinitive verbs in the speech, one refers directly to David and two are added for emphasis. But the woman's speech is characterized by incomplete sentences and dangling infinitives. At the most, she has only eight complete sentences, mixed with four incomplete sentences and thirteen dependent clauses. Though she uses twenty-four verbs, only fourteen of these are finite. The rest are verbal adjectives and infinitives, sometimes dangling without referents.

All of Nathan's sentences employ very standard syntax. Even his longer sentences remain straightforward. But the woman's sentences often employ obscure and perhaps even incorrect syntax. Particles and prefixes present more difficulties than usual in translation. Her speech presents frustrating interpretive difficulties for the king as well as for us.

Nathan employs repetition several times to create anticipation and drive home his point. But the woman's speech does not. In fact, her speech causes anticipation and then veers off in another direction, creating misreadings and necessitating re-readings.

Nathan speaks bluntly. He addresses the king as "you" and attributes eight past actions to him, ranging up to "despising Yahweh." The woman refers to the king in second person only twice, and uses royal titles eleven times in this speech alone. She only attributes one past action directly to the king, and two more indirectly. She only accuses the king of thinking, speaking, and not bringing back.

The wronged parties, Uriah and "his wife," are brought up directly and repeatedly in Nathan's speech, and David's sins are named with brutal candor. The woman, on the other hand, never mentions Absalom either by name or by relationship to the king, but refers obliquely only to the "banished one." None of the events or language of chapter 13 are recalled in her speech. In fact, as will be discussed below, all oblique intertextual clues in her speech refer not to Absalom's story but to the Bathsheba/Uriah/Nathan episode.

Both speakers describe the king in a nominal sentence. Nathan denounces the king ("You are the man," 2 Sam 12:7), but the woman says, "like an angel of God, so is my lord the king" (2 Sam 14:17), flattering him.

Thus Nathan points his finger incessantly at David's guilt, but the woman diffuses and diminishes her point in every way possible. Interestingly, as the woman's speech proceeds further and further from its main point (bringing home the outcast one), it also becomes more and more intelligible.

Not only is the speech itself more difficult to determine in this story than in the previous one, but even the speaker is more difficult to discern. Nathan came without a disguise, and he made abundantly and repeatedly clear that he was speaking for "Yahweh the God of Israel." But in the course of the woman's speech, not only is Joab's role as author of the message concealed from the king, not only is the woman's "I" diffused by such self-references as "your servant" and "your handmaid," but the woman's own identity changes more than once. Sometimes she is the mother of an endangered son; other times she is a messenger pleading with the king over his own family situation; at times she seems to be both at once. Not until later does David know for certain who is addressing him.

This adds up to an oppressive clarity for Nathan's speech, and an impenetrable fog for the woman's speech. While Nathan's sharp words sliced through the king's defenses, her speech threatens to drown the king in confusion.

In spite of all this, the king grants Joab's request. I submit that he does this, not out of conviction, but because for all its opaqueness and confusion, her speech does one thing with consummate effectiveness. It makes certain veiled allusions for the king who has ears to hear them. On one level, there are her frequent references to sin and guilt, coupled with her elaborate praise of the goodness and wisdom of the king, which neither he nor we, knowing his story, can swallow without choking. These references which juxtapose hints of guilt with declarations of elaborate praise put the king in a very awkward psychic position, especially since he does not yet know who sent the woman and whether or not she is in a position to know the damning details of his private life. But on another level, I propose, her most effective weapon is her frequent allusion to *hadavar hazeh*, "this thing." This phrase is the key to the king's granting her suit.

It is a conspicuously empty phrase waiting for content. Within the space of 2 Samuel 11-14 it occurs thirteen times, compared to a total of eight times in all the rest of 1 and 2 Samuel. In addition, variations on the phrase and its elements abound. In fact, the woman uses the word *dvr*, as a noun or a verb, thirteen times in her speeches.

The phrase is introduced by Uriah (11:11), in the speech in which he one-ups the king's morality: "As you live, I will not do this thing," that is, sleep with his wife while his comrades sleep on the battlefield. Next it is used by David in his second message to Joab after Uriah's death: "Do not let this thing be evil in your eyes" (11:25). Ostensibly David is forgiving Joab for a botched battle; only David and Joab know that "this thing" is actually the murder of Uriah.[10] Ironically, two verses later, the narrator uses almost the same sentence to sum up God's opinion: "And evil was the thing which David had done in the eyes of Yahweh" (11:27). Here the definition is set: "this thing" is a euphemism for the murder of Uriah and the violation of Bathsheba.

The phrase is used again by David in his unknowing self-accusation: "the man who did this thing deserves to die" (12:6). The phrase is thrown back at him twice by Nathan, once referring to David's deed (12:14), and once referring to the thing that God planned to do against David (12:12). Later, when David ceases mourning for his dead son, his servants ask him what is this thing that he has done—a heartstopping question for the guilty king, though innocently posed (12:21).

Only elements of the phrase are found throughout Tamar's rape and Amnon's murder in chapter 13, except at the story's midpoint, when Absalom tells Tamar not to "take this thing to heart" (13:20), and when David is told "all these things" (13:21).

Thus far, the phrase has been working its will in two ways.

First, it serves as an echo in David's mind, a reminder of Uriah, and of his desperate message to Joab, in which he entrusted his reputation forever to the general's discretion. But on another level, we have heard it used when David could not, and it has helped structure our reading, foregrounding the relationship Nathan has drawn between David's sin and the ensuing tragedies.

By the time Joab uses the phrase to coach the woman, "Speak to him in this way," or literally, "like this thing" (14:3), we get a hint of the way things will go. When the woman uses it three times straight (14:13, 15, 20), once as a plural (14:19), and four other times in variation (14:12, 15, 17, 20), she begins to work a new meaning into it: "this thing" is what David did, but it also becomes what Joab hopes that he will now do. In fact, identifying Joab's reason for the deceit, she says "in order to turn the face of the thing, your servant Joab did this thing" (14:20). In so thoroughly connecting David's guilt with Joab's request, she exercises inexorable pressure on the king in behalf of his most powerful subject. Evidently Joab knows what he has and how he can use it.

And though the story fails to entrap, the speech fails to convince, and the ruse fails to protect, the king nonetheless decides in Joab's favor. In a little ironic twist of his own, he forms this encoded answer to Joab: "I have done this thing—go and bring back the lad Absalom" (14:21). And Joab, ever quick on the draw, replies appreciatively, "the king has done the thing of his servant" (14:22).

True to his own methods, Joab persuades the king by coercion and innuendo. And David, unconvinced in heart, does exactly what he has been strong-armed to do and not a jot or tittle more: Absalom is brought home but not welcomed by his father.

If Joab's aim is to prevent a military action against Absalom, he has succeeded. If his aim is to patch up the torn family and to provide the king an heir, he fails miserably. In fact, this episode leads directly to Absalom's bid for the kingdom and to his death. If Joab's aim is to reassert his influence over the king, it backfires more than embarrassingly three times: first, when the king refuses to see Absalom; second, when Absalom's reappearance culminates in civil war and death; and third, at the end, when Joab himself must flee for his life and die on the altar of government security.

So where is the wisdom of the wise? In the very most positive sense possible, the word *hakamah* can refer merely to the woman's ability to coerce the king while keeping her own self safe, perhaps not a small accomplishment considering the mortality rate around the king.[11] But more likely the narrator addresses us ironically, playing a joke on us. By setting up a tale similar to the Nathan tale, the narrator raises our expectations for a similarly luminous outcome, but then fails splendidly to deliver. This importunate woman reads not as a second Nathan, come again to set things straight, but as a parody of his methods, fit for a king doomed to moral confusion.

Ironically, the Tekoite woman's failure is the narrator's success. When two chapters earlier the narrator wanted a crystal-clear picture of what was what, this picture was enhanced by the clarity of the story. Motives were clear, speech was clear, the confrontation's winner was clear. Even in chapter 13 we were still being provided some authorial opinion reflected in the words of Tamar ("such a thing is not done in Israel," 13:12).

But by chapter 14 all clarity has dissolved, not only for the king but for us also. Like the Tekoite woman, whose speech is unpredictable, the narrator fools us, and we never quite know what will happen next. We think Joab will speak to the king, but instead he sends a woman. We are told she is wise, but she does not play the part. We are led to think she will convince the king, but she does not. She prepares to accuse the king, but her accusation floats away in the flotsam and jetsam of unconnected words, and she ends up blessing him. She lies till she is caught and then tells absolutely all. She begins to become an identifiable, undisguised person, but then she disappears in the breaking of the truth. The king knows the ruse but he agrees anyway. No cue we pry out from one moment helps us to predict the succeeding moment. It becomes impossible even for us to do what the woman credits the king with doing: "judging good and evil" (vs. 17); "knowing all that is in the land" (vs. 20). Thus we not only observe the king's loss of control, but we participate in it ourselves.

But here is another layer of irony, this one not apparently intended: the story has been too subtle for modern readers. Countless interpreters have, with varying degrees of enthusiasm and reluctance, consented to the woman's suit, just as the king did. Yet, if the comparative dearth of literature about the story says anything, it says that this story finds no more lodging place in the souls of its interpreters than it did in the king's soul. We are, like the king, convicted and convinced by Nathan, but coerced and confused by Joab. We are, in addition, reading foreign literature in a foreign tongue, and we are still learning to trust our instincts. If we can, unlike David, take the time to judge, if we can identify the sources of chaos in the story, then we can keep the anarchy loosed on David's reign from becoming our confusion as well.

NOTES

[1] See for instance McCarter (1964), Whybray (1968), Simon (1967), Hoftijzer (1970), Ridout (1971), Hertzberg (1964), Camp (1981), Fokkelman (1981), Hagan (1979), and Waldman (1986/87).

[2] According to 2 Sam 3:2-5, Amnon is David's first-born, followed by Chileab (who is never mentioned again), Absalom, and then Adonijah. Amnon's personal influence on the king is already clearly portrayed in chapter 13.

[3] This verse reads: *vatkal david hammelek latse't 'el-avshalom ki-niham 'al-'amnon ki-met*. The feminine form of the first word renders some kind of textual emendation necessary. Keil and Delitzsch (1864:293) translate the sentence: "Und es (dies) hielt den König David zurück nach Absalom auszuziehen" ("And it held David the king back from going out"). Wellhausen notes that *david hammelek* is a highly unusual construction, and speculates that an emendation is required for "David" (Driver 1890:236). LXXL and LXXA, along with 4QSama, read *ruah hammelek*. Taken this way, the first word has been emended to the Qal form *vatekel* and translated "longed" in the sense (used fairly frequently in Pss. and other poetry) of "faded," "failed," or "pined": "The spirit of the king longed to go out to Absalom." This is the way most current English translations take it, even though *klh* is

never used in this sense anywhere else in the Deuteronomistic narratives. Rahlfs' LXX, though, using the same cue, reads "and the spirit of the LORD ceased going out after Absalom." No matter how the words are read, there seems to be a prejudice toward translating the verse so as to make David favorably disposed toward Absalom.

Ruah may be preferable textually to David here, but it still sits uneasily, because it is a very rare word in Samuel, occurring only sixteen times, and never in the court history at all. Except for one possible reference to a troubled spirit (1 Sam 1:15, although the LXX and Latin read "in hard days") the word never refers to the human spirit.

A more likely rendering of this phrase may be presented by the idiom in which the verb *klh* is frequently found in Samuel, particularly in the Saul-David stories: "evil was determined by him" (*kaltah hara'ah me'immo*; 1 Sam 20:7; cf. vs. 9; 25:17; Esth 7:7). In 1 Sam 25:17, the subject "evil" is replaced by an infinitive: "it was determined by his father to kill David." If this idiom is being used in 2 Sam 13:39, the only element missing is the *me'im*: "It was determined by the king to go out . . ."

Further ambiguities are presented by the words *latse't* and *niham*. Fokkelman (1981:127) has correctly noted that *latse't* is a military term, used many times in Samuel-Kings for armies marching out, often with the preposition *'el* or *'al*. So the phrase *latse't 'el-avshalom* could mean either "to go out to Absalom" or "to march out against Absalom."

In most other instances of the verb *niham*, God is the subject, and it is translated "repent" or "relent." When humans are the subject, it usually seems to mean "be sorry" or "grieve." In a few instances, this word has been translated as "be comforted." Yet almost all of these (Gen 38:12; Ezek 14:22; 31:16; and 32:31) can just as well, often better, be translated "grieve." So the phrase *ki-niham 'al-'amnon* could be rendered either "for he was grieved over Amnon" or "for he was comforted over Amnon."

[4] Gunn (1988:297) raises the interesting possibility that her discourse attempts to signal this fact to the king: "she has been threatened, she says, by 'the people' (the word could also mean 'army') and, in particular, by 'the hand of the man who would destroy me and my son' (v. 16)," that is, Joab. Waldman (1986/87:16) also notes that "the one who is speaking to her" is really Joab.

[5] The theme of David's failure to attend to justice is spelled out most damningly in the story of Mephibosheth, who brings to David an urgent case of slander, theft, and deceit (2 Sam 19:24-30), a case the king himself has unwittingly brought about. The king's response is no more patient than it is with the woman of Tekoa: a rude remark and a hasty compromise between undetermined good and evil (see Ackerman 1990:52). Damrosch (1987:247) points out that David "cannot be

bothered to sort out the truth."

⁶ Whether this statement is an attempt to reassure the king that she will take responsibility for this decision, or an ironic assertion that the throne will be guilty if her son dies, remains ambiguous. However, the mere mention of the word *naqiy* ("clean" or "guiltless") runs over with irony, because being *naqiy* is rather a sore spot for the king. Once he was eminently *naqiy* (1 Sam 19:5); later he was vehemently *naqiy* (2 Sam 3:28), but since Nathan's rebuke he has been by no stretch of the imagination *naqiy*.

⁷ Hoftijzer (1970:44) works very hard, through obscure and conjectural syntactic constructions, to improve her speech according to the standard he believes is called for by her supposed designation as "wise woman." His reconstruction, in turn, supports his conclusion that she is "a very wise woman indeed." Fokkelman (1981:135) calls her speech "plain language," adding in a footnote that to find such plain language we must first get through a great deal of work due to the "difference in culture and language," a difference not significant, apparently, in the rest of the court history. Camp (1981), similarly, bases much of her argument for an office of trained "wise women" (customarily and regularly granted authority in ancient Israel) on the reconstruction of the woman's speech as direct and audacious, coupled with her designation as *hakamah*.

⁸ Indeed, the last person who swore, "As your soul lives," to the king was Uriah (2 Sam 11:11), who died for turning to the right or the left from what his lord the king said.

⁹ Simon (1967:223-225), who thinks that the Tekoite woman succeeded, goes to great lengths to explain her parable as an exception to the "clear and reasonable rule" that the parabolic offense must be a lesser crime than the actual one.

¹⁰ Sternberg (1985:218) notes the ostensive message as, "Don't take it to heart," while the real message to Joab is "Good!" or "Thanks!"

¹¹ Gunn (1988:297): "Perhaps she is simply trying to stay alive in a world where men wield power ruthlessly and capriciously."

8

READING JEROBOAM'S INTENTIONS: INTERTEXTUALITY, RHETORIC, AND HISTORY IN 1 KINGS 12

STUART LASINE

According to the books of Kings, Jeroboam's decision to make two golden calves for the cult centers of his new kingdom has dire results. It not only becomes a sin for his people and for his doomed dynasty (1 Kgs 12:30; 1 Kgs 13:34), but causes the fall of the Northern Kingdom and exile beyond the River (1 Kgs 14:15-16; 2 Kgs 17:23). It is even responsible for Josiah's later sacrifice of the priests of the high places in Samaria (2 Kgs 23:20; cf. 1 Kgs 12:32; 13:2; 2 Kgs 17:32). Aaron's calf-making at Sinai has similar consequences. Like Jeroboam, Aaron brought a "great sin" on the people (Exod 32:21, 30, 31; cf. 2 Kgs 17:21). If Jeroboam's sin leads to the sacrificial slaughter of non-Levitic priests, the sin at the mountain leads immediately to the slaughter of Levites by their fathers and brothers (Exod 32:26-29).[1] Some scholars go so far as to claim that what the Deuteronomist (Dtr) is reporting in 1 Kings 12 is not merely Jeroboam's "cultic primordial sin" (Hoffmann 1980:132), but "something like an Old Testament teaching of original sin" (Debus 1967:95). Similarly, Exodus 32 is not merely reporting "Israel's prototypal sin" (Kaufmann 1972:13) but "Israel's original sin" (Scharbert 1968:83) or the "fall of man at Sinai" (Aurelius 1988:76).[2]

If the results of the calf-making are so utterly sinful and disastrous, one might expect that the intentions of the calf-makers would be sinful and suicidal as well. Yet many commentators believe that when Jeroboam made his calves and installed them in Bethel and Dan, he did so "with the best and most sincere of intentions and commendable piety" (Morgenstern

1948:485; cf. De Vries 1985:162; Jenks 1977:103). Aaron has also been said to have had "good intentions" when he made his calf (Janzen 1990:605). That explains why he "could declare in all sincerity, after making the image, that the next day would be a 'festival to the Lord'" (Sarna 1986:217). Even the people who had demanded "a god" from Aaron "intended nothing more than an appropriate object emblematic of the divine presence" (Sarna 1986:217).

If one were forced to determine the message of the golden calf narratives solely on the basis of these descriptions of the calf-makers' intentions and the results of their actions, only one message could emerge: the road to sin, exile and priestly slaughter is paved with good intentions. Yet it would seem that no road could span the vast distance between such pure intentions and such sinful results. Must we conclude that the well-meaning Aaron and Jeroboam were replaced by evil twin brothers who then proceeded to carry out the actions which led to all these sinful results? In a sense the answer is "yes," for the two sets of commentators cited above are actually talking about two different Aarons and two different Jeroboams. Those who are describing their good intentions are referring to the historical Aaron and Jeroboam, while those who outline the evil effects of the calf-makers' work are referring to the literary Aaron and Jeroboam. The former are speculating about the historical realities behind the text as it stands, while the latter are describing the consequences which follow from actions taken by characters in the text.

In what follows I will examine the manner in which diachronic studies use specific features of the present text as a basis for speculation about Jeroboam's intentions and the popular fetishism which resulted from his actions. After showing why this way of reading the narrative usually results in a distorted picture of the author and the audience for which he designed his work, I will make a detailed synchronic examination of Jeroboam's intentions as they are presented in 1 Kings 12, including those verses which reveal his intentions by alluding to Exodus 32 and other passages. I will conclude by asking how the synchronic analysis might contribute to a more precise understanding of the ancient Israelite audience for which 1 Kings 12 was intended, and by showing how the specific combination of illegitimate cult reform, mass idolatry and false leadership described in 1 Kings 12 might be related to the problems which prompted Hezekiah to undertake his cult reforms in the late 8th century.

DIACHRONIC EXPLANATIONS OF JEROBOAM'S INTENTIONS AND THE RESULTING IDOLATRY

Historians are well aware that, on one level, 1 Kgs 12:28 implies that Jeroboam attempted to attract pious followers of Yahweh to his new cult centers by introducing his golden calves with the same blasphemous declaration made by the calf worshippers at Sinai: "Behold/These are your gods, O Israel, which brought you up out of the land of Egypt" (1 Kgs 12:28/Exod 32:4). They recognize that only an insane person would seek to court loyal followers of Yahweh in this fashion, if those followers were familiar with the events at Sinai as they are reported in Exodus 32. In fact, it is for this reason that diachronic interpreters conclude that the literary Jeroboam of 1 Kings 12 is a victim of "polemical distortion" (Cross 1973:73), and propose as a realistic alternative that the presumably sane historical Jeroboam was appealing to a tradition of acceptable Yahwistic calf symbolism known to his followers in the north, a tradition which the author of Kings is attempting to obscure.

The author's desire to obscure this tradition is usually attributed to his misunderstanding of cult-images, a misunderstanding which many scholars believe is characteristic of the Hebrew Bible as a whole.[3] According to this argument, the author of Kings "completely misses the point of Jeroboam's action" (Jenks 1977:103; cf. Gray 1970:315). Others speculate that the historical Jeroboam may have caused the people to confuse Yahweh with Baal when he made the calves, "however excellent [his] intentions may have been" (Kennedy 1901:342; cf. Jenks 1977:103). It is usually assumed that Jeroboam himself was aware that the calves, like the cherubim in Jerusalem, simply represented a pedestal for the divine presence, although the difference between a pedestal and an idol would have been lost on the ordinary worshipper. Only Jeroboam and "people of a more refined religious sensitivity" could appreciate the difference (de Vaux 1971:102-103; cf. Noth 1960:233). The calves were "all too open to misinterpretation by the unsophisticated" (Nelson 1987:81). In other words, while the author misunderstands the historical Jeroboam's true intentions with the calf images, the only thing Jeroboam misunderstood was the degree of religious sophistication of the people to whom he was appealing—assuming, of course, that he was not consciously attempting to control them politically by pandering to their fetishistic proclivities. Thanks to this set of assumptions and hypotheses, historians are able to trace a plausible path from Jeroboam's innocent intentions to the resulting outbreak of popular fetishism which eventually triggered the polemic in Kings.

This line of interpretation not only assumes that Jeroboam was addressing a 10th-century audience which mistook symbols and emblems of divinity for fetishes,[4] but that the misguided 7th- or 6th-century authors of the polemic in Kings were addressing an audience which was equally misinformed about the nature of image-worship. At the same time, this interpretation presupposes that Jeroboam believed his audience to be *well-informed* about traditions of acceptable Yahwistic calf-images, if not stories which lauded an earlier occasion of calf-building at Sinai.[5] The fact that the first documented opposition to northern calf-images comes only in the 8th century with Hosea (8:4-6; 10:5; 13:2) is taken as evidence that these positive traditions remained vital long after Jeroboam's reign, in the north if not in the south as well. In addition, archaeological evidence suggests that the inhabitants of Israel and Judah were exposed to the use of a variety of bovine imagery in the worship of Hadad and Baal (if not Yahweh) throughout the monarchical period.[6] In spite of these indications that ancient readers of Kings would be at least somewhat knowledgeable about such images, the historians' alternative scenario assumes that the author of Kings is addressing an audience which was so ignorant of any tradition of laudable calf-worship, and so uninformed about the symbolic use of calf images to represent Yahweh's invisible presence or power, that they would accept as historical fact a reductive and blatantly polemical portrait of Jeroboam.

Before accepting the notion that Jeroboam's intentions were misconstrued by all concerned, one must consider the possibility that the author was actually addressing a much more sophisticated audience, one which was not only familiar with the true purpose of cult images and traditions of acceptable calf symbolism, but which was also capable of detecting the presence of subtle literary devices like irony and hyperbole. The charge that images were misunderstood as fetishes is based mainly on the seeming identification of a god and its image in biblical texts. Preuss (1971:282-85) has rightly challenged this view, claiming that the biblical writers were well aware of the difference between the gods and their images. The "identification" serves a rhetorical function; it is an intentionally compressed and reductive presentation of what the polemists believe to be the reality of the situation, namely, that image and "god" are equally vacuous. Clearly, the fact that biblical texts misrepresent image worship does not necessarily imply that the biblical authors misunderstood how the worshippers viewed the cult-images.

Similarly, one cannot simply assume that the biblical authors intentionally misrepresented other cults "in order to protect the identity and purity of Yahwism" (Carroll 1977:54). This assumes that the audience for which the polemics were fashioned was so uninformed and naive that they not only needed such prophylaxis, but could be convinced by polemics which, according to Carroll, amount to nothing more than "a ludicrous example of sheer reductionism of the grossest materialistic type" (1977:53).

If, however, the authors were speaking to audiences which were sufficiently knowledgeable about the phenomenon of image-worship to recognize that such portrayals were ludicrously reductive, the authors would expect those audiences to interpret these polemical portraits just as they would seek the message of any caricature or ironic exposé. Because "recourse to irony by an author carries an implicit compliment to the intelligence of the reader" (Abrams 1981:90), the very presence of irony in texts such as 1 Kings 12 would constitute evidence that the author was addressing an audience which possessed some degree of literary sophistication. One objective of the detailed synchronic analysis of 1 Kgs 12:26-28 and related texts offered in the next section is to determine whether irony is in fact present.

When I say that I will examine 1 Kgs 12:26-28 for clues about the audience addressed by the author, I am talking about what Peter Rabinowitz (1987:21) calls the "authorial audience." Rabinowitz points out that readers of narrative play several audience roles at any given time. The "authorial audience" is the hypothetical audience for which an author rhetorically designs a work. The author expects members of that hypothetical audience to possess a specific degree of knowledge and literary competence (e.g., knowledge of literary conventions, ability to detect the presence of rhetorical devices, knowledge about historical persons and events alluded to in the narrative). Rabinowitz believes that "even among the most jaded readers— academics—the majority still attempts to read as authorial audience" (1987:30). In what follows I will argue that the historians who assume that the ancient audience of 1 Kings 12 was incapable of recognizing the ludicrous and reductive nature of the polemic against Jeroboam have misconstrued the authorial audience.

In addition, scholars who offer the standard diachronic reading of 1 Kings 12 typically fail to acknowledge the role played by the "narrative audience" in establishing the meaning of the text. As members of the narrative audience, readers believe (or pretend to believe) what the narrator says. The "ideal narrative audience" accepts "uncritically" what the narrator has to say (Rabinowitz 1977:135). Rabinowitz points out that if we do not pretend to be members of the narrative audience, or if we misapprehend the beliefs of that audience, we are apt to make invalid, even perverse, interpretations (1987:86). Readers routinely pretend to believe what the narrator presents as real even though they simultaneously "know better." In realistic fiction this may not be a major issue, for there is a good deal of overlap between the facts presented by the narrator and what the authorial audience believes to be fact. When a narrator *does* relate facts which the authorial audience finds to be incredible or astonishing, that very incredibility becomes an indicator of how the narrator's story should be interpreted.[7] As noted by Booth (1974:57-58), when authors make glaring errors of historical fact and have speakers betray "foolishness that is 'simply incredible'" they may be signaling readers to view such elements as indicators of an ironic intent.

The words of the speaker Jeroboam in 1 Kgs 12:28 will seem incredible to the *narrative audience* of Exodus 32-1 Kings 12.[8] They will share the astonishment of R. Judah bar Pazzi (*j. Seqal.* I, 1, 45d) when he compared the people's giving up their gold for Aaron's calf with their later giving of gold for the Tabernacle (Exod 35:21-29) and then exclaimed: "Shall we read and not be confounded [or startled; *nibʻat*]?" The *authorial audience* will recognize that the narrator's picture of Jeroboam attempting to attract pious Yahwists by alluding to the apostasy at Sinai is so startling and incredible (historically as well as intertextually) that the point must be that the king was actually foolish and self-destructive enough to use such an absurd strategy. Only the *ideal narrative audience* could accept the narrator's report of Jeroboam's allusion to Exodus 32 at face value and not be confounded. One midrash about Jeroboam expresses the point of view of the ideal narrative audience quite well. In response to the people's initial demand for an idol, Jeroboam sends out emissaries who attempt to persuade pious Israelites to accept the calves by pointing out that the wilderness generation was the most cherished of all generations and was not severely punished for their idolatry. They claim that Jeroboam merely wanted to do the same thing, only twice over (*j. ʻAbod. Zar.* 1:1). This story manages to acknowledge Jeroboam's allusion to the people's apostasy as the narrator had reported it in Exodus 32 and still find a credible and even rational basis for Jeroboam's appeal to this sinful event.

SYNCHRONIC ANALYSIS OF JEROBOAM'S INTENTIONS IN 1 KGS 12:26-33 AND RELATED TEXTS

Quotation as a Way to Expose the Self-Will and Self-Deception of Idolators Like the Jeroboam of 1 Kgs 12:28-33

In 1 Kgs 12:26-27 the narrator informs readers about Jeroboam's motivations and intentions by directly quoting what he "said in his heart." This narrative technique is relatively rare in the histories (see, e.g., Long 1984:41), although it is more frequently used in the prophetic books and Psalms to expose the mentality of idolators and other complacent and deluded malefactors.[9] Before quoting Jeroboam's public proclamation "Behold your gods . . ." in verse 28, the narrator reports that the king "took counsel" (*wayyiwwâ'ats*) with himself, not with the kind of counselors upon whom his rival Rehoboam had been so utterly dependent.[10] In verse 33 the narrator calls attention to the fact that Jeroboam's newly established festival (12:32) was taking place in the month he devised alone (reading *millibbôd*, Kethib; cf. Neh 6:8), or, from his own heart (reading *millibbô*, with Qere). Finally, in 13:33 the narrator recalls the priests of high places whom Jeroboam had chosen from among all the people (12:31), remarking that those appointed were "any who had the desire" (*hehâpêts*). They, like their employer, do what they desire. Taken together, these verses suggest that the actions which resulted in an idol-worshipping kingdom were part of a self-conceived and privately planned agenda by the king, implemented without input from human advisors or guidance from God.

For readers who are familiar with Deuteronomy 12, 16, and 18, the element of self-will in Jeroboam's agenda for cult reform will be even more pronounced. In Deuteronomy 12, Moses relates Yahweh's order to destroy pagan objects (vss. 2-4) and goes on to declare that future offerings will be made "at the place Yahweh your God will choose" (vss. 5-7). This is the same place where festivals will be celebrated (Deut 16:15) and Levites will officiate (Deut 18:6). When this state of affairs is in effect, says Moses in Deut 12:8, "you" shall no longer do as "we" do presently, that is, "every man what is right in his own eyes." In a sense, when Jeroboam decides to do the right thing in his own eyes with altars, images, festivals, and non-Levite priests at Bethel and Dan, he draws Israel back from monarchical "rest" (1 Kgs 5:18; 8:56; cf. Weinfeld 1972:170) into the kind of anarchy, idolatry and internecine strife reported in Judges 17-21 (including idolatry and chaos in Bethel [20:18][11] and Dan [18:27-31]), when there is no king in Israel. In effect,

Jeroboam brings on the kind of chaos that kings were installed to prevent.

The fact that Deuteronomy includes idolatry among the "abominations to Yahweh" associated with hypocrisy and deception (7:25-26; 27:15; cf. Weinfeld 1972:268-69) suggests that it is associated with self-deception as well as with self-will. As noted by Muecke (1982:22, 35-37), irony is often used in literary works to expose the self-ignorance and "self-assured blindness" of characters. In biblical polemics against idolatry, the astonishing and fatal self-deception and obtuseness of idolaters is often revealed by presenting their private thoughts and intentions in an ironic manner. For example, in Isa 44:9-20 the idolators' topsy-turvy attitude is revealed by "quotation" of what they *should* say but *do not*. If they were not oblivious to the truth about their behavior, they would wake up and ask, "Shall I fall down before a block of wood . . . Is there not a lie [*sheqer*] in my right hand?" (44:19-20) More often the idolators are ironically "quoted" as though they *were* actually admitting the true meaning of their actions, even though in reality they remain unaware of this meaning. For example, Isaiah quotes the "scoffing proverb-makers" of Jerusalem as saying, "we have made lies our refuge" (28:15). The prophet ironically attributes to the ungodly scoffers awareness of the actual import of their actions (Blank 1977:56; cf. Wolff 1964:71 and 84). In reality, they are far from such an awareness, even though the prophet implies that the folly of their deeds (in this case, a treaty with Egypt; see below) should be blatantly obvious.

A related technique is the ironic description of the result of the idolators' actions as though it were their conscious intention, often through the use of the conjunction *lema'an*.[12] For example, Isaiah states that the "rebellious children" who do not take counsel from Yahweh do so "in order to" (*lema'an*) add sin to sin (30:1; cf. 5:19 and below). Hosea exposes the absurdity of the "calf of Samaria" in similar fashion, describing how "with their silver and gold they made idols for themselves, in order that [*lema'an*] it shall be cut off" (8:4-6; text uncertain). A less obvious example is Moses' statement to "all Israel" in his farewell address that while "you have seen all that Yahweh did before your eyes" in Egypt, "Yahweh has not given you a heart to know, and eyes to see, and ears to hear unto this day" (Deut 29:1, 3). The authorial audience of Deuteronomy cannot take these words literally, if for no other reason than the fact that Moses has repeatedly said—and shown—that the people *have* been given the faculties to know and choose life and good, but nevertheless chose death and evil. Moses' point is that they have been so unnaturally stupid and self-destructive that it is as if God did not equip them with the means to witness, understand and respond with good intentions to the obvious message.

In 1 Kgs 12:28, the narrator exposes the king's idolatrous mentality by directly "quoting" his speech and thoughts in the same way that the prophets ironically "quote" idolators as saying what they would actually *never* say or even acknowledge. For the narrative audience familiar with Exodus 32 as well as 1 Kings 12, calf-worship is so foolish, and so obviously doomed to disaster, that it is as though the king had actually been so mad as to declare "Behold your gods, Israel, who brought you up out of the land of Egypt," in spite of the apostasy at Sinai and its consequences. In addition, the narrative audience which appraises Jeroboam's other cult reforms (1 Kgs 12:31-32) in terms of the standards set up by the speaker Moses in Deuteronomy 12, 16, and 18, will again be astounded by the overwhelming folly and self-defeating nature of his actions. Jeroboam's obliviousness to the destruction which the author believes will inevitably result from this enterprise is underscored by reporting the result of the king "vexing Yahweh" as though it were his intention. Jeroboam is said to act in order to vex Yahweh (1 Kgs 14:9, 16) and to "cause Israel to sin" (14:16). The phrase *hik'îs 'et yhwh* ("to vex [or provoke] Yahweh"), which McCarthy[13] calls "the provocation formula," is used in Deuteronomy, Kings, and Jeremiah to make the same sort of ironic judgment on idolators as the ironic *lema'an*, by describing result as though it were purpose.[14] From the point of view of the author of Kings, the fact that Jeroboam and the kings who followed him persisted in "sinning," in spite of all the warnings from prophets (1 Kgs 13:2-3; 14:7-16; 2 Kgs 17:13-14, 23; cf. Hos 13:2), could well be viewed as having been intended to vex Yahweh.

Jeroboam's Intentions in 1 Kgs 12:26-27 and the Leader's Duty to Restrain Followers who "Break Loose"

Many commentators believe that 1 Kgs 12:26-27 put "words into Jeroboam's mind that must have been close to actuality" (De Vries 1985:162; cf. Talmon 1958:50). Even Hoffmann (1980:64), who dismisses as anachronistic the idea of a central cult in Jerusalem exercising a magnetic power of attraction over people in the north during Jeroboam's reign, concedes that the independence of his kingdom could only be maintained if the new state were put "cultically on its own feet." What is most striking in Jeroboam's quoted thoughts, however, is his fear of assassination by his people, as well as the understanding of his people which would give rise to this fear. His motivation for making golden calves is the thought that the heart of the people would return (*weshâb*) to Rehoboam when they went up to offer sacrifices in Jerusalem, leading them to kill him and return (*weshâbû*) to his rival. This thought occurs to Jeroboam shortly after Rehoboam had set out to make the kingship return (*lehâshîb*) to himself by force (12:21), only to be countered by the man of God Shemaiah, who informs Rehoboam that Yahweh wants him and every one of his men to return (*shûbû, wayyâshûbû*) home (vs. 24). In effect, Jeroboam is concerned that his own people might themselves do what Rehoboam and his army wanted to do against him. By inaugurating calf-worship, Jeroboam actually prompts the people to go north from Bethel in a procession to Dan, rather than returning south to Jerusalem after assassinating him (12:30).

Jeroboam's quoted thoughts in verses 26-27 imply that he views his followers as so fickle and violent that they might kill him and return their allegiance to Rehoboam, in spite of the fact that they had so recently killed Rehoboam's *corvée* officer Adoram, an act which prompted Rehoboam to rush back to Jerusalem in his chariot to avoid the same fate (12:18).[15] When Jeroboam goes on in verse 28 to announce his solution to the threat he has just pondered in verses 26-27, he does so in terms which call to mind the events surrounding Aaron's calf at Sinai. Readers who recall the behavior of the people before and after

Aaron builds his calf may find the king's fear of his followers' irrationality and violence to be well founded. The Israelites who gather against Aaron in Exodus 32 possess all the traits of mass psychology (impatience, ambivalence toward authority figures, a tendency to "deify error," an inclination to create scapegoats) which leaders must be able to control.[16] Moses' rebuke of Aaron after he destroys his brother's calf-idol shows how Moses understands mass psychology, and how he expects a true leader to cope with it. Moses excoriates his brother for having brought a great sin on the people (vs. 21): "What did this people do to you, that you have brought a great sin upon them?" Moses views the people as having "broken loose," because Aaron had "let them break loose" (pr'; Exod 32:25).[17] Moses judges Aaron by his own strict standards. He implies that it is easy for a true leader to restrain the people's tendency to break loose—so easy that Aaron's failure to do so could only be intentional, as though Aaron led them into anarchy and sin in order to pay them back for some wrong they had done to him earlier.

However, the narrator's account of Aaron's failure in Exod 32:1-6 suggests that Aaron had failed not because he chose to release his control over the people, but because he immediately surrendered to their irrational demands and so was controlled by them. In this sense Aaron resembles Saul rather than Jeroboam, who *does* intentionally lead his people to commit a great sin in the way implied by Moses.[18] When Samuel is about to encounter Saul for the first time, Yahweh tells Samuel "This one will restrain [ya'tsôr] my people" (1 Sam 9:17).[19] If Yahweh resembles Moses in His emphasis on the importance of a leader constraining his people, Saul resembles Aaron when he later leads Israel to sin by fearing the people and listening to their voice after the victory over Amalek (1 Sam 15:24).

While both Exodus 32 and 1 Kings 12 describe failures of leadership which result in rampant idolatry, Aaron and Jeroboam display two distinct types of leadership failure. In this respect the two narratives are complementary rather than identical. Exodus 32 shows the danger caused by the absence of a strong leader, when his followers are impatient, fickle, and incapable of restraining themselves. The idolatrous Israelites cannot be controlled by a passive leader like Aaron. 1 Kings 12, on the other hand, describes the danger presented by a leader who takes decisive action to control the people because he believes they are capable of turning against him and killing him. However, in his effort to control and constrain the people from harming him, Jeroboam seductively "draws them away" *into* idolatry (*nâdah* Hiph., 2 Kgs 17:21 Qere; cf. Deut 13:6, 14) instead of fulfilling his true task of constraining them *from* idolatry.

CONCLUSION: SYNCHRONIC ANALYSIS AND HISTORICAL INTERPRETATIONS OF 1 KINGS 11-12 AND RELATED TEXTS

In an influential study, Perlitt (1969:208) suggests that Exodus 32, like 1 Kings 12, was composed during Josiah's reign, in order to show the Judean audience that all the later problems stemming from Jeroboam's actions had occurred in spite of the early warning and prohibition reported in Exodus 32-34. While my synchronic analysis does not point to any specific date of composition, it does clarify what the narratives are *specifically* warning against, namely, the disastrous consequences which occur when leaders fail to restrain the people from idolatry. Aaron fails because he passively surrenders to the mob, allowing them to break loose, while Jeroboam restrains the mob from assassinating him by actively drawing them into idolatry. The seriousness of the religious anarchy which results in both cases is underscored by repeated reports that at least some of those who had served the calves were themselves sacrificed because of that service—by the Levites (Exod 32:25-29; cf. Deut 33:9), by Josiah (1 Kgs 13:2; 2 Kgs 23:20), and by the narrator implicitly criticizing Jehu for sacrificing Baal priests but failing to do away with the golden calf cult as he had done away with the Baal cult (2 Kgs 10:29).

The synchronic analysis has also provided support for the notion that 1 Kings 12 is aimed at an audience which possesses enough knowledge and literary sophistication to recognize that the narrator's account of Jeroboam intentionally reproducing the fiasco at Sinai is a blatant misrepresentation designed to expose the king's self-defeating willfulness through the use of irony and the absurd. At the same time, the fact that these texts focus on the chaos which ensues when people are allowed, or encouraged, to break loose into fetishism, suggests that the author and the well-educated authorial audience might believe that the majority of their less sophisticated fellow citizens were just as capable of mistaking cult-images for fetishes as were the character Jeroboam's followers—and therefore just as likely to be seduced into disaster by another false leader.

For their part, historians who assume that the author of 1 Kgs 12:26-32 is writing for an audience which would take the narrator's incredible statements at face value are guilty of mistaking the *author's* intentions. This is not to deny that there are certain elements shared by 1 Kings 12 and Exodus 32 which are difficult to characterize as authorial inventions designed to be taken as ironic or incredible by the authorial audience (e.g., the fact that Jeroboam's ill-fated sons bear the same names as Aaron's doomed sons Nadab and Abihu; see n. 1 above). It only means that the specific concept of idolatrous calf worship and false leadership projected by the narratives is communicated through the use of literary devices which require the audience to use their knowledge of the actual use of cult-images in their people's history to gauge how radically the author misrepresents such usage in order to make his point.

While the sychronic examination of 1 Kings 12 and Exodus 32 demonstrated that the authors of these texts believed the problems of illicit cult-images of Yahweh, mass chaos, and false leadership were intimately related, it could not determine at what point in Israelite history this specific cluster of problems would have been of most vital importance to Israelite religious and political authorities. However, Dtr also mentions this specific set of problems in his report of a cult reform about which historians are somewhat better informed. Interestingly, this is not the account of Josiah's reform (2 Kings 22-23) which explicitly refers back to the Jeroboam narrative, but the account of Hezekiah's reform in 2 Kings 18. By comparing 1 Kings 12 with 2 Kings 18—and taking into account what is known about the historical context of Hezekiah's reforms—one can better understand the kinds of social and political forces which might have led the author of 1 Kings 12 to characterize Jeroboam's reforms as he does.[20]

Dtr's polemic against Jeroboam had condemned the king's new calf-centers and other reform measures as apostate by defining the only legitimate cult-center as Jerusalem and by branding as illegitimate the rural *bamôt* and cult-objects like the calves. Among the forces which seem to have fostered this definition of the true cult in the 8th century BCE were the instability of monarchic succession in the north following the death of Jeroboam ben Nebat's namesake Jeroboam II, and Assyrian intrusion into Syria-Palestine (which ultimately led to the fall of Samaria and the reduction of Judean-controlled territory to Jerusalem during Sennacherib's campaign[21]). For prophets like Hosea and Isaiah, and for later writers like Dtr, political alliances with other nations against Assyria, cultural assimilation with Assyria, and cult practices which were deemed syncretistic threatened to reduce to chaos the religious and social order they were struggling to conserve in the face of the possible loss of national autonomy and identity. One way to cope with these threatening influences was to condemn them as foolish and corrupting innovations. The fact that these cultic actions and objects may have been as firmly grounded in Yahwistic tradition as those located at the central Temple (if not more so) was not important; what mattered was that those still in control used their remaining power to (re)define what was tradition and what was anathema.

Because illicit cult practices and ill-advised international alliances were perceived as invitations to chaos, it is not surprising that they became associated with other forms of "chaos" dreaded by those in power, including the chaos of mob action prompted by false leaders who "seduced" the people or were overpowered by them. Thus, when Hosea and Isaiah condemn Israelite leaders for attempting to protect themselves against the Assyrian threat by making alliances with other untrustworthy foreign powers, they use ironic quotation and the result-intention switch to depict those leaders as idolators who are just as self-deceived and death-devoted as the run-of-the-mill image-worshippers who bow down to calves, pledge themselves to Baal, or frequent rural *bamôt* (e.g., Isa 28:15; 30:1; cf. Hos 7:8-11; 8:4; and above).

If Dtr links the problems of "centrifugal" cult reforms and mob pressure when he reports how the divided monarchy began with Jeroboam, he shows the relationship between the Assyrian threat, "centripetal" cult reform and the leader's need to restrain the people when he recounts how Hezekiah reformed Judah after Jeroboam's sin ended the divided monarchy. While the narrator's direct report of Hezekiah's reform in 2 Kgs 18:4 is extremely brief (especially in comparison with 2 Chronicles 29-31), it does include a remarkable notice that the king crushed (*kâtat* Piel) Nehushtan, the bronze serpent long ago fabricated by Moses. Ironically, the artifact crafted by Israel's prototypal true leader and "crusher" of calf-idols (*kâtat* Qal; Deut 9:21) had apparently begun to draw the people away from Yahweh like the idols made by Aaron, Jeroboam, and other false leaders. This would be particularly ironic if the people were burning food offerings to it *because* it was made by Moses. In contrast to the standard inventory of *bamôt, matstsêbôt*, and *'ashêrâ* destroyed by the king (see 1 Kgs 14:23; 2 Kgs 17:10; 21:3; and 23:14-15), the unique and relatively lengthy account of the smashing of Nehushtan stands out precisely because it links cult offerings, idolatry, and the issue of proper leadership.

The few remaining references to Hezekiah's reform in Kings also connect his actions with the problem of the people's tendency to be seduced into idolatry. Ironically, these references occur in the speech of an Assyrian diplomat as part of *his* attempt to seduce and mislead the people of Judah by telling them that Hezekiah is attempting to mislead *them*. Speaking to the assembled people in their own language, the Rabshakeh warns his audience not to let the king "beguile" them (2 Kgs 18:29) by implying that he could deliver them, or "incite" them (18:32) by convincing them that Yahweh could be trusted to deliver them (cf. vs. 30). The verb used by the Rabshakeh in verse 32, *sût* (Hiphil), is used by Moses in Deut 13:7 in reference to those who entice family members to follow other gods. Before speaking to the people as a whole, the Rabshakeh had told Hezekiah's three representatives that they should not think of using trust in Yahweh as a counterargument, for Hezekiah had radically reduced the quantity of Yahweh's *bamôt* and altars, and had told Judah and Jerusalem to worship before the Jerusalem altar (18:22). The Rabshakeh implies that the king's reforms and centralization measures have offended Yahweh, so that Yahweh could not be trusted to deliver them. The implied connection between the reforms and the king's alleged misguidance of the people is made explicit in the Chronicler's summary version of the Assyrian argument (2 Chr 32:11-12).

The authorial audience of Kings is of course expected to recognize that the Rabshakeh has things upside down; the reforms and the centralization would please Yahweh, not offend Him. Hezekiah is not seducing the people by preaching trust in Yahweh after having committed cultic apostasy; on the contrary, his actions were "right in the eyes of Yahweh" (18:3). The king depicted by the Rabshakeh resembles Jeroboam, not Hezekiah. The Assyrian imagines an apostate Hezekiah telling his assembled people, "You shall worship before this altar in Jerusalem" (2 Kgs 18:22), just as Jeroboam told the assembled Israelites to worship at the altar in Bethel (and Dan) rather than in Jerusalem (1 Kgs 12:28; cf. 12:32-33). From Jeroboam's topsy-turvy perspective, he is just as much an advocate of cult "centralization" as any southern king. From the Judean point of view, on the other hand, both Jeroboam and the Rabshakeh need to reverse their understanding of what constitutes the center of legitimate worship for Yahweh's people. From Dtr's perspective, centralization of the cult in the Temple, the smashing of false cult objects, and alliance with Yahweh rather than foreign powers, are the only ways to stave off political and social chaos and invite deliverance. By placing their trust in these measures Hezekiah and his restrained people (2 Kgs 18:36) have found the true antidote to the seductive spell cast by smooth speakers like the Rabshakeh and the Jeroboam of 1 Kgs 12:28 and 2 Kgs 17:21.[22]

NOTES

[1] If one accepts the notion that Exod 32:34 alludes vaguely to the fall of the Northern Kingdom (see Perlitt 1969:209; and the scholars cited by Hahn 1981:99 n. 612), then both narratives would also be similar in projecting exile as a result of calf apostasy. Yet another similarity is the fact that both Jeroboam and Aaron have sons named Nadab and Abijah/Abihu who die prematurely (Lev 10:1-3; 1 Kgs 14:17; 15:27).

[2] Although I would argue that the concept of original sin is alien to these stories, and to the Hebrew Bible as a whole, such theological characterizations do make the point that it is difficult to exaggerate the author's assessment of the negative repercussions of the calf-images.

[3] For example, Carroll (1977:53) argues that Israel's understanding of reality, and particularly of its God Yahweh, was so different from that of other ancient Near Eastern peoples that image worship could only be misunderstood.

[4] Kaufmann's influential argument (1972:7-20) that the images were inevitably mistaken for mere fetishes is accepted by Carroll (1977:53) and many others. The most extensive critique of this view is Faur's (1978:3-5). Faur himself believes that Israel's neighbors viewed consecrated images as "living idols" or personifications of the god (1978:5-12). According to Jacobsen (1987:29), the images offered the potential and incentive for a theophany because the god "participated" in the image.

[5] See, e.g., Cross (1973:74-75) and the many scholars cited by Hahn (1981:215 and n. 19) and Moberly (1982:162, 221 n. 21).

[6] See, e.g., Mazar (1982) for a discussion of the Iron Age I bronze figurine of a bull found at the so-called "bull site" in the Land of Manasseh, the "few bronze bull figurines . . . known from the Levant" (1982:29) at the time of his article, and the stelae from Arslan Tash and other locales which depict the storm god Hadad (Ba'al) standing on a bull. For a description of the Middle Bronze Age silver calf figurine found in Canaanite Ashkelon in 1990, see Stager (1991).

[7] E.g., the egregious anachronisms in Judith and Tobit signal readers that, while what follows may convey an important message or truth, it is not based on historical fact.

[8] Because biblical narrators tend to be self-effacing, the narrative audience of Exodus-Kings will assume that the same voice is reporting the entire continuing story. Hearing Jeroboam's quoted words in 1 Kgs 12:28 after having read Exod 32:4 will lead the narrative audience of Exodus-Kings to radically revise their understanding of Jeroboam's description in 1 Kgs 11:26-12:27, as they simultaneously reconsider the "holistic sense" of the two stories in the larger context of Exodus-Kings.

⁹ This is true of all but one occurrence of this phrase in the prophets and Psalms listed in BDB (Isa 14:13; 47:8-10; Hos 7:2 [text difficult]; Pss 10:6, 11, 13; 14:1; 35:25), although the phrase is not used so regularly in other biblical books to expose the mentality of sinners.

¹⁰ See Hahn (1981:270-72) for references to some of the many scholars who take the Niphal imperfect of y'ts here as indicating that the king took counsel alone, that is, with himself.

¹¹ Admittedly, some commentators (e.g., Boling 1975:285) believe that bêt-'êl here simply means "the sanctuary" and not the place Bethel. Moreover, the reference to Bethel in 20:26 occurs in connection with an appropriate action taken by the Israelites, not the foolish action reported in verse 18. Yet the fact remains that the mention of Bethel verse 26 is part of a larger context involving grotesque and unholy civil strife.

¹² For a list of passages in which lema'an is used ironically, see BDB (775); Koehler and Baumgartner (549); and Driver (1902:325-26).

¹³ McCarthy (1974:100); cf. Driver (1902:72); and Weinfeld (1972:340 #6).

¹⁴ In fact, hik'îs and lema'an appear together in Jer 7:18; 25:7; 32:29.

¹⁵ Thus, the rivals "Jeroboam" and "Rehoboam," whose throne-names express a desire for the people to be great and to expand, share a fear that the people of Israel might use their expanding power to assassinate them.

¹⁶ It is Le Bon (1960:110) who observes that "the masses . . . turn aside from evidence that is not to their taste, preferring to deify error, if error seduce them." The Greek historians continually note the combination of irresponsibility, violence and lack of restraint which characterizes humans in groups (e.g., Herodotus 3, 81; Thucydides 3.84; cf. Freud 1959:9-10). For a discussion of René Girard's views concerning the operation of the scapegoat mechanism in communities, and an application of his ideas to the Pentateuch, see Lasine (1992).

¹⁷ The most recent studies of the verb pr' are those of Janzen (1989; 1990). While his understanding of pârua' in Exod 32:25 (1990: 603-605) differs from that given here, I would agree with his translation of yippârа' in Prov 29:18 as "fall into anarchy" (1989:396). Janzen believes that the Chronicler's reference to King Ahaz breaking loose in Judah and bringing Judah low (2 Chr 28:19) implies "not simply that the king personally acted wantonly, but that—as the Hiphil form indicates, and like Aaron—he as king had been responsible for forms of social behavior in Judah that went against the rule and the order of Yahweh the divine king" (1989:400). It must be noted, however, that Exodus 32 does not imply that Aaron himself shared the mentality denoted by the verb pr', unlike Ahaz, who is accused of

walking in the ways of the kings of Israel, and "making molten images [massêkôt] for the Baalim" (2 Chr 28:2) among other sins, and who ultimately infects the people with his own idolatrous lack of restraint.

[18] I would therefore disagree with Aberbach and Smolar's view (1967:135) that Aaron and Jeroboam are "to all intents and purposes identical."

[19] For a discussion of this unique use of the verb 'âtsar to describe the leader's duty to constrain the people, see Edelman (1991: 48-49).

[20] Of course, such general analogies do *not* constitute evidence that a version of 1 Kings 12 was composed during the early years of what Weinfeld (1985:89; cf. 91) calls "the period of Hezekiah-Josiah."

[21] According to Weinfeld (1985:86), "the Hezekian reform was born out of dire circumstances at the time of Sennacherib's expedition against Judah, when only Jerusalem was left free. It was therefore easy to proclaim Jerusalem as the only legitimate place of worship." However, Cogan and Tadmor (1988:219) argue that the reform should be dated prior to 705 BCE, on the grounds that it would have been unwise to disrupt social and religious stability by altering the cult while provisioning for war. They suggest instead that Hezekiah's reform was directed at preventing the idolatrous practices held responsible for the fall of the Northern Kingdom in 722 BCE from leading Judah to the same fate (1988:220). While Halpern agrees that the reform antedated Sennacherib's assaults, he also associates the reform with Hezekiah's preparations for revolt, his "hedgehog defense" against Assyria, and his overall programme of "centralized urbanization" (1991:19, 27, 47).

[22] In the end, the Rabshakeh's quoted words serve only to expose his topsy-turvy logic, as do the words of the Assyrian king quoted by Isaiah (Isa 10:8-11; cf. 2 Kgs 18:22, 34-35) and the quoted speech of all other biblical idolators.

9

THE FALL OF THE HOUSE: A CARNIVALESQUE READING OF 2 KINGS 9 AND 10[1]

Francisco O. García-Treto

> "I saw a topsy-turvy world," he replied, "the upper [class] underneath and the lower on top."
> "My son," he observed, "you saw a clear world."
> — Pesahim 50a

When the story of Jehu's destruction of the House of Ahab and of the House of Baal in Samaria (2 Kings 9 and 10) is read as an integral part of the large narrative design of the Deuteronomistic work (DH), an instance of intertextuality appears in which motifs with dramatic, even tragic, intent are now "carnivalized."[2] The central motif so dealt with is "house," well-known as the integrating motif in the structure of the Davidic story in Samuel. The House of Ahab becomes, in fact, a negative, or antithetical, allusion to, or "re-presentation" of, the Davidic House. Therefore, awareness of intertextuality allows a rich reading of DH as a narrative meditation on the rise and fall of the House—in all the senses of "house"—of David, even in passages where the overt reference is to the House of Ahab.

"HOUSE" IN 2 KINGS 9 AND 10

I begin by observing that "house" (*bêt*) appears to be a *Leitwort* in these two chapters, where it actually occurs eighteen times. The most common combination is in the expression "House of Ahab," relatively rare in 2 Kings,[3] with the great majority of its occurrences in chapters 9 and 10. Next in frequency is "House of Baal," found five times in chapter 10 out of the total of ten occurrences in the Bible.

Not only does Jehu go "inside" the house (*habbaytah*) with

the young prophet who anoints him in the crucial scene of initiation, but all the scenes in the two chapters involve a series of variations on an "inside/outside" theme which keeps the reader aware of house/non-house contrasts, even at points where "house" is not mentioned. For example, the word does not occur in 9:30-37, but the scene is unimaginable without the house where Jezebel first holds a commanding position at the window while Jehu stands outside, only to be cast outside to her death as he goes inside to eat and drink. The proud Queen Mother had just sarcastically identified the rebellious general (who is in process of destroying her dead husband's "house") with Zimri, the hapless rebel whose capture of his master Baasha's house had only furnished him with the instrument for his suicide: "and burned the king's *house* over him with fire, and died."

From *within* the house, Jehu sends his people to "see to this damned woman, and bury her, for she is—after all—a king's daughter," but his servants return to him to report that they could only find bits and pieces. *Without* her house, Jezebel has literally become dirt. Other uses of "house" in these chapters include *asher 'al habêt* ("the one over the *house*") for "palace steward" in 10:5, and two topographic references associated with accounts of the killing of members of the Judean royal family (9:27; 10:12, 14). Granted that it is not easy to avoid running into place names compounded with *bêt*, these names nonetheless add to the cumulative effect that the variations and repetitions of that theme create in 2 Kings 9 and 10.

But it is now time to return to a consideration of "house" as a motivic constellation in the text at hand. What, in the first place, is the meaning of "House of Ahab" in our text? The first three occurrences of the expression (2 Kgs 9:7, 8, and 9) punctuate the young prophet's commissioning speech to Jehu, each time with a definite and different nuance. In verse 7, the prophetic voice tells Jehu to "strike down the House of Ahab *your master*," and both the rest of the verse and the anticipatory use of "your master," the very word which Jehu will hear from Jezebel's scornful lips in verse 31, identify her here as being in some sense "the House of Ahab."[4] Next, the male progeny[5] of

Ahab's line is identified as "House of Ahab" in the prophet's speech (vs. 8). Finally, in verse 9, "House of Ahab" means "dynasty," in explicit comparison to the "houses" of Jeroboam ben Nebat and Baasha ben Ahijah. This prophetic speech is a programmatic statement for the ensuing narrative: the stories of Jehu's massacres at Jezreel and Samaria are precisely the accounts of the destruction of Ahab's progeny and kin, of Jezebel, of Ahab's dynasty. Part of the same motivic constellation that Joel Rosenberg (1986) and others have identified for the senses of "house" in the Davidic dynastic oracle of 2 Samuel 7 has emerged in the structure of the fall of the House of Ahab in 2 Kings 9 and 10 (see also Regina M. Schwartz 1991:192-210).

The story of the destruction of the House of Baal in chapter 10 caps off the series of narrative events in Dtr's presentation of Jehu's destruction of the House of Ahab. Two "houses"—of a king and of a god—are linked in the narrative of their fall as, *mutatis mutandis*, divine and royal. "Houses" are also coupled in the Davidic dynastic oracle of 2 Samuel, and in other texts, such as 1 Kings 8, where the same motivic framework is apparent. The latter is of particular interest, since the main structural elements in the account of Jehu's destruction of the House of Baal actually mirror those of Solomon's consecration of the House of YHWH. A royal convocation of the people to the royal city, the identification of special classes of participants, and the offering of sacrifices unusual in their number or nature, are all prominent elements in both accounts. The placement of the Ark in the inner sanctuary of the House of YHWH signals the building's consecration as a noble shrine,[6] while the removal of the "pillar" from the inmost recess to the outside of the House of Baal marks its desecration into a latrine.

Once recognized, the prominent function of the "house" motif in 2 Kings 9 and 10 raises by implication questions about the relationship of this use of the motif to the larger design of the Deuteronomistic History's view of kingship. It also raises questions about how allusions to the Davidic "house" present in the narrative of Jehu's destruction of the House of Ahab may be read.

CARNIVALIZATION

But of course, in order to answer those questions the reader must first construe a sense for the text at hand. Is Jehu, the destroyer of the "house," praised or criticized? Northrop Frye (1982:40) reads the following:

> Ahab . . . is portrayed in the main as a kind of sinister clown, whose effete and corrupt dynasty was wiped out by Jehu in a whirlwind of righteous fury.

Paul Hanson (1986:147), on the other hand, reads the same text differently:

> . . . what strikes one in the Jehu story in 2 Kings 9-10 is how this king transferred the authority divinely conferred on him within the carefully formulated conditions of the covenant into a personal authority, and how he exploited both the reform zeal of Yahwism and the power of his office to his own benefit. Moreover, he accomplished this with an unflinching vehemence and cynicism.

What are we then to make of Jehu? Speaking of the use of gaps in biblical narrative—what he calls "aspect[s] of the world . . . that the informational omissions and discordances blur, ambiguate, reduce to hypothetical status"—Meir Sternberg (1985:232-33) lists Jehu as an example of narrative "gapping" with respect to character: "Is Jehu a madman or a zealot?" George Savran (1987:155) has more recently posited a narratorial strategy in 2 Kings 9 and 10 which is "to speak approvingly of the destruction of Ahab and Baal but to cast doubts upon Jehu's motives as well as his methods," through devices such as showing Jehu's increasing "enthusiasm for killing" as the story progresses, presenting him in "complimentary contrasts" with his victims, and placing unflattering comments on the lips of other characters in the narrative (152-55).[7] Even Saul Olyan, who argues that Jehu is presented as Yahweh's instrument for restoring *shalom*, so that the narrative "can hardly be taken as a condemnation,"[8] agrees that he is presented "with much irony."

I propose that a category in some ways akin to irony, Mikhail Bakhtin's "carnivalization," provides the key for a valid reading of 2 Kings 9 and 10.⁹ To begin, I quote Bakhtin's characterization of carnival and carnivalization.

> The problem of carnival . . . —its essence, its deep roots in the primordial order and the primordial thinking of man, its development under conditions of class society, its extraordinary life force and its undying fascination—is one of the most complex and most interesting problems in the history of culture . . . What interests us here is . . . the determining influence of carnival on literature and more precisely on literary genre.
> Carnival itself . . . is not, of course, a literary phenomenon. It is syncretic pageantry of a ritualistic sort . . . Carnival has worked out an entire language of symbolic concretely sensuous forms—from large and complex mass actions to individual carnivalistic gestures. This language, in a differentiated and even (as in any language) articulate way, gave expression to a unified (but complex) carnival sense of the world, permeating all its forms. This language cannot be translated in any full or adequate way into a verbal language, and much less into a language of abstract concepts, but it is amenable to a certain transposition into a language of artistic images which has something in common with its concretely sensuous nature; that is, it can be transposed into the language of literature. *We are calling this transposition of carnival into the language of literature the carnivalization of literature.* (1984b:122; italics mine)[10]

Bakhtin identifies four basic carnivalesque categories (1984b:122f). First, there is *"free and familiar contact among people,"* the result of a carnivalistic suspension of "laws, prohibitions and restrictions that determine the structure and order of ordinary, that is noncarnival, life," including "all hierarchical structure and all the forms of terror, reverence, piety and etiquette connected with it—that is, everything resulting from socio-hierarchical inequality or any other form of inequality among people (including age)."

Second, carnivalization involves *"a new mode of interrelationship between individuals,* counterposed to the all-powerful socio-hierarchical relationships of noncarnival life. The behavior, gesture, and discourse of a person are freed from the authority of all hierarchical positions . . . defining them totally in non-carnival life, and thus from the vantage point of noncarnival life become eccentric and inappropriate."

The third category is "*carnivalistic mésalliances* . . . Carnival brings together, unifies, weds, and combines the sacred with the profane, the lofty with the low, the great with the insignificant, the wise with the stupid."

Finally, there is *profanation*: "carnivalistic blasphemies, a whole system of carnivalistic debasings and bringings down to earth, carnivalistic obscenities linked with the reproductive power of the earth and the body, carnivalistic parodies on sacred texts and sayings, etc."

Bakhtin also identifies as "the primary carnivalistic act . . . the *mock crowning and subsequent decrowning of the carnival king*," an act which reveals "the very core of the carnival sense of the world—the *pathos of shifts and changes, of death and renewal*. Carnival is the festival of all-annihilating and all-renewing time" (1984b:124). Precisely because of the ambivalent duality represented by this quintessential carnivalistic act, it is easy to misunderstand the carnivalesque as merely parodic. Julia Kristeva (1980:80) warns that "there is a tendency to blot out the carnival's *dramatic* (murderous, cynical, and revolutionary in the sense of *dialectical transformation*) aspects, which Bakhtin emphasized." Peter Stallybrass (1985:113-14), arguing that "we should analyze the carnivalesque as a set of rhetorical practices within the social, a set which includes, but is by no means limited to, linguistic devices," proposes a "tentative morphology" which may serve to supplement Bakhtin's categories in identifying carnivalization:

1. The replacement of fast by feast.

2. Transgression of spatial barriers. For example, the marketplace as the locus of public life encroaches upon the privacy of houses. Locked doors are broken down; windows are smashed (see Thomas 1967:16, 27). At the same time, the boundaries of the village or town may become permeable, the inhabitants processing out into the fields, woods and forests.

3. Transgression of bodily barriers. The carnivalesque emphasizes those parts which rupture the "opaque surface" of the classical body: "the open mouth, the genital organs, the breasts, the potbelly, the nose" (Bakhtin 1984a:15-17). The head is subordinated to "the lower bodily stratum." The mouth and nose are foregrounded because they are equated with the anus and the phallus.

4. The inversion of hierarchy. The servant rules his master, the child rules his parents, the wife rules her husband.

5. The degrading of the sacred.

6. The transgression of the linguistic hierarchy. The languages of billingsgate (oaths, curses, obscenities) are privileged over "correct" speech.

I suggest that it is precisely to these categories of the carnivalesque that we may look for guidance in reading 2 Kings 9 and 10. The excesses of violence, the grotesque acts, the scatology—in sum, the strangely repulsive features of this text—may be read as indices of carnivalization. And the dualism of crowning/decrowning—the carnivalesque act *par excellence*—can be seen throughout the narrative of the "Fall of the House."

2 KINGS 9 AND 10: A CARNIVALESQUE READING

The Shape of the Text[11]

The structure of the two chapters, from 9:1 to 10:31, becomes evident once it is recognized that 9:1-14 and 10:29-31 serve as a "crowning/decrowning" set of brackets. Jehu is anointed (the functional equivalent of crowning) in the former, and the latter criticizes and relativizes his reign, placing him (despite some praise for destroying the House of Ahab) under the baneful sign of those kings who persisted in the sins of Jeroboam. This judgment plants on his brow the Deuteronomistic kiss of death, negates the blessing of his anointing, and effectively decrowns him.

Within those brackets, then, the narrative proceeds in two symmetrical parts. Each part has a threefold structure in which two events take place while Jehu is on his way to the place at which he arrives in the third (Jezreel in the first part, Samaria in the second). Similar sequences of violent acts occur in the two parts, except that in the first part those killed are individuals, whereas in the second part they are groups: first Israelites (Joram in 9:15-26; Ahab's kin in 10:1-11 [17]), next Judeans (Ahaziah in 9:27-29; Ahaziah's kin in 10:12-14), and finally aliens or "alienated" Israelites (Jezebel in 9:30-37; Baal and his followers in 10:15-28). The last scene in each sequence is marked not only by Jehu's direct involvement, but by scatological references to the results of that action (Jezebel's corpse becomes "dung upon the field," and Baal's house is a "latrine"). The Jezebel scene also represents, as we shall see, another scene of crowning/decrowning.

The structure I propose may be sketched as follows:

A. JEHU IS KING (9:1-14)   CROWNING

    (from Ramoth-Gilead to Jezreel)

  1a Joram is killed (9:15-26)   King of Israel
  2a Ahaziah is killed (9:27-29)   King of Judah

    (in Jezreel)

  3a Jezebel is killed (9:30-37)   Alien Queen
                                              Symbolic Crown-
                                              ing/Decrowning
                                              Dung

    (from Jezreel to Samaria)

  1b Ahab's kin are killed (10:1-11 [17]) Israelites
  2b Ahaziah's kin are killed (10:12-14) Judeans

    (in Samaria)

  3b Baal worshipers and temple destroyed (10:15-28)

B. JEHU'S RULE IS CRITICIZED   SYMBOLIC
                                                        DECROWNING

Five Scenes of a Carnival

1. ". . . wherefore came this mad fellow to thee?"
Immediately striking in the presentation of this story is that Elisha the prophet, though the initiator of the chain of events which ensue in Jehu's bloody suppression, remains a prologue figure, absent from the narrative of subsequent events. Not only does Elisha set in motion Jehu's military coup through an intermediary, but that intermediary is deliberately presented as a character of marginal, even risible status. In the preceding chapter, Elisha the renowned "man of God" is shown in direct interaction with Hazael, crown prince and soon-to-be monarch of Syria, who comes to him with presents and entreaties from King Ben-Hadad, whose doom the prophet seals with his oracle.

In 2 Kgs 9:1-4, however, Elisha makes an appearance only to commission a nameless, junior (called "boy" or "young lad" in 9:4) and apparently somewhat ridiculous (called "crazy" in 9:11) "son of the prophets" as his messenger to Jehu. Elisha's speech of commissioning, with its prolonged paratactic series of specific and seemingly superfluous commands, reads as if the prophet were carefully instructing a dim-witted or completely inexperienced agent on how to carry out an anointing.[12] There is, in fact, an almost comical effect to the last three commands: "and open the door, and flee, and don't wait," as if to emphasize that the emissary is not aware of the import, or needs to learn of the likely consequences of his mission. That is, it is Elisha's commission and not his messenger which is to be taken seriously.

It is then significant that this marginal character, while ostensibly carrying out his master's instructions, in fact disobeys him by adding to Elisha's terse message ("Thus says YHWH: I anoint you king over Israel") the programmatic lines of verses 7-10a, adumbrating the violent events to come, and telling Jehu to "strike down the House of Ahab your master."[13] The student prophet calls Jehu to overthrow his master, echoing not Elisha but Elijah.[14] The effect is incongruous, as if a masquerading "sorcerer's apprentice" has unwittingly pronounced a spell he cannot control. That incongruity is underlined by Jehu's associates' characterization of the prophet as a "madman" (*m-sh-g-*ʻ, 9:11),[15] as well as by Jehu's use of a word connoting something like "ranting"[16] to deprecate the speech of the by-then-escaping "fellow" (lit. "the man" in 9:11). When Jehu reports the words of the prophet to his companions, he omits the "ranting"—off-handedly referring to the addition to the prophetic message as "thus and so," and repeating, word for word, only Elisha's original formula of anointing.

The scene closes in an informal, *ad hoc* proclamation of Jehu as king by his cohorts which almost restores a sense of normal "expectedness" to the proceedings. At this point, only Jehu and the reader know what happened "inside," but we have had a glimpse of the violent overturning of the world, of the carnival that is about to erupt into the "houses" of Ahab and Baal.

In accomplishing the anointing or "crowning" of Jehu, the story underlines the mismatch, the *mésalliance*, between the general and the "nobody" who anoints him. The protagonist on whom the spotlight will fall for the rest of the narrative is one who has just had kingship thrust upon him by a novice "madman." And this madman's transgressive intrusion of Elijah's curse into Elisha's explicit instructions vests on Jehu not only kingship, but "madness" as well. As the first of many transgressions of hierarchy punctuating this narrative, the young man's supplanting of his master is an infectious call to Jehu to supplant his. The wild ride is about to begin.

2. "*. . . for he driveth furiously.*"
Not only hierarchical, but spatial transgression is also a prominent feature in the narrative. The shofar blast and royal shout of 9:13 signal the start of a headlong race in which Jehu drives to Jezreel and on to Samaria. The root *rkb*, which forms the verb "to ride," the noun "chariot," and the name Jehonadab ben Rechab, appears 16 times in the two chapters. Clearly it is a *Leitwort* that binds and flavors the text. Three times in conjunction with forms of *rkb*, and once by itself, we also find the noun *sus*, "horse."[17] In 9:20, moreover, the watchman's recognition of Jehu's wild style of driving yields, in a single verse, three instances of the root *n-h-g*, "to drive" or "lead," along

with "furiously, madly" (*beshigga'on*). Apart from two occurrences (in 9:3 and 10), forms of *nus* ("to flee") appear on three other occasions (once in 9:23, and twice in 9:27, along with an occurrence of *r-d-p*, "pursue").

The pace is breathless as Jehu's cavalcade sweeps along, demanding on the way that commoners or menials join it—plain soldiers (9:18, 19), eunuch servants (9:32)—but overcoming and destroying royalty as it passes. In the final episode of each series, the "ride" intrudes symbolically into a house, and an exchange of "inside" and "outside" signals destruction. Jezebel begins inside her house and above the road, but dies outside, trampled by Jehu's horses as he goes inside. Jehonadab ben Rechab, taking the ominous *Leitwort* in his very name, goes with Jehu into the soon-to-be demolished House of Baal, which Jehu's men will penetrate as far as the inmost recesses in order to bring outside the "pillar of Baal."

3. "... for she is a king's daughter."

The unassuming, diffident Jehu of the anointing and proclamation scenes[18] undergoes a change as the action progresses. His discourse takes on a sort of importure, demanding authority—for the most part he will speak in imperatives, or in interrogatives that either deny another the right to question him (e.g., 9:18, 19) or demand allegiance (e.g., 9:32; 10:15). The crucial scene of the encounter between Jezebel and Jehu in 9:30-37 finally brings together the carnivalizing "madness" embodied in the latter with the former as the emblematic object of its fury; and, at its end, Jehu makes the only purely indicative speech (10:24, though functionally this is an imperative) since his anointing. As if resuming his indicative statement of 9:12 (except that now the content he refused to disclose before by dismissing it as "thus and so" is made explicit), Jehu recognizes in the fate of Jezebel "the word of YHWH, which he spoke by his servant Elijah the Tishbite." The name of Jezebel appeared first in the prophetic curse in 9:7 and 10, on the lips of the young prophet: accused of murdering the prophets and other servants of YHWH, Jezebel is fated to be eaten by dogs and lie unburied in the field of Jezreel. Jehu's allusion to this oracle in 9:36, however, adds a coarse element not found in 9:7-10: "and the corpse of Jezebel shall be as *dung on the face of the field* in the territory of Jezreel, so that no one can say, 'That is Jezebel'" (9:37).[19]

Jehu's coarse reference here is not unprecedented. Another characteristic that his discourse develops is *the use of course language, of curses, of insults*. Jezebel's name comes from Jehu's lips, for instance, in a direct personal insult to Joram. When the king and his rebel general meet, it is not over the reading of a formal ultimatum for surrender or a similar procedure dignified by custom for such occasions. Rather, it is a pungent insult, a bit of "mother-swearing," that rude Jehu hurls at the king: "What peace, with all the whoring and witchcraft of your mother Jezebel?"[20] Prophetic curse and barracks billingsgate have anticipated her appearance, and after her death Jehu's striking valedictory, "see now to this *cursed woman*, for she is a *king's daughter*" (9:34), simultaneously recognizes and negates her status in carnivalistic "praise-abuse" (see Bakhtin 1984a:432f).

That praise-abuse signals a symbolic "decrowning" of Jezebel, since when she finally appears in person to confront Jehu (9:30), it is as a queen, not as a murderer, a whore or a witch. There is a clear "crowning" (or perhaps better, anointing) allusion in her coiffure and eye-paint preparations, and her position "looking out of the window" recalls other royal persons (e.g., Michal in 2 Sam 6:16 and Abimelech in Gen 26: 8).[21] Her challenge to Jehu, in which she calls him "Zimri, murderer of your master," is a reminder of the fate of one who, like him, transgressed the barriers of hierarchical difference and destroyed himself in the process. Crowning herself to put Jehu in his place, however, Jezebel is in the end the subject of a sudden and drastic "decrowning." From below, Jehu calls for her overthrow, and it is her newly "carnivalized" menials— perhaps the very ones who had just dressed her hair—who toss her out the window.

What Bakhtin calls the "lower body stratum" becomes suddenly dominant at this point. Jehu goes in to eat and drink, that is, to fill his belly, quite literally over Jezebel's dead body, which concurrently is transformed into excreta. Her blood, the narrator points out, splatters "the wall" (9:33), an allusion to the crude Deuteronomistic idiom for males used in 9:8 ("those who piss against the wall"). While her blood is allusively turned into urine against the wall, her body, eaten by dogs, is literally to become dung on the ground (9:36, 37). The fate of the "cursed woman"/"king's daughter" is also a presage of what is to happen to the house of her god.

4. *". . . but who slew all these?"*
Most notable in the narrative of the slaughter of Ahab's descendants is the theme of the reshuffling of alliances, of the inversion of hierarchies, of the creation of a new social order in Samaria. Much of this happens not by Jehu's direct action, but while he is still at a distance, in Jezreel and on the way. Although "Jehu slew all that remained of the House of Ahab in Jezreel, all his great men, and his familiar friends, and his priests" (10:11), as well as "all that remained to Ahab in Samaria" (10:17), the slaughter of the seventy "sons of Ahab" is specifically the act of their Samaritan guardians. Challenged by Jehu's letters, the rulers, the elders and the guardians of Ahab's descendants promptly switch their allegiance and kill the "sons of their master," one of whom would normally have become their king. Just as the common soldiers sent out from Jezreel to challenge Jehu fell in behind him, and just as Jezebel's eunuchs became her executioners as soon as Jehu confronted them, so the Samarian authorities, with a minimal amount of fearful consideration (10:4), become Jehu's "servants" (10:5). The previously unthinkable action, not only of murdering their wards but of sending Jehu grotesque confirmation of their allegiance in the form of seventy severed heads in baskets, suddenly becomes thinkable.

As Jehu's influence spreads, however, so spreads the blame or responsibility. Jehu's remarkable speech in 10:9 summarizes these themes: "Are you blameless? True, I conspired against my master and killed him; but who struck down all of these?" "All of these," of course refers to the seventy members of the House of Ahab whose heads have just been delivered to the gate of

Jezreel. At this point in the narrative, we begin to sense that something larger than Jehu is active. Jehu begins to seem as much borne along as leading the movement. And also from this point on, the violence will escalate in numbers of victims, as whole groups are slaughtered without a single personal name remembered.

5. "... *and broke down the House of Baal."*
Jehu's ride ends in the House of Baal. Accompanied by Jehonadab ben Rechab, Jehu lies when he offers, in fact, to enthrone Baal in ritual homage: "Ahab served Baal little; Jehu shall serve him much." This deception eventually involves actually offering the requisite "sacrifices and burnt offerings." Ironically, of course, the worshipers of Baal are themselves to be the sacrifice Jehu really meant in his misleading speech. The use of "great sacrifice" (*zebah gadol*) in 10:19 gives the reader an ironic hint of what is to come. The phrase recalls its only other occurrence in the DH, Judg 16:23, where it is the lords of the Philistines who prepare to sacrifice to Dagon, with similar results—a destroyed temple and a massacred congregation.[22]

Just as their god suffers the humiliation and destruction of his house in a sudden reversal, so the worshipers of Baal, rather than being rounded up, imprisoned, and killed as wretched jail inmates, go to their deaths still in the festal garb in which they were moments before celebrating the feast—a carnivalesque turn which echoes the fate of Jezebel. And just as in that turn the lower bodily stratum imposed itself as the regal "mock queen" fell to her death, so here the house of the "mock god" is profaned, destroyed, and turned into a latrine "until this day."

CONCLUSIONS

This study has confirmed the significant presence of a "house" motif in 2 Kings 9 and 10. A "motivic constellation" which includes the House of Ahab and the House of Baal in a variety of related senses represents in those chapters the monarchy, the family, the dynasty—in a word, the institution of Ahab—as well as the religious establishment of Baal. The linkage that Rosenberg and others point out between the same elements in reference to the Davidic House and the Temple in 2 Samuel also holds true here, with respect to the House of Ahab and the Samarian Temple of Baal.

While the "house" motif furnishes a sort of stationary target, the dynamic rush of Jehu's activity in bringing about the "Fall of the House" provides the action in 2 Kings 9 and 10. The narrative is bracketed by the account of Jehu's anointing, which is marked by a strong emphasis on the marginal status of the one performing it, as well as by his striking transgression of Elisha's explicit orders, and by the ambiguous judgment rendered on Jehu at the end of the narrative. I suggest that it is possible to recognize, in this and in many other features of the narrative, a complex of the characteristic signs of "carnivalization." The structure of the narrative within those brackets was charted as two parallel series of overthrows (of individuals and of groups), the first ending in Jezreel and the second ending in Samaria, each with a sequence involving Israel/Judah/alien. The last event in each series is especially "carnivalistic" in character, including a "crowning/decrowning" and highlighting the "lower bodily stratum."

A question which immediately arises from this analysis concerns the referential ambiguity of the "house" theme in 2 Kings 9 and 10. Behind the House of Ahab and the House of Baal, is there possibly a reference to the House of David and the First Temple seen from an exilic perspective? Parallels between David and Ahab—and between David and Jehu—have been noticed by other readers of this narrative (e.g., Damrosch 1987:244-46). It is most significant, in my opinion, that the Deuteronomistic oracle against Jerusalem, occasioned by the evil deeds of Manasseh and particularly by this most wicked of Davidides' imitations of Ahab (2 Kgs 21:3) in cultic apostasy, explicitly identifies the downfall of David's city with that of the House of Ahab: "And I will stretch over Jerusalem the measuring line of Samaria, and the plummet of the house of Ahab; and I will wipe Jerusalem as one wipes a dish, wiping it and turning it upside down" (2 Kgs 21:13). Does Dtr, or better, Dtr^2, offer in the narrative of 2 Kings 9 and 10 a critique of the Northern monarchy alone, or rather of all monarchy? Is it a critique of the Northern cult, or of all Yahwism? Does it univocally condemn the Northern monarchy and cult alone, or is this a "dialogic" text in which all human authority is carnivalized and thus opened to criticism—both the House of Ahab and Jehu its destroyer, but, in powerful allusion, the House of David as well? 2 Kings 9 and 10 shows us the very line and the actual plummet that will mark Jerusalem's fate, even as it signals Samaria's.

But using "carnivalization" as a heuristic device for reading 2 Kings 9 and 10 also yields the possibility of reading in this text, with its gruesome excesses of violence and its crude and abusive language, much more than simply repulsive hostility toward the long-gone House of Ahab. Speaking of "praise-abuse," a characteristic carnivalistic trait in the work of Rabelais, Bakhtin writes in terms which ultimately apply to all truly "carnivalistic" human events, political, literary or whatever:

> The old dying world gives birth to the new one. Death throes are combined with birth in one indissoluble whole. This process is represented in the images of the lower bodily stratum; everything descends into the earth and the bodily grave in order to die and to be reborn. This is why the downward movement pervades Rabelais' entire imagery from beginning to end. All these images throw down, debase, swallow, condemn, deny (topographically), kill, bury, send down to the underworld, abuse, curse; and at the same time they all conceive anew, fertilize, sow, rejuvenate, regenerate, praise, and glorify. (1984a:435)

And again, speaking directly of "carnivalization," Bakhtin pleads for a vision of carnival as

> . . . past millennia's way of sensing the world as one great communal performance. This sense of the world, liberating one from fear, bringing the world maximally close to a person and bringing one person maximally close to another . . . with its joy at change and its joyful relativity, is opposed to that one-sided and gloomy official seriousness which is dogmatic and hostile to evolution and change, which seeks to absolutize a given condition of existence or a given social order. From precisely that sort of seriousness did the carnival sense of the world liberate men. But there is not a grain of nihilism in it,

nor a grain of empty frivolity or vulgar bohemian individualism. (1984b:159f)

The narrative of the "Fall of the House" is, to be sure, critical and negative, even at times repulsive, and it is not easy to discern in it positive, life-giving elements. But is that the final word, or may it, along with much other exilic writing of similar crude and violent negativity, not perform a positive and hope-bringing function, even as it relativizes and profanes the past? Does it not say, emphatically, that the old world is dead, so that out of its grave the future may be born? As in R. Joseph's encounter with a higher level of reality, is not the "topsy-turvy world" actually the "clear world" of life-giving hope?

NOTES

[1] This paper appeared originally in *JSOT* 46 (1990:47-65). It appears here, in revised form, by the kind permission of the editors of *JSOT*.

[2] The work of Mikhail Bakhtin, along with that of his followers and critics, is the source of the concept and terminology of "carnivalization" which I propose to utilize. "Intertextuality" is also derived from Bakhtin, or more precisely from Julia Kristeva's presentation of Bakhtin (see Todorov 1984:60).

[3] It occurs only eleven times in nine verses: 8:18, 27; 9:7, 8, 9; 10:10, 11, 30; 21:13. Six of those are in 2 Kings 9 and 10.

[4] A similar identification of the king's wife with his "house" appears in 2 Samuel 6:20.

[5] The crude Hebrew expression "those who piss against the wall" echoes not only Elijah's curse of Ahab in 1 Kgs 21:21, but also the curse on Jeroboam in 1 Kgs 14:10. The first expression also recalls Zimri's destruction of the House of Baasha in 1 Kgs 16:11. Outside prophetic discourse, the phrase appears only in David's salty threat to exterminate the household of Nabal in 1 Sam 25:22 and 34.

[6] In 1 Kgs 8:12-13, after the placement of the Ark in the "Holy of Holies," Solomon prefaces his consecratory discourse with the majestic formula: "YHWH has said that he would dwell in thick darkness. I have built thee an exalted house [*bêt zebul*], a place for thee to dwell for ever." The presence of the hapax legomenon (*zebul*) in this verse may be related to the parodic perversion of a probable Phoenician *'i-sebul*

into "Jezebel," where Baal's epithet meaning "prince, stately, noble" is turned into "dung." Rather than agree with John Gray that this is a "scribal perversion" (368), I take the pejorative deformation of the name of Ahab's queen as deliberate. Jezebel does become "dung on the ground" in 9:37, and the House of Baal is desecrated into a latrine in 10:27.

[7] Savran's analysis calls to mind the words of Jacques Ellul (1972:98f): "All Jehu's work is done in a situation of ambiguity and misunderstanding. He is anointed by God, but in the long run he does nothing but evil wherever he goes. He fulfills prophecies, but he is condemned for so doing. He is a man of God, but he uses all methods of the devil."

[8] Saul Olyan (1984:652-68; esp. 654). Savran, on the other hand, says of the same motif that "the mention of *shalom* is the kiss of death" in the story (1987:154). Olyan's reading, moreover, does not apply to chap. 10, where the *shalom* motif does not appear. He thus leaves both the massacre of Ahab's progeny ("your master's *house*") and the destruction of Baal's house out of his schema.

[9] Definitions of what constitute irony vary widely. On one hand, e.g., Good's classic work (1981:30) defines it as "criticism, implicit or explicit, which perceives in things as they are an incongruity," but distinguishes it from satire, sarcasm, invective or parody by adding that irony's distinctive marks are understatement and a "stance in truth from which perception comes" (31). On the other hand, Barbara Babcock (1984:107), focusing on the grotesque, obscene and violent antics of Pueblo ritual clowns, suggests that "both clowning and criticism are 'sanctioned disrespect,' ways in which society paradoxically institutionalizes doubt and questioning. Both . . . are also forms of irony . . . irony is not a matter of seeing a 'true' meaning beneath a 'false'; but of seeing *a double exposure on one plate.*" My own view tends toward Babcock's.

[10] Bakhtin's presentation of carnival and the carnivalesque may be seen primarily in chap. 4 ("Characteristics of Genre and Plot Composition in Dostoevsky's Works"), and in *Rabelais and His World* (1984a).

[11] Had Burke O. Long's *2 Kings* (1991) been available when this paper was being written, it would have been helpful to compare his form-critically oriented analysis of the text with mine.

[12] Cf. the role of Samuel in 1 Sam 16:1-13, the anointing of David. Even though YHWH gives multiple instructions, these are presented in a dialogue in which Samuel's autonomy and authority are reinforced.

[13] The verses are, of course, part of what traditional biblical scholarship considers editorial additions to Dtr. See Olyan (1984:655f).

[14] It is interesting that Targum Jonathan consistently renders the MT's *beney-hannabi'im* (lit. "sons of the prophets") as "students of

the prophets," as in this passage. In vs. 4, where the MT reads *hanna'ar hanna'ar hannabi'* ("the young man, the young man, the prophet"), the Targum translates "the young man, the *student* of the prophet." Thus the Targum, correctly in my judgment, renders the second *na'ar* as "student of" (in construct), reading in the MT the intent to convey the neophyte, "apprentice" status of this character.

[15] See Olyan (1984:663). Olyan notes the striking use of a word of the same root to characterize Jehu's driving in vs. 20, and judges that the writer is using this device to associate Jehu with the "the Elijah-Elisha school." Further, for him the *sh-g-'* words are "symbolic of the service of Yahweh. Both the prophets and Jehu are instruments of Yahweh's restoration of *šālôm*."

[16] So in TANAKH, but note the use of the same word in Elisha's probably scatological reference to Baal in 1 Kgs 18:27.

[17] Forms of *rkb* occur in 9:16, 17, 18, 19, 21 (twice), 24, 25, 27, 28; 10:2, 15 (twice), 16 (twice), and 23. Forms of it in conjunction with *sus* or *susim* occur in 9:18, 19; and 10:2.

[18] Note his question to the young prophet in 9:5, and his reply to his companions in 9:10 and 12.

[19] That pungent metaphor is found nowhere else in the book of Kings. The majority of its occurrences are in Jeremiah (8:2; 9:21; 16:4; 25:33). Ps 83:11 is the only other instance.

[20] In contrast, Jehu addresses the Samarian authority in a tough but not insulting tone in the ultimatum for surrender he sends to them in 10:2-3.

[21] Simon Parker (1978:74) has argued that Jezebel's preparations represent an attempt to seduce Jehu: "she makes herself up and stations herself conspicuously at a window, hoping to capitalize on her sexual charms." I agree, rather, with Olyan (1985:206), who argues, *contra* Parker, that, while women preparing for lovemaking would apply makeup and make up their hair, "regal women appearing in public probably did the same thing."

[22] *Zebah gadol* appears only one other time in the MT, in Ezek 39:17, once again in reference to a "sacrifice" of human beings offered to the birds and the beasts, in this case after battle.

10

JEHOIACHIN AT THE KING'S TABLE: A READING OF THE ENDING OF THE SECOND BOOK OF KINGS

JAN JAYNES GRANOWSKI

With 2 Kgs 25:27-30, the books of Kings as well as the Deuteronomistic History (DtrH) end. This terse, enigmatic conclusion has disappointed many readers. It has also engendered an unresolved debate concerning its theological significance. As the "final word" of the Deuteronomistic historian (Dtr), the verses are as remarkable for what they omit as for the little they include. The task of this study is to explore the theological and literary facets of these closing lines in order to make sense of the ending they provide. The question of the ending's function for Kings and for the DtrH will guide this study throughout.

THE THEOLOGICAL IMPASSE

Martin Noth's pessimistic assessment (1981 [1957]) of the final four verses of the DtrH has provoked an unfinished discussion among Hebrew Bible scholars. He interprets this conclusion, in the aftermath of divine judgment, as "something final and definitive," in which the Dtr has "expressed no hope for the future, not even in the very modest and simple form of an expectation that the deported and dispersed people would be gathered together" (97). Many agree, with varying degrees of qualification, that Noth's understanding of the negative tone of the verses is accurate (e.g., Gray 1963:42, 705-6; Friedman 1981:191; cf. Begg 1986:49-56).

Other scholars side, instead, with Gerhard von Rad (1984 [1966]) in perceiving the end of the DtrH as hopeful, even optimistic. From the perspective of his gospel/law or promise/judgment schema, von Rad is certain of the "particular theological significance" of "the very end of the deuteronomist's work." He writes (220):

> Obviously nothing is said here in strictly theological terms, but a carefully measured indication is given: an occurrence is referred to which has immense significance for the deuteronomist, since it provides a basis upon which Yahweh would build further if he so willed. At all events the reader must understand this passage to be an indication of the fact that the line of David has not come to an irrevocable end.

Even in his *Old Testament Theology* (1962:343), von Rad's assessment evinces none of the "messianism" for which it has been criticized (cf. Wolff 1982:85). Rather, he presents a realistic acknowledgment of the "openness" of the final four verses of Kings. In von Rad's eyes, Dtr simply leaves the history of ancient Israel open to the future; he does not seal it in final judgment.[1]

THE LITERARY DIMENSION

The debate concerning the theological significance of the ending of 2 Kings has failed to provide a generally accepted interpretation. Even Richard D. Nelson (1987:265-66), in his newer literary-critical approach, concludes his study with the same fundamental questions: "Is this last paragraph vital to the theology of Kings or simply a postscript? Does it advocate hope or merely underscore despair?"

Neither has the discussion of the redaction history of Dtr's final passage produced a decisive clue to its significance. Whether the four concluding verses came from the hand of Noth's Dtr, or from a Deuteronomistic school, or from a Babylonian Jew intent on shoring up the story with one more brief report, an aesthetically and theologically satisfying account for 2 Kgs 25:27-30 has yet to appear. Nelson's key questions still call out for answers. How do these verses function?

I wish to approach this long-standing question from an alternative tack. I propose here a reading of DtrH's closing passage from the perspective of narrative criticism. My close examination of these verses will focus on their literary attributes, especially in terms of *closure* and *intertextuality*.

A QUESTION OF CLOSURE

Whether or not 2 Kgs 25:27-30 served as the original conclusion for the DtrH, the verses do constitute the ending of Kings in its present form. Perhaps simply because of their placement—at the end of a substantial historical narrative—the verses have long intrigued but often disappointed readers. Readers usually have great expectations for endings. A reader may seek a summary, a show of justice or of mercy, a resolution in death or marriage or revelation, or, what Henry James has termed "a distribution at the last of prizes" (in Kermode 1966:22). Nevertheless, human beings have a "deep need for intelligible Ends" (Kermode 1966:8).

Commenting on the newness of literary methodologies for the study of endings, Mikeal Parsons (1987) notes,

> Despite the importance of endings for stories, only recently have literary critics turned their attention to the task of developing a methodology which allows critical examination of narrative endings.

Literary critics Shlomith Rimmon-Kenan (1983), Barbara Herrnstein Smith (1968), and Marianna Torgovnick (1981) have all defined essential components of a methodology for the study of closure. A summary of their theories will precede their application to 2 Kgs 25:27-30.

Rimmon-Kenan (1983:119-20) opens her discussion of closure with an observation on the nature of language:

> ... language prescribes a linear figuration of signs and hence a linear presentation of information about things. Not only does it dictate progression from letter to letter, word to word, sentence to sentence, etc., it also imposes upon the reader a successive perception of bits of information even when these are meant to be understood as simultaneous in the story.

Therefore, according to Rimmon-Kenan, "the text can direct and control the reader's comprehension and attitudes by positioning *certain* items before others." When this linguistic fact applies to narrative endings, she terms it "the recency effect." By her definition,

> The recency effect encourages the reader to assimilate all previous information to the item presented last. Thus, placing an item at the end may radically change the process of reading as well as the final product.

Rimmon-Kenan's notion of the recency effect recalls Herrnstein Smith's "retrospective patterning" (1968:119). The closural process of retrospective patterning, according to her, involves the reader's realignment of certain thematic elements within their understanding of the text they have finished reading.

> . . . that is, connections and similarities are illuminated, and the reader perceives that seemingly gratuitous or random events, details, and juxtapositions have been selected in accord with certain principles.

Both the recency effect and retrospective patterning describe the ways endings aid and influence readers in making sense of entire texts, as well as of the endings themselves.

If the reader of DtrH formed her finalized understanding of the theological history from the perspective of its concluding four verses, what would her retrospective patterning be? Or, how would the recency effect of these verses contribute to her overall sense of the DtrH? Torgovnick's methodology for the study of closure (1981) proves quite useful in answering these questions.

Torgovnick sets forth a thorough model for the critical analysis of narrative closure. Although her method is designed specifically for the novel, the fact that it applies to narrative discourse renders her method valuable for a historiographical narrative like DtrH as well. The sense of an ending that she identifies with closure "designates the process by which a novel reaches an adequate and appropriate conclusion" (1981:6). And such a conclusion, in turn, leaves in the reader the "sense that nothing necessary has been omitted from a work." These definitions indicate the reader-orientation of Torgovnick's notion of closure. Her evaluative model has five sets of elements, each of which may be applied to the text of 2 Kgs 25:27-30.

First, Torgovnick gives two major patterns of ending—*epilogue* and *scene*. But the closing passage of 2 Kings does not fit smoothly within either of them. Part of the difficulty in classifying DtrH's conclusion stems from its sheer brevity. The three sentences of verses 27-30, however, align more closely with her definition of an epilogue with (1) its shift in perspective (in time scale or orientation) and (2) its "element of *nachgeschichte* (after-history) for the major characters" (1981:11). Verse 27 marks a definite shift in both time and place from the verses that immediately precede it. And although Jehoiachin is not a "major character" in DtrH along the lines of Samuel or David, he is the last living king of Judah. Thus, the narrative of Jehoiachin's fate in Babylon comes as near as possible to providing the *nachgeschichte* for a major character in a narrative which has no more truly major characters after the death of Josiah.

Verse 28, however, also conveys the sense of a cameo scene which presents, if from a distance, "a final dialogue between two or more characters" (Torgovnick 1981:11). After all, the reader witnesses Evil-merodach speaking kindly to Jehoiachin and giving him new clothes and an elevated throne. Thus while it lacks full conformity to either pattern, the ending of 2 Kings partakes of elements from both patterns and thus demonstrates its general conformity to formal patterns of narrative closure.

Second, Torgovnick lists five closural strategies—*circularity, parallelism, incompletion, tangential,* and *linkage* (13-14). These five terms describe the relationship of a narrative's end with its beginning and middle. The final four verses of 2 Kings demonstrate different closural strategies according to the various possible delimitations of the full text to which they belong. If the verses conclude DtrH, to which Deuteronomy 1-3 is the beginning (so Noth), then they evidence a degree of incompletion. Deuteronomy opens with a stirring speech by Moses—"These are the words that Moses spoke to all Israel beyond the Jordan." This lengthy speech by a major character recounts for the people their history since leaving Sinai. Kings, in contrast, closes with a brief report by an anonymous narrator. The report does not include a single well-developed (much less major) character. The only speech contained in the closing pericope of 2 Kings is that of the Babylonian king, on which the narrator only comments, "and he spoke kindly to him" (vs. 28a). For the reader, the Judean king exists in silence. Thus the narrative of DtrH tapers off into the minimal and then into nothingness, giving the reader no clear sense of an ending.

If, on the other hand, 2 Kgs 25:27-30 forms the closing scene of the Genesis-Kings corpus (so Peter Miscall 1986:viii), then the passage reads with more parallelism. It hearkens back to other royal exiles (Hoshea's in 2 Kings 17), to other imprisonments and releases by foreigners (Joseph's in Genesis 40-41), and to other kingly acts of mercy and patronage (David's in 2 Samuel 9). These parallelisms will receive further attention in the section on intertextuality.

If, however, the end of 2 Kings functions primarily within the books of Kings, then the final verses attest to the closural strategy of circularity. That is, they clearly recall the beginning of 1 Kings, which opens with four poignant verses portraying an enfeebled King David. The once strapping youth is now "old and advanced in years." The formerly mighty warrior can no longer "get warm" (1:1). The king who has loved many beautiful women and fathered many children has now been reduced to lying in helplessness and impotence while the lovely Abishag acts only as his nurse (1:4).

The Jehoiachin depicted in the final four verses of 2 Kings is a similarly enfeebled monarch. His impotence, however, is political. Jehoiachin has been released from prison and is provided for by a pagan king. He sits on a throne, but he is "king" in name only. He is beholden for his freedom to the son of his captor Nebuchadnezzar. He lives out his days in the humiliation of exiled vassalage, while relying on the condescension of a foreign monarch for his daily bread. In this way the narrator of Kings brings his story full circle—from one powerless monarch to another—with only the briefest sketch of the concluding situation of each.

Third, Torgovnick assesses the implied author's relationship with the reader at closure. By "implied author," she refers to Wayne Booth's definition (1961:71; quoted in Torgovnick 1981:16): "The 'implied author' chooses, consciously or unconsciously, what we read; we infer him [from his novels] as an ideal, created version of the real man; he is the sum of his own choices." Torgovnick's method, therefore, may apply even to texts with unknown authors, such as DtrH. She then offers three possible classifications for the author/reader relationship during closure—*complementary, congruent,* and *confrontational* (17-18). In the concluding passage of 2 Kings, the implied author does not manifest any overt rhetoric to coax the reader into accepting his conclusion (congruent). In one sense, he seems to confound reader expectations by omitting a speech or a summary statement (confrontational). In yet another sense, the unspectacular events and characters which close off DtrH in 2 Kings do not merit the pomp and circumstance of a grander ending.

From this perspective, the implied author has tailored his narrative form to the nature of the events and actors that populate his history. Thus, the grand-scale figures like Moses and David and Elijah garner speeches and narrative elaboration appropriate to their characters. The epic evil of Ahab and Jezebel earns them relatively large stretches of DtrH narrative. For such diminutive figures as the unimpressive final king of Judah, Dtr reserves minimal treatment—a two verse negative assessment of his reign (2 Kgs 24:8-9), the barest details of his surrender to the Babylonians (vss. 12 and 15), and a succinct four verse report on his last days (25:27-30).

In a historical narrative such as DtrH, the implied author has a powerful effect on how readers perceive the characters in the narrative. He may inflate the influence of some, overstate the negative impact of others, and consign still others to historical oblivion. Nevertheless, portraits of historical characters are not the implied author's exclusive creations. The roots of his characters sink deep into the sod of tradition and history. Their narrative existence therefore reflects, to a greater or lesser degree, their historical existence. Had Jehoiachin been a more impressive person, he would have no doubt cut a wider swath on the pages of DtrH. As DtrH's final narrative stands, however, content seems to have suggested form. The end result is a short narrative report that reflects a basically complementary (trusting) relationship between implied author and reader.

If this analysis is correct, it points toward a fourth kind of relationship analyzed in Torgovnick's model of closure—the implied author's relationship with his or her own ideas at the narrative's end. Torgovnick defines this relationship as either *self-deceiving* or *self-aware*. With respect to 2 Kgs 25:27-30, this classification presents a problem, because it generally requires "extratextual information and statements of intention" by the actual author (19). Such evidence from the author of DtrH's final passage is obviously beyond current reach. Whether the implied author of our text is self-aware or self-deceiving is, finally, impossible to conclude in this instance.

Torgovnick's fifth aspect of closure concerns "the author's and reader's viewpoint on the novel's characters and major action" at the narrative's end (14-15). The two possibilities are, according to Torgovnick, *overview* and *closeup*. 2 Kings 25 fits neither classification with much ease. Insofar as it focuses on the single character of Jehoiachin at the time of his "rehabilitation," however, the narrative may be regarded as a closeup. The ending remains, nevertheless, at a significant distance from Jehoiachin's character. The conclusion produces only the situational facts about Judah's last surviving king. No interior or emotional details clutter this stark and distant portrait.

Although such a final perspective may mystify some readers, Torgovnick stresses the intentionality inherent in all narrative "arrangements."

> The implied author or the narrator may pretend to be at sea about the ending, like the characters. But as the 'arranger of collocations' in the novel (to use Kermode's phrase), the author only disingenuously pretends to be 'in the middest.' He usually has very good and very precise reasons for ending at a chosen point. (1981:15-16)

While this statement strays perilously close to the "intentional fallacy,"[2] Torgovnick makes a credible and modest point, because she only assumes the artfulness of the implied author (which in biblical texts shades into "the final redactor"). In order to apply her proposal to DtrH narratives, however, one must modify her comment about the implied author pretending to be "in the middest." Actually, where historical narratives are concerned, and when the history's conclusion coincides with the lifetime of the implied author, this author *is* "in the middest."

In summary, 2 Kings closes with a brief *epilogue*. The epilogue provides the reader with a final distant glimpse of Jehoiachin, the last surviving king of Judah. As the reader has no real reason to mistrust the implied author, the closural strategy suggests a *complementary* reader/author relationship. The implied author seems to be *self-aware*, which in turn indicates the purposiveness inherent in the form and content of DtrH's closing moments.

AN INTERTEXTUAL READING

The final pericope of 2 Kings evinces several key closural features, according to Torgovnick's model. Yet the degree of satisfaction—the real sense of an ending—which this passage gives the reader depends upon the reader's ability to integrate it into the whole of DtrH. Thus, I will next explore 2 Kgs 25: 27-30 with a view to its intertextual features—those features that link it, by means of form or content, with other portions of DtrH, as well as with the entire Genesis-Kings corpus.

"Intertextuality" is currently a fashionable term among literary critics. According to Thaïs Morgan (1989:240), "the notion of intertextuality emerges from the cross-fertilization among several major European intellectual movements during the 1960s and 1970s, including Russian formalism, structural linguistics, psycho-analysis, Marxism, and deconstruction, at the least." With its roots in the ideological battleground of Paris in the sixties and seventies, intertextuality is no neutral term. Because of its colorful origins, however, the insights of such contemporary literary theory can provide the biblical critic with a refreshing set of perspectives and interests with which to approach the biblical text.

While he credits Julia Kristeva with originating the term "intertextuality," Roland Barthes (1981:39) provides one of the more helpful descriptions of the concept:

> Any text is a new tissue of past citations. Bits of codes, formulae, rhythmic models, fragments of social languages, etc. pass into the text and are redistributed within it, for there is always language before and around the text. Intertextuality, the condition of any text whatsoever, cannot, of course, be reduced to a problem of sources or influences; the intertext is a general field of anonymous formulae whose origin can scarcely ever be located; of unconscious or automatic quotations, given without quotation-marks. Epistemologically, the concept of intertext is what brings to the theory of the text the volume of sociality.

As Barthes' reference to a "general field" suggests, critics who utilize intertextuality often perceive of the text in spatial rather than linear, historical terms.[3] Such a shift of perspective allows literary critics to rethink literature and literary history "in terms of space instead of time, conditions of possibility instead of permanent structures, and 'networks' or 'webs' instead of chronological lines or influence" (Morgan 1989:274). This novel perspective, in turn, proves very valuable to the critic who is interested in discussing—unimpeded by questions of historical development and influence—the various elements within one text that derive an extra dash of significance from their allusion to another text.

In his perceptive article on intertextuality, Owen Miller (1985:21) defines the intertextual relationship "metaphorically as a form of citation in which a fragment of discourse is accommodated or assimilated by the focused text."[4] Miller emphasizes the metaphorical aspect of this definition because he understands that "the text itself is complete and the intertext merely an addition brought by the reader making, in his engagement with that text, connections with his own repertoire" (33). According to Miller, "it is the reader, then, who establishes a relationship between a focused text and its intertext, and forges its intertextual identity" (21). A text only "demands" an intertext when the reader perceives that text as "incomplete, in need of some 'supplementary' text" (33).

What intertexts, then, does the closing passage of 2 Kings

accommodate or assimilate? Three texts present themselves as likely and suggestive candidates: 2 Samuel 9, the story of David's beneficent gesture towards Mephibosheth;[5] Genesis 40-41, the story of the imprisoned and then exalted Joseph; and Genesis 11, the story of God calling Abraham out of the land of the Chaldeans.

2 Samuel 9

The narrative of David's kindness to Mephibosheth differs in several notable ways from the account of Evil-merodach's kindness toward Jehoiachin. First, the 2 Samuel 9 narrative is more extensive than 2 Kgs 25:27-30. The 2 Samuel narrative contains a fair amount of dialogue, while the 2 Kings narrative consists of a narrator's monologue. In the Mephibosheth story (2 Sam 9:7), the reader hears the exact words of kindness from the king, along with the king's professed motivation for his generosity:

> And David said to him, "Do not fear; for I will show you kindness for the sake of your father Jonathan, and I will restore to you all the land of Saul your father; and you shall eat at my table always."

Certainly, one reason for the narrator's expansiveness in 2 Samuel 9 is the concern in DtrH to portray David as favorably as possible. This motivation would not carry over to the final verses of 2 Kings, where a Davidic scion stands indebted to a foreign king. That the implied author means to denigrate the Babylonian king, on whose charity Jehoiachin lives out his days, is clear from the adjustments to the king's name. Historically, Nebuchadnezzar's son and successor bore the name Amel-marduk, "man of Marduk." In the DtrH text, however, the Babylonian king receives the name Evil-merodach (*'ewîl merodak*). The Hebrew adjective *'ewîl* means "foolish." And *merodak* is simply the Hebrew rendering of the Babylonian deity Marduk. In 2 Kgs 25:27, therefore, the Babylonian king's name functions as a polemic against both the god of Babylon and the character of Jehoiachin's benefactor.

Despite these distinctions, the text of 2 Kgs 25:27-30 and its intertext in 2 Samuel 9 share the crucial element of a triumphant king having mercy on a member of a defeated royal house. In both instances this mercy takes the form of life-long provision for the patronized by the patron. And, in both cases, this provision translates into the graphic image of the humbled royal personage dining at the king's table:

> So Mephibosheth ate at David's table, like one of the king's sons. (2 Sam 9:11b)
>
> So Mephibosheth dwelt in Jerusalem; for he ate always at the king's table. (vs. 13a)
>
> And every day of his life he dined regularly at the king's table. (2 Kgs 25:29b)

This significant similarity between the two narratives heightens the implications of their differences. The terseness of the 2 Kings narrative, and its punning insult to the Babylonian king and his god, underscore the Judean humiliation beneath the surface of the text. David's house has met a fate more brutal than the house of Saul. The chosen line of David has concluded its reigning days beholden not to another king of Yahweh's anointing, but rather to a king whose very name raises up the absurdity of a false foreign god—Evil-merodach, foolish Marduk. And yet, what could be a more fitting end for the royal representative of an idolatrous Judean people, than to sit daily as the honored guest at a pagan court banquet?

Genesis 40-41

When the scope for possible intertexts broadens to include the Pentateuch as well as DtrH, wider intertextual connections appear. The presence of the exile/imprisonment/exaltation motif in 2 Kgs 25:27-30 conjures up the Joseph stories in Genesis. In particular, Jehoiachin's fate in Babylon seems a distant mirror of Joseph's fate in Egypt. For both characters, imprisonment in a foreign land precedes a more favorable, even exalted situation in that land.

Although 2 Kgs 25:27-30 echoes Genesis 40-41, the two narratives maintain several key distinctions. Again, the intertextual narrative is more extensive, more detailed in its presentation. The narrator draws the characters in the Joseph story with more depth and definition. Also, in Genesis 40-41, Joseph captures the attention of the Pharaoh by way of the Pharaoh's butler. Joseph impresses both men with accurate dream interpretations after claiming, "Do not interpretations belong to God?" (Gen 40:8b) In other words, God's gift of dream interpretation gains Joseph his freedom. Jehoiachin's freedom, by contrast, is unearned and unexplained. Here, God's instrumentality is nowhere apparent.

A second important difference between the Genesis 40-41 story and the 2 Kings 25 pericope lies in what becomes of the released captives. Joseph's release leads to his political empowerment: "And Pharaoh said to Joseph, 'Behold, I have set you over all the land of Egypt'" (Gen 41:41). In contrast, Jehoiachin's release culminates in a sham of his political power: Evil-merodach places Jehoiachin on "a throne above the thrones of the kings who were with him in Babylon" (2 Kgs 25:28b). In other words, Jehoiachin takes the place reserved for the preeminent vassal, the chief puppet king. This ironic significance reflects the most negative aspect of this intertextual reading.

But Jehoiachin's powerlessness is only implied, never stated. By hearkening back to Joseph's tale, 2 Kgs 25:27-30 may signify a tacit recognition of Jehoiachin's vastly improved status and influence. As a prominent vassal in Evil-merodach's court, Jehoiachin may hold a degree of sway. Still, the brevity of the final 2 Kings narrative renders this possibility inconclusive. An ironic interpretation appears more plausible.

A more hopeful implication emerges from a longer chronological perspective on this intertextual relationship. Joseph's tenure in Egypt prefaces the Egyptian enslavement of his people; yet their enslavement precedes their liberation and their entry into the promised land of Canaan. The intertextual implication for the ending of the DtrH is, therefore, in the long range, optimistic. When seen as a variation on the Joseph theme, the final Jehoiachin pericope recalls not only Genesis but also Exodus and the ensuing conquest narratives. An air of (eventual) renewal thereby enlivens the gloom of exile in the narrative of Jehoiachin's elevation.

Genesis 11

More hopeful still are the intertextual implications of the setting of the final four verses of DtrH. Between verses 26 and 27, the scene shifts from Judah to Babylon. In verse 26, however, the narrator explicitly identifies the Babylonians as "the Chaldeans," thus implicitly tagging Babylon as "the land of the Chaldeans." In this association, the implied author beckons the reader to remember Abraham, whom God called out "from Ur of the Chaldeans to go into the land of Canaan" (Gen 11:31). In the exiled Jehoiachin, the Davidic line has made a full circle and united itself with the patriarch Abraham's place of birth. Does this signify a cruel pilgrimage? The confluence of Davidic and Abrahamic covenants? Or the beginning of a new historical cycle? Surely the exilic reader could only wonder and hope. The contemporary reader, on the other hand, knows of the hope as well as the heartbreak that lie in store for the people of ancient Israel, who emerge from the Exile into the Restoration as a reconstituted people.

CONCLUSION

An intertextual reading confirms the theological judgments of both Noth and von Rad. In 2 Kgs 25:27-30, pessimism coexists with optimism; judgment stands side by side with hope. As Nelson (1987:267) suggests, the brief narrative of Jehoiachin's fate is "richly ambiguous rather than merely negative." The DtrH narrative has taken the reader to the end of an era. As the poet Wallace Stevens suggests, "the imagination is always at the end of an era" (in Kermode 1966:31). And yet, for historical communities (unlike characters in novels), endings generally translate into new beginnings. Dtr can guide the reader through what has been. As to what will be, who can say?

The larger canonical context of DtrH, which 2 Kgs 25:27-30 does not conclude, militates against a finally pessimistic theological reading of these final four verses. After all, Jehoiachin's death in exile is not "the end" of the people of God known as Israel. Nor does his death mark the extinction of the Davidic line. This same canonical context, however, also argues against a finally optimistic reading. Jehoiachin's end does toll the death knell for the monarchy. After Jehoiachin, no more Davidic kings will rule in Judah. His grandson Zerubbabel will return to Jerusalem to assume political leadership of sorts, but he will not be a king. 1-2 Kings ends as it began (an appropriate note of closure) with the last days of a king. Even more appropriately, it ends with the last days of the last king. 2 Kgs 25:27-30 provides what careful readers seek—"an intelligible End" to a story ripe with intertextual possibility.

NOTES

[1] Wolff (1982:86-88) finds fault with both Noth and von Rad. Noth's is too negative, while von Rad's is too positive. In reality, however, Wolff only differs from von Rad's interpretation when its positive elements are exaggerated. Wolff simply rejects von Rad's gospel/law and promise/judgment schemas in favor of his apostasy/turning-to-Yahweh schema (88). In other words, Wolff emphasizes what God requires (repentance) over what God offers (promise/gospel).

[2] The intentional fallacy "identifies what is held to be the error of interpreting or evaluating a work by reference to the intention—the design or plan—of the author in writing the work" (M. H. Abrams 1971:79).

[3] Kristeva (1980:65) credits Mikhail Bakhtin with this shift in perspective, which she further develops: "What allows a dynamic dimension to structuralism is [his] conception of the 'literary word' as an *intersection of textual surfaces* rather than a *point* (a fixed meaning), as a dialogue among several writings: that of the writer, the addressee (or the character), and the contemporary or earlier cultural context."

[4] Miller's definition differs in some basic respects from those of Barthes and Kristeva. This reflects the plurality among critics in their understanding of intertextuality. I find Miller's understanding helpful because it is not interwoven into a larger and complicated ideological program, as are Barthes' and Kristeva's. Although ideological interests are always implicit, the discussion of an ideological program would serve only to detour this study from my interest in formulating an intelligible ending for 2 Kings.

5 I am indebted to Peter D. Miscall (1986:22) for the notion of 2 Samuel 9's connection with 2 Kings 25. Miscall suggests that 2 Samuel 9, in which David invites a grandson of Saul to dine at his table, ironically foreshadows the similar fate of the Davidic line depicted in 2 Kgs 25:27-30, in which Evil-merodach invites a scion of David to dine at the royal table in Babylon.

PART III

GENESIS TO KINGS AND BEYOND

11

A BLESSING CURSED:
THE PROPHET'S PRAYER FOR BARREN WOMB AND DRY BREASTS IN HOSEA 9

Deborah Krause

Despite their wide variety, theories of intertextuality share interests in the power of reversal.[1] Such theories translate into methodological procedures which are often intentional (even strategic) about the broadening effect of reading texts in relationship rather than as isolated units of meaning. In biblical studies, intertextual methods are often used to challenge the objectivist claims of "Higher Criticism," and therefore to question its authority to produce *the* interpretation of a particular text.[2] As such, intertextual reading strategies are often double-edged. On the one hand, a particular text is placed in relationship with others to produce a fresh reading. On the other hand, this new reading is often aimed at displacing the text's dominant interpretation according to critical consensus.

Such is the case with this paper. Specifically, I take issue with the form-critical reading of Hos 9:14 offered by both Hans Walter Wolff (1974) and James L. Mays (1969). They read the prophetic interjection, "Give them O Lord—what will you give them?—give them a miscarrying womb and dry breasts," as an intercessory prayer for mercy on behalf of Ephraim. My contention with this reading arises from its assessment of the sterilization of women as an act of mercy. This is fueled, moreover, by my suspicion that some interpreters may move too quickly to such conclusions. Hence, in order to challenge the interpretation offered by Wolff and Mays, I will broaden my reading of Hos 9:14 in relation to a different network of intertextual relationships—relationships that draw out more fully the literary and thematic depth of the text. Overall, this strategy will serve a reading of the prophet's prayer as *ironic* and *judgmental* rather than as genuinely intercessory. Each area of intertextual relationship shows how the theme of judgment is played out through the vehicle of ironic reversal.[3]

One network of intertextual relationships (with other second person intercessions in Hosea and elsewhere) demonstrates how the imperative to "give" is employed ironically in the request for dry breasts and a miscarrying womb. Another intertextual relationship, with Gen 49:25, reveals how the prayer for dry breasts and miscarrying womb comprises an ironic reversal of an ancient blessing of the breasts and womb. Finally, when the prayer is read intertextually as the centerpiece of a unit (Hos 9:10-17), it is clear that this is one of several thematic reversals. These reversals are undergirded by a reflection on the tradition of Israel, and announce overall the infertility of Ephraim and its removal from the LORD'S care.

The detection of ironic reversal demands that the reader see texts in tensive relationship with one another. It is important to note that Wolff and Mays also draw on textual comparisons in order to establish their reading of the prayer as intercessory. Their comparisons, however, seek to establish *similarity* between the forms of the various texts. The intertextual comparisons of this paper will draw out the dissimilarities and tensions between texts, and thereby will enable the reader to recognize their ironic content. It is hoped that my expansion of the horizons around 9:14 will not only discredit interpretations of the prayer as genuinely intercessory, but will also draw attention to its horrific qualities, and open up its interpretive possibilities in relation to the ancient tradition of the LORD'S care for Israel.

COPING WITH THE FORM OF HOSEA 9:10-17

The form of Hos 9:10-17 is problematic. Thematically, the unit flows nicely from 9:9 where the prophet announces that the LORD will "remember" the iniquity and "punish" the sins of Ephraim. And indeed, this is precisely what transpires in 9:10-13. But 9:14 presents form critics with a problem in that the prophet, without benefit of introductory formula, directly addresses the deity: "Give them O LORD—what will you give them?" In 9:15, again without a concluding formula, the deity resumes the remembrance of Ephraim's iniquity, and the judgment of its sin. This oracle continues up to 9:17, when the prophet speaks again, and summarizes the divine judgment: "My God will cast them off, because they have not listened to him; they will become wanderers among the nations."

Wolff and Mays attempt to cope with this problem by comparing the unit with similar phenomena of prophetic interjection in Isa 6:11, Amos 7:2 and Amos 7:5. All three of these texts share a pattern of alternation between divine and prophetic speech, and in each case the prophet directly addresses the deity in the midst of an oracle of judgment.

> How long O LORD? (Isa 6:11)
>
> O LORD forgive [O LORD Cease] . . .
> How can Jacob stand? He is so small. (Amos 7:2, 5)
>
> Give them O LORD—what will you give them?—give them a miscarrying womb and dry breasts. (Hos 9:14)

The comparison may be helpful in establishing a general pattern; but Mays and Wolff press it too far when they bring the tentative formal similarities to bear on determining and limiting the content of Hos 9:14. After all, Hos 9:10-17 is unlike Amos 7:2, 7:5 and Isa 6:11, for in Hosea the LORD does not engage the prophet's interjection with a response. As such, Hos 9:10-17 is not dialogical.[4] Because both Isaiah and Amos ask the deity for mercy, however, it seems that these readers would have Hosea do the same. They each claim that given the list of judgments in 9:11-13 (dispersion, abandonment, feminine infertility, and infanticide), the prophet (with great angst) chooses feminine infertility—the barren womb and dry breasts. Wolff (1974:166) states that this is a choice of the "least evil" option. And Mays (1969:135) maintains that the prophet's choice is a comparably "merciful blessing."[5] In both cases, the interpretation of Hosea's prayer enters into psychological speculation about the prophet, and understands his primary concern to be staving off the slaughter of innocent children.[6]

There are several problems with this reading. First, the "list" of horrors which Wolff and Mays find in 9:11-13 is not a review of options in which the *ki 'im* ("even if") of verse 12a functions as a choice between feminine infertility and infanticide. As Buss (1969:63, 123; employing Hillers) has demonstrated, the *ki 'im* introduces a futility curse. Throughout Hosea, futility curses are employed to underscore judgments of death and barrenness (8:7; 4:10; 5:6). Hence, *ki 'im* in 12a does not establish a condition for escaping the infertility trap of 11b: "No birth, no pregnancy, no conception!" Rather, it broadens the scope of the LORD'S judgment in verses 11-13 (and later in vss. 15-16) over the entire spectrum of the possibility for life. The prophet's prayer for a barren womb and dry breasts, therefore, is not a choice for a comparably merciful blessing. Instead, it reiterates the harsh divine proclamation for feminine infertility at the locus of fertility: womb/breast. In this sense, Hosea does not intercede for Ephraim as do Isaiah and Amos. Rather, he *affirms*—much like the chorus in Greek tragedy—the portrait of doom offered in the divine oracle.[7]

Second, Wolff and Mays do not adequately account for the prophet's "change of heart," from his alleged request for mercy in 9:14, to his clear affirmation of the LORD'S abandonment in verse 17. In their discussion of the problem, they enter into further psychological speculation and rationalization. Here Hosea is tortured. He struggles. His mediatory position between the people and the LORD is taxed. He is torn; yet finally he is won over to the LORD'S side. If this text were not being read in light of Isa 6:11, Amos 7:2 and Amos 7:5, would such an interpretation be possible?

Third, according to this reading, the only function of the interjection is as an unheard plea for a dubious and highly qualified form of mercy. As such, the verse is denied its thematic depth in relation to the issue of the LORD'S giving and Ephraim's denial of the LORD'S gifts. It is also denied its literary depth in relation to the surrounding unit and the larger tradition. And finally it is denied the possible rhetorical impact of its ironic reversal. Another kind of intertextual reading of Hos 9:14 is possible, one better attuned to the dynamics of ironic reversal within Hosea.

HOSEA 9:14 AND THE IRONIC REVERSAL OF INTERCESSION

The interjection of Hosea in the midst of divine judgment places him in the role of an intercessor on behalf of Ephraim. As such his three-fold use of "give" (*ntn*) would appear to plead for the well-being of his people. However, an examination of the use of this word in other biblical intercessions to the LORD, especially within the book of Hosea, reveals its ironic formulation here. This irony arises out of the discontinuity between the prophet's intercessory prayer for the LORD to "give," and the content of that request: barren womb and dry breasts.

In the Psalter, when the deity is asked to "give" on behalf of Israel, the request is usually for divine salvation (e.g., Ps 85:7) or, in negative formulations ("do not give"), it demands deliverance from enemies (Pss 27:12; 74:19). In light of this larger context, the imperative that God "give" dry breasts and a barren womb in Hos 9:14 is incongruous with other intercessory prayers. As such, it is not a genuine intercession for divine mercy. Rather, it functions ironically as an intercession for divine judgment.

Thematically, within the book of Hosea as a whole, the three-fold repetition of *ntn* in 9:14 points to the larger claim that the LORD is the one who gives, and that Israel/Ephraim is denying this source. The issue is highlighted in chapters 2 and 13, and (most compellingly for Hos 9:14) in Hos 11:8.

Hos 2:12 (2:14) provides a startling link with 9:10 in that the wife considers her fig tree (*te'enatah*) to be given (*ntn*) to her by her lovers. Earlier, in 2:5, the issue is also at hand. There, the woman considers her bread, oil, drink, etc. to be given to her by her lovers. In 2:9 the LORD complains, "she did not acknowledge that I gave her bread . . . and gold and silver which they used for Baal."

In chapter 13 the issue of what Ephraim has been given in a king and princes is mocked by the prophet's report of divine speech. In 13:10 the LORD notes the lack of a king and princes for Ephraim's defense, and mocks Ephraim's request to be given such leadership. In turn the LORD responds, "I have given you kings in my anger, and I have taken them away in my wrath,"

(13:11). Here the issue is clear: the LORD gives and the LORD takes away—even kings and princes.

In Hosea 11:8, the prophet reports a divine cry of self doubt in the midst of a harsh proclamation that the LORD will return Israel to Egypt. Verses 1-7 demonstrate the LORD'S care for Israel, Israel's disobedience, and the LORD'S punishment. Verse 8 marks a turning point: "How can I give you up [*'etenka*] Ephraim? How can I give you up [*'etenka*] Israel?" Here, most poignantly, one can see the thematic connection of the LORD and Ephraim through the verb *ntn*. In all ways Ephraim belongs to the LORD. The LORD is the source of all Ephraim's gifts, and the LORD cannot give her over (*ntn*). In fact, through the thematic connection of *ntn*, it is as if the LORD'S cry in 11:8 answers the prophet's request in 9:14. To give Ephraim dry breasts and a barren womb would be to give up Ephraim and to make Ephraim like Admah and Zeboim in Genesis 19—desolate.

The intercessory words "give . . . give . . . give" in 9:14 do not serve merely to intercede ironically for Ephraim. They also incorporate into the intercession for infertility the assertion that the LORD is the source of all giving, and that Ephraim is denying this source. By recognizing the *intertextual tension* between this intercession to give and others in the Psalter and Hosea, the ironic interplay between the *form* of the request and its *content* has a particular rhetorical force. Hosea does not only confirm the LORD'S punishment of Ephraim; he offers a crystalized statement of its cause: the LORD is the source of Ephraim's gifts, yet Ephraim has denied this source. Hence, Ephraim will be given that which cuts off all of its future yield.

HOSEA 9:14 AND THE IRONIC REVERSAL OF BLESSING (GENESIS 49:25)

The ironic interplay of Hos 9:14 is further intensified by the prophet's employment of the phrase "miscarrying womb and dry breasts." Contrary to the formulations of Wolff and Mays, the phrase is no benign reference to infertility. Rather, it constitutes a *reappropriation* and *reversal* of an ancient blessing.

The words "womb" (*rehem*) and "breasts" (*shadayim*) appear together in a couplet only in Hos 9:14 and Gen 49:25

(Catlett 1988:179).[8] In Genesis, Jacob blesses his son Joseph (the father of Ephraim). He begins in verse 22, "Joseph is a fruitful [*porat*] bough, a fruitful vine." He continues, "by God almighty who will bless you . . . with blessings of breast and womb" (Gen 49:25). Von Rad (1974:421), Speiser (1964:371) and Skinner (1925:507) all maintain that the poetry in this blessing is ancient. Skinner (1925:529) maintains that this unit might even be Northern in origin.

The unique sharing of the breast and womb couplet, and the similarity of the surrounding catchwords for Ephraim (e.g., "fruitful" [*porat*] and the root of Hos 9:16 that will bear no fruit [*peri*]) suggest a relationship between the two texts. Hosea's reference to, and reversal of, this ancient blessing has been noted by others (Trible 1978:61; Catlett 1988:178-181). In the context of Gen 49:25, the content of Hos 9:14 is clearly not concerned with a plea for mercy. Rather, it starkly reverses an ancient blessing of fertility and reformulates it into a curse.[9]

The possible basis for Hosea's use of the Genesis tradition has also been explored. Michael Fishbane (1985:377) makes a case for Hosea's use of the Genesis tradition regarding Jacob (or a reflection of that story) and suggests that Hosea transforms it for later Israel. Catlett (1988:166-188) includes an entire section on the prophet's references to Genesis.[10] While the early date of Hosea makes a difficult case of arguing for literary dependence, there seems at the least to be evidence of shared tradition between Hosea and Genesis at several points. Hosea 12 and 9:14 seem to offer a particularly clear use of Genesis (or the tradition behind it); in both cases Hosea reverses the traditional elements of promise and election in his prophecy against Israel/Ephraim. Such a technique of reversing tradition is an effective means of making the assertion that the LORD has withdrawn traditional support from Israel/Ephraim, and has altered the heretofore accepted relationship. By appealing to the ancient blessing of breast and womb lexically, the prophetic interjection pulls up (from its root) the entire tradition of the LORD'S sovereign care as the one who gives breast and womb, and allows the tradition to judge Ephraim's current denial of the source of its fertility. The LORD, who once gave breast and womb, will now give miscarrying womb and dry breast. Through the ironic interplay, again, the judgment and its basis in the tradition are made present. Within the prophet's ironic intercession for barren womb and dry breast, all who have ears to hear the ancient tradition stand aware that the previous order of the LORD'S relationship with Ephraim has been reversed: the blessing is now a curse.

HOSEA 9:14 IN ITS CONTEXT: THE CENTER OF IRONIC REVERSAL

The ironic intercession of 9:14 is located at the center of the larger unit 9:10-17.[11] This larger unit forms a thematic *inclusio* which contains the contrast between the LORD'S care for Israel/Ephraim and the LORD'S rejection of Ephraim. The reversal is underscored by a tradition-historical reminiscence of the cultic malpractices of Baal Peor (9:10) and Gilgal (9:15). These remembrances serve to present the motivation for the judgment of 9:14—Ephraim has denied the source of its fruitfulness.

The inclusio is formulated in the reversal of Ephraim's salvation history: the LORD *found* (*m-ts-'*) Israel ("your fathers") in the wilderness (10A); Ephraim will be *cast off* (*m-'-s*) among the nations (17A). Metaphorically, this is matched in the reversal: Israel/your fathers were like *grapes*, and *fig tree* (9:10Ab); but Ephraim's *root is stricken*, and *will bear no fruit* (9:16B). In the first case, the former condition of the LORD'S care is contrasted with the subsequent rejection; and in the second case Israel/Ephraim's fruitfulness is contrasted with its barrenness.

This inclusio is undergirded by a reminiscence of history which plays out the theme of Ephraim's denial of the LORD'S gifts through cultic malpractice. In 9:10b the LORD remembers Baal Peor, and the way Israel strayed away (Numbers 25). In 9:15 the LORD reflects on the evil (*ra'*) of Gilgal. In light of the other cultic references to this place name in Hosea (4:15 and 12:11), the reference to cultic malpractice is clear. However, a political allusion may also be present (1 Samuel 11-15).[12] Whatever the specific content of the malpractice, in both cases it evokes the LORD'S revulsion. At Baal Peor the people became *detestable* like the ones they loved. At Gilgal the LORD began to *hate* them.

In the center of the unit stands the prophet's prayer. In light of the inclusio of reversal, and the historical remembrance of Israel/Ephraim's cultic malpractice, the ironic intercession in 9:14 serves as the locus of the LORD's rejection of Ephraim. Throughout the unit the tension between Ephraim's fruitfulness and Ephraim's denial is present. But in 9:14 that tension receives its ultimate expression. The LORD (the source of fruit) must give to Ephraim (the fruitful one) a "gift" of ultimate infertility. Within the context of 9:10-17, the result of this ironic intercession is that the fruitful one (who has denied its source) is in turn denied its fruit.

CONCLUSION

A reading of Hos 9:14 (9:10-17) which is attentive to its literary and thematic depth can interpret the prayer as a call not for mercy but for judgment. The formulation of the prayer produces several ironic reversals: the found ones are cast off, the fruit is dried up, the blessing is a curse. Finally, even the intercession is a judgment! These reversals function to indict. But they also remind Ephraim that it was once found, that it was once fruitful, that the blessing of breast and womb did once stand, and that the prophet did once genuinely intercede.

A reading that allows Hos 9:14 its full thematic and literary play—and thereby its most condemning tone—allows the full rhetorical effect of Hosea to be heard. Certainly, as Wolff himself notes (1974:169), by the end of the unit of 9:10-17, judgment more than ever has become a central theme. This judgment, however, is managed in such a way that a more central theme of instruction can be offered, in order that Ephraim might yet hear (vs. 17) and acknowledge the one who gives life.[13]

At the end of the book, one sees the centrality of the teaching regarding the LORD as the source of Ephraim's gifts. In 14:9, the final verse of divine speech reported in Hosea, the teaching is reformulated from an ironic intercessory curse into a statement of assurance—yet another reversal.

> O Ephraim, what have I to do with idols?
> It is I who answer and look after him.

I am like an evergreen cypress.
From me comes your fruit.

The double-edged program of this paper is complete. Appraisals of the prayer for barren womb and dry breast as genuinely merciful require the reader to equate unlike forms (i.e., Hos 9:14 with Isa 6:11, Amos 7:2 and Amos 7:5). I have therefore suggested another intertextual approach, emphasizing other intertexts and focusing on the *tension* these intertexts create within Hos 9:14. A reading of the interjection in light of these texts has enabled a more profound appreciation of the ironic depth of the prayer. In this appreciation, the prayer is not only ascribed its appropriate horrific quality, but is also understood within the larger program of Hosea's tradition-dependent judgment.

NOTES

[1] For example, Harold Bloom (1981:16) understands the intertextual relationships between texts to demonstrate a linear tension between poets and their precursors. Each of Bloom's categories of "misreading" traces how "strong" poets use the words of their precursors in order to reverse their relationship with them. Hence, in the final category (Apophrades, or return from the dead) the poem reads "not as though the precursor were writing it, but as though the later poet had written the precursor's characteristic work." Julia Kristeva (1980; 1984), on the other hand understands intertextual relationships not in a linear sense, but rather as a "mosaic." Yet, in her theory, texts always involve the "transgression" of the boundaries of other texts.

[2] E.g., Daniel Boyarin's work (1990:12) challenges (in part) the historical-critical oriented understanding of midrash *ha'aggadah* with an intertextual, "dialogical" understanding of midrash.

[3] Literary theorist D. C. Muecke (1970:35) describes three basic features of irony: "i) a contrast of appearance and reality, ii) a confident unawareness (pretended in the ironist, real in the victim of irony) that the appearance is only an appearance, and iii) the comic effect of this unawareness of a contrasting appearance and reality." The reversals in 9:10-17 hold together the apparent meaning of salvation history with the incongruous reality of Ephraim's behavior, and the incongruous plan of the LORD for Ephraim. The word play on "Ephra-

im" (literally "the fruitful one") in this sense is itself ironic, as in this context "Ephraim" appears to be fruitful, but in fact is dried up. For a clear discussion of irony in the context of biblical interpretation, see Gail R. O'Day (1986:esp. 11-32).

[4] Wolff attempts to cope with this formal discrepancy by insisting upon the jussive force translation of 9:17 ("My God, cast them off . . ."), thereby creating a more dialogical character for the passage. This translation does effect more alternation in speech between deity (vss. 10-13), prophet (vs. 14), deity (vss. 15-16), prophet (vs. 17); such alternation alone, however, does not create a dialogue. At no point in the unit (or anywhere in Hosea) is there an account where the deity directly responds to the prophet's questions or calls.

[5] Both Wolff and Mays note that barrenness in general is a curse; in this situation, however, the prophet is forced to see it as "a sign of God's gentleness" (Wolff 1974:167), or as "a kind of blessing for which he could pray" (Mays 1969:135). In both cases their readings maintain that the prayer is a genuine intercession for mercy.

[6] Never does the prophet demonstrate the kind of sentimentality which Wolff and Mays anachronistically ascribe to him. In fact, in the midst of prophetic speech in 13:16 (14:1) the metaphors of infanticide and feminine mutilation are drawn out as a prediction of judgment (the final decree of judgment in the book): "their little ones will be dashed into pieces, and their pregnant women will be ripped open."

[7] The particular chorus which comes to mind is that of the "Old Men" in Sophocles' *Antigone*. Throughout the tragedy the same dynamic of the chorus' address and encouragement of the gods (who are not scripted) offers the audience guidance as to the gods' position in the conflict between Antigone and Creon.

[8] The appearance of *baten* (another word for womb) and *shadayim* occurs in Ps 22:10, but Catlett is correct that nowhere other than Gen 49:25 and Hos 9:14 are *rehem* and *shadayim* coupled.

[9] Catlett (1988:180) uses this very language (blessing-curse) with regard to this reversal in 9:14: "what appeared in Genesis as a blessing to Joseph becomes in Hosea a curse to Ephraim." Surprisingly, Catlett still appropriates both Wolff's and Mays' reading of the verse as a genuine intercession (226 nn. 24 and 25). This is especially surprising as Catlett's work attempts to be particularly attentive to the *ironic* content of reversals in Hosea. Here he is aware of the irony of a blessing as a curse, but misses the irony of form in the condemnatory effect of the intercessory prayer.

[10] Catlett claims allusion to Genesis tradition in Hosea 12 (Jacob), Hos 1:2 (Gen 28:1-2), 1:9 and 2:1 (Gen 13:16; 15:5; 26:24; 28:14), 4:3 (Gen 1:20-28), 2:20 (Gen 1:30), and 11:8 (Genesis 19). In all of these connections he establishes lexical linkages.

[11] Anderson and Freedman (1980:539) argue for a tight chiastic structure of Hosea 9:10-17 in which verse 14 stands at the center.

Their argument is compelling, but the chiastic structure they present is too neat. The thematic inclusio of the reversal of Ephraim's relationship with the LORD, and Israel/Ephraim's fruitfulness, maintains the strengths of their observations without demanding the forced one-to-one relationships they draw in each verse.

[12] Von Rad (1972:114) claims that the "apparent split between religion and politics in Hosea is a modern distinction." It does seem as though the efforts to parse exclusively political or religious significance out of Hos 9:15's reference to Gilgal are futile. This is especially the case in that the tradition used for the political argument (1 Sam 15) contains a clear element of cultic malpractice as well (1 Sam 15:21).

[13] The rhetorical effectiveness of the barren womb and dry breast metaphors in Hos 9:14 in no way excuses the use of images of violence against women (or anyone else for that matter) in Hosea's judgment against Israel. For an extensive treatment of this hermeneutical issue in relation to the marriage metaphor in Hosea, see Renita Weems (1989:87-104).

12

JOB AND JACOB:
THE INTEGRITY OF FAITH

ELLEN F. DAVIS

The subject of this study is the question of Job's integrity, and it will be argued that there is a fundamental relation between the two senses in which that phrase may be understood. The first sense has recently been the subject of considerable scholarly attention. Arguments for the literary integrity of the book seem now to have prevailed over attempts to discredit or sheer off those parts (i.e., the narrative frame, the poem on wisdom in chap. 28 and the Elihu speech in chaps. 32-37) which previous generations of critical scholars thought beneath the inspiration of the great poet of the dialogue.[1] They have demonstrated the vitality and sophistication of a literary style that, by holding different theological perspectives in sustained and acute tension, discloses the limitations of each but also the degree of truth present in them all.

The other sense in which one may speak of Job's integrity—namely, as a character trait of the *man*—points to a major theme of the book. That Job is a person of integrity is the first thing we learn of him (*wehayah ha'îsh hahû' tam*, 1:1), on the authority of the apparently disinterested narrator, and that characterization is subsequently reinforced as the persistence and consequences of Job's *tummah* ("integrity") are asserted or called into question by parties on every side of the controversy surrounding him: in God's boasts to Satan (1:8; 2:3), in the challenge posed by Job's wife (2:9), in his own speeches (9:20-22; 27:5; 31:6; cf. 21:23) and those of his counsellors (4:6; 8:20). Yet it is curious that a theme which occurs repeatedly within both the narrative and the poetic sections has not occupied a more central place in study of the book's structure and message.[2]

It is the aim of this essay to show, first, that the matter of Job's *tummah* is indeed the central question of the book and provides the perspective from which the complex unity of its message may be discerned. Contrary to those who argue that the prose narrative is preserved merely to provide fodder for the poet's cannon,[3] I maintain that the narrative characterization of Job is never contradicted and that the appearance of contradiction which troubles many readers is due to an inadequate understanding of the word *tam*, commonly translated "blameless"[4]—a translation which probably approximates the primary sense the word conveyed to the poet's original audience. It is a major task of the poem to deepen and complicate the meaning of that key term and thus bring the audience and Job himself to a new sense of what it means to be a person of integrity.

Second, this study will consider why that one word should have been so important as to warrant such extensive reinterpretation. One may grant the likelihood that the four-fold characterization of Job (*tam weyashar wîre' 'elohîm wesar mera'*, 1:1) was the "heroic epithet" conventionally associated with this man of legendary piety.[5] But if the poet had rejected this traditional characterization—that is, if it were correct to see a disjunction between the narrative and the poetic representations of Job—then we should expect to find the inconvenient linguistic inheritance undermined or at least glossed over in the portrayal of outraged Job. Yet, far from neutralizing the (presumably) conventional language, the poet takes up the first element of the epithet in such a way that, rendered prominent through repetition, it becomes central to the whole revised history of the furious sufferer. I shall argue that the indispensable significance of the word *tam* for understanding Job's character derives from its association with another person of integrity—namely, with Jacob—who likewise struggles with God and with humans (Gen 32:29) and at last is granted a vision whereby he is fully transformed into the effective vehicle of divine blessing.[6]

THE IMPLICATIONS OF INTEGRITY

The function of the word *tam* within Israelite wisdom literature is important for understanding the ordinary connotations which the word would have had for the poet's contemporaries. Walter Brueggemann (1977:242) has noted that the terms *t-m* and *'-q-sh* ("integrity" and "perverseness") occur numerous times in the wisdom traditions, both singly and as a pair, denoting alternative "direction[s] and style[s] of conduct." Throughout, usage of the terms reinforces the sapiential conviction that consequences follow reliably upon behavior: "The one who walks in integrity [*battom*] walks securely, but the one who perverts [*me'aqqesh*] his ways will be found out" (Prov 10:9; cf. Prov 28:18; *et al.*). The judgment implied in the terms is not abstract but expresses the effect of public conduct upon community life: "acting or speaking in devious ways which undermine the well-being of others or acting in ways that enhances [sic] the well-being of others, i.e., edifies the community" (239).

Brueggemann sees in the narrative of Job the dramatization of integrity as it is embodied in "the one who acted for the community according to the norms of the community" (251).[7] Moreover, he draws a basic distinction between the narrative frame and the poem with respect to God's own faithfulness to that value. In his view, the divine speech leaves in terrible doubt the question of whether God shares Job's commitment to the order and value of community life—that is, whether God is *tam*. Brueggemann's study is valuable for its recognition that this word draws the book of Job *in its entirety* into dialogue with Israel's wisdom tradition. Nonetheless, by restricting the operation of integrity to the social sphere, he precludes the possibility of producing a satisfactory reading of the poem; for it is precisely such an understanding which the poet means to challenge. Brueggemann's treatment of Job is curiously truncated:

> So far as the question of integrity-perversity goes, Job has the last word in ch. 31. And he retains the last word; the final statement of Job ($42_{1\text{-}6}$) concedes nothing on this central issue. Perhaps God is if not just, at least shrewd enough not to get drawn into that discussion. (255)

Job's peroration in chapter 31 is surely the fullest expression of his original understanding of integrity, and it is wholly in accord with the orientation toward community life which Brueggemann discovers in Proverbs. Job in his self-righteousness is thoroughly conventional, satisfied that his public conduct was such that it should have assured human regard (cf. Prov 29:10) and divine favor (Prov 11:20).[8]

Yet, contrary to Brueggemann, God does not remain ominously or shrewdly silent with respect to Job's central claim. I shall argue that the divine speech is a direct response to that claim and that Job acknowledges it as such, that God affirms his claim to integrity and yet also reveals the inadequacy of Job's own conception of it, disclosing a dimension of "integrity" which transcends but does not devalue responsibility to human community. Moreover, as the next section will show, the prior usage of the word outside the wisdom tradition—specifically, in the ancestral narratives—prepares the way for such a reconceptualization of *tummah*.

It is Job's wife who first points toward that transcendent aspect of his integrity. Her challenge (2:9a) is commonly heard as a mocking question ("Do you still persist in your integrity?"), implying that Job's vaunted integrity has availed him nothing. But it may also be read as a statement rather than a question: a sad affirmation that integrity is the one thing of value which Job has left, and that very integrity demands that he now curse the God who has senselessly destroyed everything else.[9] In either case, she asserts that it is solely in relation to God that Job's integrity is meaningful, and she urges him now to discard it as wholly delusory or else to prove it in the severing of that poisonous bond.

Although Job rebuffs his wife's challenge, still his answer accepts the theocentric terms in which she posed it: "Will you speak like one of the impious women (*hannebalôt*); shall we accept good from God and not accept evil?" (2:10). S. R. Driver (1921:26) has shown that *nebalah* (cf. 42:8) does not mean "folly," as it is frequently translated, for "the fault of the *nabhal* is not weakness of reason but moral and religious insensibility, an invincible lack of sense or perception, for the claims of either

God or man." The term is applied to those who have a settled incapacity to perceive the blessings or demands of Israel's God: the heathen (Deut 32:21; Ps 74:18, 22) or the practical atheist (Ps 14:1). What seems to be emerging in the exchange between Job and his wife is the basis for a new understanding of integrity, one that God's speech will confirm. Integrity is primarily a theological virtue and only secondarily a social one. *Tummah* is the polar opposite of *nebalah*: a heightened sensitivity to God's presence and action and the ability to live in accordance with that sensitivity, even when it controverts previously settled convictions about the just ordering of the world. The person of integrity is not only morally upright but also humble and resilient in faith, socially responsible but also responsive to the God who is free to change the terms of the relationship and the conditions under which faith must be practiced.[10]

The challenge of Job's wife is further significant for its allusion, albeit indirect, to the important theme of blessing. The quadruple repetition (1:5, 1:11, 2:5, 2:9) of the otherwise rare "antithetical" usage of *brk* (cf. I Kgs 21:10, 13[11]; Ps 10:3) indicates at the outset that the very nature of blessing is at issue in this tale. And indeed, God's final vindication of Job's truthful speech (42:7) reveals that, in ironic fulfillment of the Satan's predictions, Job is to the end one who "blesses God to [his] face" (cf. 1:21). Unlike his counsellors, who are content to theorize about God, Job insists that God appear to hear his claim and answer his accusation. If blasphemy is taking God's name in vain, invoking that power for validation of a position or action *apart from any genuine encounter with God*, then it is these garrulous theologians and not Job who must be charged with that offense. Job may, as he finally admits (42:3), have too small a view of God's ways, but he presses always for a personal hearing, never doubting before whom his integrity must be vindicated. Even with his railing, Job speaks truly to and about[12] God, for in anguish and in hope of deliverance, he holds responsible to him the God whose essential nature it is to hear and answer the cry of distress.[13] Indeed, maybe now Job understands God better than before, for suffering makes him incautious and thus pushes him into a posture in which he is open to awe.[14] Rightly despairing of the egotistical attempt to control God through good conduct (cf 1:5), he becomes through his very rage more radically theocentric in perspective. In view of this transformation, which will be complete only when God has spoken, there is nothing facile about the epilogue's affirmation that Job's end is blessed even above his beginning (42:12). For through relinquishing his pretensions to control, he becomes more receptive to blessing, and not only for himself. The man who once shadow-boxed with the imagined sins of his children is now called to the far more spiritually demanding task of making atonement for his enemies (42:8, 10). The full measure of Job's transformation is the astonishing divine charge to set his prayer as a hedge against the threat of God's own "insensibility" (*nebalah*) to the need for mercy. Thus Job becomes as in the past (cf. 29:13, 31:20), yet more profoundly, a channel for the reciprocal flow of blessing between heaven and earth. As will be shown below, this theme of blessing is another important link between the histories of Jacob and Job.

INTEGRITY AND BLESSING

The setting of the Joban narrative evokes Israel's earliest memory: Job, like Abraham and his descendants, is a desert sheik, a tent-dweller who prospers (Job 29:4).[15] The nomadic setting "in the land of Uz" recalls the ancestral period before Israel became a people settled in their own land. Yet the Joban poet makes no explicit connection between Job's history and the mainstream tradition. Rather the reverse: the Gentile atmosphere of the poem is underscored by the fact that God appears almost throughout as a foreigner. The peculiarly Israelite Tetragrammeton (YHWH) is found only in the narrative frame and the divine speech; elsewhere pre-Mosaic names (El, Elohim, Eloah, Shaddai) are used.

Gordis (1965:213) suggests that the choice of a non-Israelite protagonist reveals the Joban poet to be "an exemplar of the universalism of spirit which existed in Second Temple Judaism side by side with more particularistic views." Yet if the poet wished to avoid particularism, then it is strange that the God whose appearance marks the climax of the book is identified as

YHWH, more strikingly because the appellation was previously avoided. The poet does finally anchor Job's experience in a distinctively Israelite tradition—but the "finally" is all-important to the message of the book.

Nonetheless, the fact that pious Job of legend was not an Israelite may have commended him to the poet's use. For if indeed the poem reflects the experience of exile,[16] then it is surely apt that the model of faith offered here is a man stripped of wealth, family, influence, health, and (from an Israelite perspective, worst of all) bereft of any claim to God's special favor. For Job stands outside the covenant promises to Abraham and David, and God is under no prior obligation to bless him. Moreover, Gentile Job, like Israel in exile, has no recourse to the institutional apparatus of Temple and priesthood to assure him of God's presence and mediate reconciliation. Job shows us the struggle and the reward of faith in its starkest form: where God's blessing is reduced to what Karl Barth called "the cheerless minimum of actual preservation" (1961:405), only the persistent hope of standing before God sustains the person of integrity, whose determination is answered and longing satisfied when YHWH speaks out of the whirlwind.

Gordis (1965:149) argues that the spirit of the book is not only universalistic but also "single-mindedly" individualistic, reflecting a trend of thought that dominated Israelite religion in the post-exilic period. But the epic proportions and ancient setting of the drama indicate the opposite. Job's story, like that of the eponymous ancestors, is larger-than-life, large enough to encompass the experience of the whole people, as a people. Job is Israel in exile: radically alienated from God, and yet unable to separate himself from this God who seems bent on destroying him. It was fitting, at a time when the success of Judah's enemies had wreaked havoc with the notion of blessing on Abraham's seed and David's house, for the poet to give the drama of betrayed and renewed faith an antique and foreign setting. Moving outside the arena of salvation history, back to a time before the blessings of land and offspring had been fulfilled, the Joban poet evoked a fictive world mirroring the existential reality of the sixth century. Perhaps only the land of

Uz was far enough from stricken Jerusalem to permit a fearless and unsentimental re-examination of the possibility for faith, of what it means to bless God and experience God's blessing, even in the midst of the most dreadful suffering.

Yet in one respect the legend of pious Job does not seem to accord with the situation of exilic Israel. For the folktale told of a man who was ethically perfect, "blameless," and Israel was not. I suggest that this is precisely the problem which prompted the one who was perhaps Israel's greatest poet to an imaginative probing of Job's history, and that an element of Israel's ancestral tradition provided the link between the legendary model of innocence and Israel's own flawed history and character.

In Israel's earliest history, the concepts of blessing and integrity belong together. There is an echo of the proverbial assurances of reward for virtue (e.g., Prov 20:7; 28:10) in the language of Gen 17:1, where Abraham is charged to walk before YHWH and behave with integrity (*wehyeh tamîm*) in order that he may be worthy of the covenant which God is about to make and the blessings that derive from it. Brueggemann rightly sees the story of Abraham, "the man of integrity [who] receives blessings," as providing a clue to the meaning of the Joban narrative (241 n.); yet the Genesis text itself supports the theocentric interpretation of "integrity" for which I argued (contra Brueggemann) above. For Abraham as for Job, the chief measure of integrity is a constant awareness of God—an awareness that amounts in each case to obsession. Appropriate action in the social sphere is a derivative and not invariable aspect of that awareness.[17]

Weinfeld's study (1970:186; cf. 200) of the royal grant in the ancient Near East provides extra-biblical support for the interpretation of "integrity" as being in the first instance a disposition toward God. He asserts that the phrase *wehyeh tamîm* (Gen 17:1) is equivalent to the Assyrian (*ittalak*) *shalmish*, "which conveys the idea of perfect or loyal service" and thus validates the character of the recipient of royal favor.[18] By analogy, it is the quality of devotion to the divine sovereign which must be proven in Abraham and Job and which is the essential qualification for blessing.

There is one other place in the patriarchal narratives that this theme of integrity appears, although it is not commonly recognized as such; and significantly, it occurs in the segment of the narrative which may be described as an extended agon of blessing.[19] I refer to the designation of Jacob as 'îsh tam (Gen 25:27). As with Job, the first thing we learn of the grown Jacob is that he is "a person of integrity"; but the phrase poses a conundrum, for if indeed tam denotes ethical integrity, then Jacob is not an obvious candidate for that accolade. Here the word characterizes a disposition and lifestyle sharply distinct from that of Esau, who is "a man experienced at hunting, a man of the open country." Translations of tam ("mild" [NJPS], "quiet" [RSV], "simple" [NAB], "retiring" [Speiser]) attempt to clarify the distinction, yet none of them can be correlated with its usage in other contexts.[20]

The best clue to the meaning of tam in this passage is the continuation of the verse: tam marks the character of the tent-dweller, one who lives with others and recognizes the demands of the social order. Scripture portrays Esau as an idiot, in the classical sense (Greek idios, "one's own"). Completely absorbed in his own immediate needs and pleasures, giving no heed to consequences, he sells his birthright for beans and pursues the genealogical dead-end of marriage with Hittite women (Gen 27:46; 28:6-9). Jacob, by contrast, although perhaps not altogether respectable, is "civilized."[21] He craves the rewards of a settled life: property, domestic pleasure, and perhaps prestige; he does not scruple at hard work, years of waiting, or deception in order to secure them. Unlike his brother, who is, in Thomas Mann's phrase, "a feckless insignificant child of nature," Jacob is well-adapted to the *mores*, if not the morals, of society.[22]

The targumic rendering of Gen 25:27 is intriguing: *weya'-aqob gebar shelîm meshamesh bêt 'ûlpana'*.[23] Tam is taken as pointing to Jacob's educability. Although hardly a translation, that interpretation has a logic of its own which sheds light on the received text. Education makes civilized life possible, for it literally leads us out (*educo*) beyond ourselves, introducing us to perspectives other than our own, imposing concerns that do not come naturally, disciplining us to know and care (however "academically") about people, causes, ideas that are completely outside our personal experience.

The Targum suggests that Jacob, though assiduous in his self-serving, is nonetheless susceptible to being drawn out beyond himself. It is this susceptibility to transcendence which develops as the narrative progresses and shows Jacob to be not only chosen but qualified to bear God's blessing. The young Jacob displays in crude form the unattractive, dangerous, but essential quality of the religious person: the capacity for a particular kind of obsession, for being seized and devoted to what lies infinitely beyond one's own ambition and control. What marks him as a person of integrity, then, is the object of his obsession, God's blessing, which he can never possess as fully as it possesses him; and his fitness to bear it is proven by his capacity to sustain that obsession until at last he is transformed by the weight of glory.

The two theophanies that frame the account of the sojourn in Haran (Gen 28:10-22; 32:23-33) establish God's protective commitment to Abraham's descendants as the horizon for Jacob's self-aggrandizement. The first encounter comes as a surprise: Jacob's journey to Bethel was a flight, not a pilgrimage; yet his response to God's appearance is crucial. His conditional pledge of allegiance to YHWH, contingent upon his own well-being and safe-conduct home, bespeaks exactly the sort of shrewd piety that Weinfeld has identified as the qualification for receiving a royal grant, and it would seem to be sufficient for the divine purpose. But only after the encounter at the Jabbok, when Jacob, by his own account, "saw God face-to-face" (Gen 32:31), is the quality of Jacob's devotion to God really tested and the change in his character evident. When Jacob—now Israel—at last enters fully into the blessing for which he connived and wrestled, settling in the land of promise, he comes *shalem* (33:18)—"safe[ly]" (RSV, NJPS) perhaps, but it may be valid to see here an allusion to a disposition ("guileless, loyal, the contrary of everything crafty"; von Rad 1972:328) which contrasts significantly with his own former behavior as well as with the deception practiced by his sons (34:13). The "interlude"[24] in Genesis 34 widens the perspective from which we view Jacob's history. His anger at Simeon and Levi's revenge of their sister's rape shows that his own concern for personal honor has been subordinated to the need to secure the safety of his household (35:30), now seen not so much as a family as the nation *in nuce* (35:11).[25]

The clearest indication of the change in Jacob is the fact that he now begins to recede into the background of the larger story of the nation. The wrestling at the Jabbok transforms a personality—Jacob, the first fully developed character in Scripture—into the human institution Israel, who is of less narrative interest, if greater spiritual significance. The brief glimpses which the narrative gives of the mature Jacob shows how profound is the change. He returns to Bethel, this time with his household, to build an altar of dedication; now he knows that this God alone affords protection in the inhospitable land of promise (35:4-5). Jacob will later offer sacrifices of a more personal kind: he sends his youngest, dearest child to Egypt as hostage for famine relief, and at last himself makes the hard journey in order that he may bless Joseph, his sons and, perhaps not incidentally, Pharaoh (Gen 47:7; cf. Gen 12:3), suffering the ultimate deprivation of death far from home. Gone is the characteristic self-assertion and skillful manipulation. Israel is named as one who has struggled and prevailed over adversaries divine and human. But at the end of his life, what is more conspicuous, and crucial for his paradigmatic status, is simply the power to endure adversity.[26] It is hard to recognize the egocentric youth in this careworn old man, rendered almost transparent by surrender to the demands of the blessing he once stole.

INTEGRITY AND EXILIC HOPE

It is my contention that the histories of Job and Jacob are linked by themes of integrity, blessing, and transformative vision, and that, against the background of Israel's greatest political and theological crisis, this linkage became a matter of the most acute existential importance. That it was deliberately if subtly forged is suggested by the particularity of the biblical text as well as what we know of the practices of ancient interpreters and the style of the Joban poet.

It is a curious fact that Jacob and Job are the only two characters in Hebrew Scripture to whom the term *tam* is applied,[27] although, as noted above, *tam* commonly appears in the generalized representations of virtue in the Psalms and Proverbs. Although the word *tamîm*, used of Noah (Gen 6:9) and Abraham (17:1), may be semantically identical, a poet's keen ear might well distinguish between a close echo and a precise one.[28] And such a convergence in the leading element of the two characterizations, preserved perhaps in similar phrases (MT: *'îsh tam*, Gen 25:27; *wehayah ha'îsh hahû' tam*, Job 1:1) is exactly the kind of thing that the allusive imagination of the Joban poet would be likely to find or make significant.[29] I have already suggested that the conventional understanding of *tam* as "blameless" was inadequate, if Job's suffering and persistent faith were to be offered as a model for exilic Israel, and that the Jacob narrative provided a vehicle for re-examining the essential nature of integrity. The fact that this element of the Jacob narrative itself begs commentary—being prominently located, linguistically clear and yet contextually problematic—makes it all the more likely that the connection is deliberate. At a time when the history of Israel's relationship with God was being combed for clues to the meaning of the disaster and seeds of hope, it would be natural to press for illumination of the riddle of the character of Israel's most important ancestor, a riddle which was already ancient by the Joban poet's time.

This kind of rumination on the tradition is one category of what Fishbane (1985:410) calls "aggadic exegesis": namely, that which "involves the reinterpretation or transformation of a specific element of the traditum." The Joban poet's expansion on that comfortable word *tam* echoes back through the tradition, revealing that the choice of that first person of integrity was rightly made. Jacob is qualified to bear God's blessing because, seized by a high sense of destiny, he ironically devotes himself to the one cause that will finally subdue his rampant egocentricity.

Likewise, exilic Israel is chosen, against all the evidence and in the face of its own guilt, to bear God's blessing into the future. That the figure of Jacob stands behind that of Job is the more probable because the prophets of Israel had already evoked Jacob as a paradigm in time of crisis (Hosea 12; Jer 9:3-5[30]), although with an intention opposite to that of the Joban poet. The prophets justified the people's punishment on the basis of the ancestor's deceit; the poet explored his essential character trait in order to disclose the full dimensions of the life of faith and to ground the assertion that the divine blessing was still in force.

The book of Job is a profound, many-sided, and finally open-ended exploration of what it means to be *tam*. Drawing out the implications of a word that might otherwise seem to be ill-chosen (Genesis) or hopelessly idealistic (Job), the poet (who, by virtue of both style and sympathy, may well be the T. S. Eliot of the Hebrew Bible) reveals the hidden wisdom of the tradition and, what is far more, establishes Israel's capacity for self-transcendence and thus the validity of its claim to be God's servant people. With respect to the unity of the book, it remains to be shown that the notion of integrity provides a clue to the enigma of the divine speech and Job's surrender.

This matter of Job's surrender poses the most important question with which any reader must reckon: Is there any genuine resolution to the book? Job demanded personal vindication and yet, when God answers with a cosmological and zoological *tour-de-force*, Job professes satisfaction (42:5-6). If that surrender is to be taken as sincere,[31] then it must be possible to show that God does indeed speak directly to Job's demand and convinces him that he has not fully understood his own claim to integrity. I shall argue that the divine speech accomplishes this, not by negating the connection between justice and cosmic order, but rather by factoring a new term into the equation.[32]

Up to the time when God appears, Job subscribes to the conventional notion of integrity as ethical impeccability and demonstrates his own virtue in adhering to a high moral standard, further implying that God shows far less regard than Job himself for the welfare of a servant (31:13). All Job's actions and words, from the pre-emptive sacrifices for his children to his final defense speech, reveal that the key element of his worldview is predictability. He assumes that God does or should observe the reasonableness of the social order, where punctilious behavior generally meets with respect. That assumption proves to be the weak point in his argument, at which God takes aim.

God confronts Job with a non-anthropocentric view of the world. As Robert Alter has brilliantly shown (1985:94-110), the divine speech in chapters 38-41 is a careful refutation of Job's egotism, the "diastolic" expansion of vision that corresponds to the sharp contraction of chapter 3. Moreover, both Job's speech and God's stand in counterpoint to the fundamental biblical statement about the world in Genesis 1. In his first burst of anguish, Job would have undone creation, blotting out with a curse the light of a world that has become unbearable to him (3:8). If Job denies the essential goodness of creation, God's reply magnifies its splendor, while yet exposing the partiality of a representation that places humanity at the pinnacle. The ease with which God sets the monster Behemoth alongside the man (40:15) makes Job's own egalitarianism (31:15) seem paltry; Adam's dominion is reassigned to Leviathan, who is "king over all the children of pride" (41:26).

Job's urgent question of just deserts is of only passing interest here. God admits that the wicked persist and even prosper (40:11-14) but directs Job's attention elsewhere, to the exquisite order of the universe—an order that, not incidentally, does not depend on Job or any other human being. The divine speech reveals that what seemed to Job to be moral chaos is in fact one facet of an order whose underlying principle is gratuitousness, the direct contrary to the predictability he had assumed.

That gratuitousness sounds the most surprising note of the assault on Job's understanding in chapter 38. Alter is right that the celebratory images of light (37:7, 13-15) and birth on a cosmic scale (38:8-9, 28-30) correspond to elements of Job's first outcry and expose its egotism. Yet in large part, the beginning of God's speech confirms what the sages—and Job himself is no exception here—already knew with respect to the inability of human wisdom to probe to the root of things, including its own origin (Prov 30:18-19; Job 28:20-28[33]). Job is outraged, not as a speculative philosopher, but as a moralist; it is consequences rather than origins for which he demands a reasonable explanation. And in view of that demand for reasonableness or predictability, there is a calculated offense in God's question of who it is that ventures

> to make it rain on earth with not a person in it,
> desert with no human there,
> to satisfy the wild waste
> and bring forth a crop of grass? (38:26-27)

The answer is obvious: in the arid climate of the Middle East, flinging water on the wasteland is the most extravagant of gestures. It points to the peculiar character of the divine economy, whose logic is that of overflow and free gift.[34]

As nonsensical as watering the desert is God's delight in the wild creatures (chap. 39). Proudly God displays the mountain goats that give birth in (humanly speaking) impenetrable recesses, the ass that roams far from the herdsman's shout, the wild ox that scorns to plow a field, the ostrich whose careless treatment of her own eggs is the ludicrous antitype to Job's own overcautious parenting. All the creatures in the divine photo album have one thing in common: they are completely untamable. Again, this can only be a deliberate affront to Job's rationalism. Every animal in which God glories is utterly useless, except the war horse (39:19-25); and even that is the exception that proves the rule, for it is precisely his wildness that makes him useful.

This whole picture plays havoc with Job's notion of the way things ought to be—which is to say, sensible, well adapted to human purposes. Yet, far from being arbitrary, each element has been set in place as carefully as one of Leviathan's scales, in conformity with God's rule (*mishpat*, 40:8) for the world. Viewed from that cosmic perspective, it is Job who is out of order with his demand that the world be other than it is: a place of wild beauty and great danger, where God rules with fearful freedom, and only those who relinquish their personal expectations can live in peace. That is the world in which the person of integrity must claim a place.

God's expression of free delight returns to a theme that has figured in the book from the very beginning, when the Satan posed the question that gave rise to all Job's suffering (1:9): "Is it for no reason [*hinam*[35]] that Job fears God?" The Satan denies the possibility of gratuitous service, given without regard for gain but simply out of delight in the One served. In other words, the heavenly Adversary rejects the possibility of genuine love for God. Now, in light of the divine speech, it is clear why that question goaded God so deeply and how thoroughly this sceptic is opposed to God's way with the creatures. For the economy of self-interest espoused by the Satan is undermined at its base by the unpredictable element of gratuitousness, which is, paradoxically, the controlling factor in every loving relationship.

Job's final words indicate that he accepts the correction implicit in the vision and at last claims his integrity on God's terms, surrendering to a wholeness that he can never comprehend:

> With the ear's hearing I had heard of You,
> but now my eye has seen You.
> Therefore I recant and reconsider
> about dust and ashes. (42:5-6)

The standard translation (RSV: "Therefore I despise myself,/and repent in dust and ashes"), which would find here an expression of shame, fails to see in the phrase '*apar wa'eper* a metaphorical reference to the human condition as contrasted with God's majesty (cf. Gen 18:27).[36] The verbal phrase *nhm* (Niphal) '*al* is used here, as always elsewhere (Exod 32:12; Amos 7:3; Jer 8:6, *et passim*), to denote a change of attitude.[37] Job does not heap literal or metaphorical ashes on his head. With humility and dignity, he attests to his new understanding of the human condition, as befits one whom God has honored with a vision. Job accepts the fact that God's unsentimental and exquisite regard for the creature is bestowed as freely and no more reasonably on Job than on Leviathan. And with that acceptance, the transformation of the saint is complete. Stripped at last of the final defense of his ego, Job claims full affinity with the world as God's creation.

The integrity to which Job attains is in fact a kind of innocence. It is not the original innocence of Paradise or of childhood, born of inexperience and easily corrupted to arrogance, but rather that which comes, after much pain, as an unlooked-for gift to the few. In his first innocence, Job played by the rules as he knew them and expected God to follow suit. In his second, more radical innocence,[38] Job gives himself up, without reservation or expectation, to the God whose uncircumspect generosity regularly ignores the matter of deserving and thus allows the world to exist (cf. Matt 5:45).

That such a surrender must ramify into the world is the reality to which the epilogue attests. Job's acceptance constitutes not just a ratification but a perfection of creation, for God's work would be compromised if the one stamped with the divine image could not imitate God's essential attribute of charity.

To all appearances (or nearly all), the tale ends where it began, with Job reinstated as a full member of the community, heavy as before with children and livestock. The ending is often judged to be a surprisingly cheap divine ploy, an unlikely attempt to repristinate the idea of retributive justice, retained perhaps for ironic purposes by the Joban poet. But I suggest that the correct perspective from which to judge the religious value of the epilogue is from Job's side rather than God's. From this angle it is seen to be, consistent with the rest of the book, a portrait of tenacious faith, stunning not so much for its reward as for its cost. For what must it have cost Job, who had been stripped to the bone and borne it, found the blessing in the bareness, to "reinvest" in family and community life, with its obligations, ethical ambiguities, and terrible risks?

Job's restoration is in fact a highly probable ending to this story of a saint, hard to accept precisely because it reveals how modest is the life of the person wholly disposed to God. When the great trial of the spirit is over, what remains for Job are the ordinary tasks of living in responsibility, hope, and gratitude: offering prayer that extends the active domain of God's mercy even to the quack healers (13:4) who showed him such limited compassion, and—surely his greatest act of courage—bringing more children into a world he knows to be dangerous and unpredictable. It is appropriate that the encumbered life is the form that Job's holiness takes. The sweeping God's-eye view of the world taught him humility, that is, it connected him more profoundly with the earth (*humus*). Like Jacob, Job at the end of his life ceases to be a dramatic figure and becomes a responsible one, offering himself as a sign and channel of blessing. His abundance is a mark of God's favor, but more importantly, it signals the crucial human response without which the effect of the blessing is lost. Job's material restoration testifies to his willingness to accept God's commitment to the world just as it is offered: not on calculable terms of reward or guarantee, but as a free effusion of pleasure in the work of God's own hands.

There is a final hint that Job comes at last to resemble the God to whom he surrenders.[39] The book ends as it began, with a portrait of Job the Parent; but this second rendering is peculiar in two details. First, Job's daughters (and not his sons) are named; and their names are unabashed celebrations of their loveliness: Dove, Cinnamon, and Horn-of-Eyeshadow (42:14). Second, and completely contrary to biblical custom, they receive an inheritance alongside their brothers, apparently for no other reason than that they are exceptionally beautiful (42:15). The anxious patriarch who once feared the possibility of his children's sin now takes revolutionary delight in their beauty. These final odd details are far from gratuitous—or, in a deeper sense, they are entirely gratuitous, and that is exactly the point. In this unconventional style of parenting we see how deeply Job has comprehended and adopted as his own the principle that underlies God's *mishpat*: the freely bestowed delight which is in fact the highest form of causality in the universe, the generosity that brings another into free being.

NOTES

[1] Recent major treatments which argue for the coherence—if not necessarily the original unity—of the book as a whole are Norman Habel (1985), Robert Gordis (1978), and J. Gerald Janzen (1985); cf. (in briefer compass) Yair Hoffman (1981:160-70), and Christopher

Seitz (1989:5-17). It is regrettable that the otherwise admirable translation by Stephen Mitchell (1987) is of limited use because it fails to observe this coherence, omitting chaps. 28 and 32-37. Bruce Zuckerman (1991) presents a sophisticated argument against literary unity yet still considers how the various layers of the book stand in contrapuntal relationship, like the parts of a fugue.

[2] Exceptions are the studies of Rick D. Moore (1983:17-31) and Walter Brueggemann (1977:234-58); cf. the following note and the discussion of Brueggemann's work below.

[3] Athalya Brenner (1989:41) speaks of the "cluster of superlatives" as an "'unrealistic' element" within the traditional story, whose fundamental ideas the poet "proceeds to challenge and demolish" (48). Similarly, Moore (1983:31), who correctly connects the question of literary unity to the issue of Job's personal integrity, considers that "the narrative Job" rebuts the words of "the poetic Job" and concludes: "The poet has denied integrity to his character, and we should deny thematic integrity to the book."

[4] So RSV, NAB, and NEB (cf. KJV "perfect"), following the LXX *amemptos* in Job 1:1. The Jerusalem Bible is more satisfactory with its translation "sound."

[5] Ezekiel's reference to Job (14:14) indicates that a form of the legend was common knowledge among his hearers. Gottwald (1959: 478) comments: "Probably the popular tale of Job was so well known to his public that the poet told it as everyone knew it and then went on to develop his own interpretation and analysis of the great sufferer." Cf. the seminal study by Shalom Spiegel (1945), wherein he demonstrates that the folktale underlies the prologue and epilogue of the present narrative.

[6] The suggestion that the poem of Job has been influenced by the story of Jacob obviously assumes that the former is later. I follow the wide consensus that the book comes from the exilic or post-exilic period. On the discussion of date, see Robert Gordis (1965:216); Gordis himself dates the book between 500 and 300. Gordis and Janzen comment (contra Pfeiffer) on the poet's knowledge of the Second Isaiah. Avi Hurvitz (1974:17-34) has demonstrated the existence of post-classical elements within the prose narrative, strengthening the case that a single authorial intention informs both the extant version of the narrative and the poem.

[7] Cf. Terrien's similar view (ad Job 1:1; 1954, III:909): "Job was not only well rounded, self-possessed, and balanced, he was also well adapted to his social environment."

[8] In 31:6 and 25:5-6, Job explicitly connects "integrity" (*tummah*) with "righteousness" (*tsedeq/tsedaqah*); the speech in chaps. 29-31 indicates that both terms denote the perfect fulfillment of religious and social obligations.

[9] Such an understanding could inform the words of J. B.'s wife Sarah in the play by Archibald MacLeish (1956:110):

I will not stay here if you lie—
Connive in your destruction, cringe to it:
Not if you betray my children. . . .
If you buy quiet with their innocence—
Theirs or yours. . .
    I will not love you.

[10] Moore's interpretation (1983:29) of integrity accords with the one offered here: "integrity implies right relationships and especially a right relationship to God," although he concludes that Job of the poem lacks this kind of integrity vis-à-vis God.

[11] The usage here confirms the point about Job. The use of *brk* to designate a curse is not so much antithetical as ironic: in adhering to the tradition of ancestral inheritance, Naboth indeed "blesses God and king," at least as the latter office is rightly understood in Israel. He, and not Jezebel and Ahaz, shows the spirit of genuine humility (which includes self-regard) that the root *brk* implies.

[12] Both possible senses of *'elay* (42:8) are apt.

[13] On the central significance of the cry of distress which moves God to act, see Claus Westermann (1974:20-38). Job 27:2-6 indicates that, like the psalmists', Job's own notion of *tummah* is fully compatible with expression of outrage.

[14] The meaning of the third term of Job's conventional characterization (*yere' 'elohîm*) is also complicated in the course of the book, as caution (1:5) becomes profound reverence.

[15] The fact that the rest of Job's final speech, like the folktale, suggests a settled kind of existence indicates there may be more nostalgia than quotidian reality in this reference to the tent (cf. the practice of modern Bedouins who maintain desert encampments while living in city houses).

[16] See note 6, above.

[17] The story of the binding of Isaac (Genesis 22) provides the clearest evidence that it is Abraham's "appalling" (Kierkegaard) responsiveness to God rather than his sense of social responsibility that is the grounds for his blessing (see vss. 16-18). That the connection may be more than fortuitous is suggested by the cluster of phrases which appear in both Genesis 22 and the prologue of Job: *'ûts* (Job 1:1; Gen 22:21), *y-r-' 'elohîm* (Job 1:1 et al.; Gen 22:12; elsewhere only Exod 1:21), *sh-k-m baboqer* (Job 1:5; Gen 22:3), *sh-l-h yad* (Job 1:11, 12; 2:5; Gen 22:12), *n-s-' 'et-'ên[ayîm] merahôq* (Job 2:12; Gen 22:4); for these references I am indebted to an (unpublished) paper by Victoria Hoffer. The implication that the prose frame has been shaped to some degree by the poet does not contradict the earlier suggestion that Job's "heroic epithet" is traditional language. Yair Hoffman (1981:160-70) argues that the prose frame, while based on a popular

legend of righteous Job, nonetheless shows evidence of having been reworked with the dialogues in mind.

[18] The semantic equivalence of the two phrases is supported by Targum Onqelos' rendering of *tamîm* as *shelîm* in Gen 17:1 (the same rendering is given for *tam* in Job 1:1 and Gen 25:27; cf. discussion below).

[19] Fishbane (1979:50) notes that the verbal stem *brk* ("bless") occurs twenty-two times in Gen 27:1-28:9.

[20] The NEB's paraphrase ("Jacob led a settled life") is closest to my own interpretation. In general, commentators do not contribute to a solution, and "explanations" only underscore the problem. E.g., S. D. Luzzatto (1965:105) argues that Jacob is only called *'îsh tam* relative to Esau; whereas his actions may occasionally be vile, "according to the need of the hour," the hunter's are habitually so. His approach is in line with early rabbinic commentary, which portrays Esau's character as thoroughly reprobate.

[21] This is exactly the connotation of *hemeros*, the Greek word with which Philo renders *tam* in Gen 25:27 (in Delitzsch 1853, II:6).

[22] Von Rad's translation of *'îsh tam* as *ein ordentlicher Mann* (1953, II:230) is close to the mark, although he construes the notion of order too narrowly, associating it with moral respectability: Jacob is *anständig* (231).

[23] "Jacob was a man of integrity, attending the schoolhouse" (Onqelos; similarly Neofiti).

[24] Cf. Fishbane's treatment (1979:46-48).

[25] This is the earliest indication of a change that becomes clearer in the later narrative. Jacob's own ambivalence at this point is suggested by his uncharacteristic hesitation on hearing of the rape (34:5).

[26] Cf. Fishbane (1979:54). It is noteworthy that endurance rather than meekness is the kind of "patience" (*hupomone*) for which Job is commended in Jas 5:11.

[27] As far as I can determine, this fact has not been noted by modern scholars. However, it may well be this verbal echo which prompted the post-biblical tradition that the two patriarchs were "double kin": according to the pseudepigraphical *Testament of Job* (1:6), Job was both "from the sons of Esau" and Jacob's son-in-law, for Dinah was his second wife and the mother of his second family (cf. Ginzberg 1968:396; and 1969:225, 241).

[28] Cf. Joel Rosenberg's comment (1986:67) on biblical narrative: "Because both biblical and rabbinical literature are founded at least in part in a kind of plea for traditional literacy, it is no accident that the reader's *verbal* literacy is exercised and trained, as well—by which I mean the reader's ability to distinguish subtle differences between key words and their puns, assonances, repetitions, and even anagrams, as guides to narrative meaning." It is the central tenet of this essay that the Joban poet is practicing what Rosenberg terms an "art of irony," in which "quotation of either a word or a traditional unit . . . aims to subvert, by complicating, the quoted material's conventional meaning,

and to supplant it with deeper levels of meaning" (ibid.).

[29] On "the rhetoric of allusion," see Gordis (1965:190-208).

[30] Fishbane (1985:376-79) comments on the typological reuse of Jacob's story.

[31] The ironic reading of David Robertson (1973:446-69) is based on the opposite assumption.

[32] It will be evident that I am in partial disagreement with Matitiahu Tsevat (1966:73-106). He is right that the content of the divine answer, and not just the fact of God's speaking, is crucial. In an argument that was anticipated by Maimonides, he suggests that the laws of the natural order and the moral order are different, and that the concept applicable to the extrasocietal sphere is neither justice nor injustice but "nonjustice." I believe that God's answer is in fact compatible with a concept of divine justice, but one that is grounded in God's sovereignty and freely given love, rather than in a predictable system of reward and punishment.

[33] The meditation on the impossibility of discovering the source of wisdom (chap. 28) is so placed that it seems to be continuous with Job's speech. This placement is apt (contra Gordis and Pope), for it suggests that Job already has the tolerance for mystery that makes plausible his ultimate surrender. But far more importantly, the interlude of wisdom hymn lapsing back into tirade casts into relief Job's central concern, which is not with arcana but with the plain disjunction between his God-given sense of right and the facts of his experience.

[34] Daniel Hardy and David Ford (1985) offer an extended exploration of the "logic of overflow." Similarly, Paul Ricoeur (1975:114-22) names the extravagance in Jesus' parables as the element which points to the Kingdom of God.

[35] Wilhelm Vischer's treatment (1947) demonstrates the central significance of this term within the book.

[36] The only other occurrence of this phrase is in Job 30:19b, where it seems to be ambiguous, suggesting both literal dirt (cf. vs. 19a) and the most debased condition of humanity (cf. vss. 1-8).

[37] For a fuller discussion of translation possibilities, see the treatment by J. Gerald Janzen in his theologically sensitive commentary. It is an open question whether the first verb is $m's$ I ("reject"), the implied object being Job's own argument, or $m's$ II ("melt"), indicating the complete dissolution of his previous understanding of himself and the structure of reality. The basic sense is the same in either case.

[38] Cf. Mitchell's treatment (1987:xx) of "the innocence of a mind that has stepped outside the circle of human values."

[39] The resemblance between God and Job is an insight of the artist and mystic William Blake, who, in his *Illustrations to the Book of Job*, gives them the same face. The point is underscored by Illustration No. XVII (the theophany), for which the inscription is I John 3:2: "We know that when He shall appear we shall be like Him, for we shall see him as He is."

13

SAMSON OF SORROWS:
AN ISAIANIC GLOSS ON JUDGES 13-16

DAVID M. GUNN

Samson has been getting a bad press:

> A kind of simpleminded, muscle-bound boy, who . . . forces his decisions on others whether they like it or not, one of whose main interests is women—Philistine women at that . . . petulant, conceited, immature. (Gros-Louis 1974:157-8)
> An over-sexed muscle-man. (Klein 1988:134)
> A boastful rogue . . . [with a] ribald, impetuous nature. (Greenstein 1981b:240, 244).
> A rogue male who . . . bullies his way into bizarre relationships . . . a "dumb palooka." (Freeman 1982:155-6)

The man is without doubt self-centered and lacking in any worthwhile vision: he is "a self-indulgent egocentric" (Klein 1988:135); his choices "rather too narrowly serve his self-interests" (Humphreys 1985:69); his "sporadic and often trivial" exploits are too often "motivated by his personal whims and impulses" (Gray 1967:236). "Here is no charismatic quickened and directed by the spirit of God to a sober end . . . [no] devoted charismatic consciously co-operating with God . . . devoted wholly to the high enterprise of the liberation of the people of God." He is rather a negative example, "a tragic example of the abuse of a high calling." His story exemplifies "the over-ruling divine exploitation of human ineptitude" (236).

Comparing him unfavorably with Saul, a figure of tragic dimensions, Cheryl Exum writes:

> Saul has a lofty purpose. He is chosen by Yhwh to "save my people from the hand of the Philistines" (1 Sam. 9:16). Though little in his own eyes, he is head of the tribes of Israel . . . with all the responsibilities that office entails. His purpose is thwarted by challenges unsuccessfully met. In contrast,

> Samson occupies himself with personal vendettas and only unwittingly serves God's purpose ... Not even at his death does Samson show any deeper understanding of his role or of God's purposes. In his dying prayer, Samson asks not that he might bring glory to God or to Israel, but for personal vindication "for one of my two eyes" (16:28). (Exum 1992:42-43)

Yet Exum also acknowledges that Samson could be characterized with more complexity than as a man of personal vendettas. Samson is "the instrument of a divine plan." "Everything that happens to Samson seems determined by God without his knowledge or consent, leaving Samson with little, if any, control over his own life" (43). Her reading of the story as comedy works well enough if the reader is content to adopt YHWH's agenda and to savor the divine manipulation of his (this god is male) human agent (instrument?). Regard Samson, however, "as a *victim* of forces beyond his control" and the comedy palls—as I have suggested to her elsewhere (Gunn 1985:121-22). Such a reading, of course, problematizes the role of YHWH in the story: "Perhaps most disturbing," she concludes, "is the fact that Samson is dispensable in God's plan ... Is he then also betrayed by Yhwh?" (43-44).

Exum's purpose is to nuance, but reaffirm, her earlier position (Exum and Whedbee 1985) on Samson and her main topic, tragedy. Thus, even given a reading of Samson as victim, she maintains, the story would still not count as tragic: "Where there is no struggle, no awareness of fatedness, there can be no tragedy, though there can be despair" (44).

I do not intend to debate the terms comedy or tragedy. Though valuable as heuristic tools, these binary categories seem to me to sit uneasily with most biblical narrative (Gunn 1985). Nevertheless, I believe my interpretation disturbs not only Exum's comic reading but also some of her reasons for rejecting a tragic one. In particular it questions what counts as a "lofty purpose" and whether Samson is unaware of, and offers no struggle against, his place in YHWH's plan.

In its broader scope the paper fleshes out the kind of reading Exum alludes to in her excursus on Samson as victim. It presents a view of this character that differs markedly from the derogatory depictions quoted. It also frames an account of

YHWH which, ironically, could easily borrow some of Samson's usual labels. Who bullies whom in this story?

I well understand conventional "comic" accounts of Samson and can read along similar lines. Yet my present reading has proved tenacious and will not easily leave me alone. It took its basic shape over a decade ago[1] in company with interpretations of other texts that seemed in curious ways to be its soul sisters—especially the stories of Saul's rejection and of the hardening of Pharaoh's heart (Gunn 1980, 1982). These, too, are narratives of divine control and human freedom. These, too, seem to collapse rather than clarify simple distinctions between divine goodness and human evil—too often the frame in which their readers have cast the stories.[2]

Since the paper's genesis, I have pondered it in light of my growing appreciation of both the coherence and complexity of Judges and of the place of the Samson narrative in it (cf. Gunn 1987; Beal and Gunn 1993). If, for example, Judges is a degenerating cycle and the Samson narrative is not simply the story of a degenerate, what then is the narrative doing in the book? But here I wish to take a different step, into the intertexts beyond the immediate contexts of Judges or Genesis-Kings. Some time ago, Edward Greenstein, having (on the whole) been convinced by my work on David, had a rather different view of my reading of Saul (1980): "Building on what I suspect to be a Christological paradigm, Gunn contends that God dooms Saul to personal and dynastic failure in order to expiate the people's sin for requesting a flesh-and-blood monarch. Gunn's interpretations constantly strain . . ." (Greenstein 1981a:207). His reading of my text intrigued me and his text illuminated my text in a way I had not considered before, though I suspect that my interpretation of what he saw was more problematic for me than what he might have imagined. If there were a christological subtext to my reading it was, I venture to say, not straightforwardly a Christian apologetic—though how could I be sure since the subtext was, if a text at all, subliminal? At any rate I then found myself with an interpretation of Samson that could also be construed as having christological dimensions. Indeed I later discovered that, although not my own inheritance, a longstanding interpretive tradition made explicit just such a connection. (See the Biblia Pauperum illustration, below, p. 251.)[3]

How then may I better understand what I am doing? My present tactic is to place my text, that is my own reading of Samson, in an implicit dialogue with a more distant text. This is one that has played a key role for Christians in mediating between the "Old Testament" and the "New Testament" (especially the Gospel passion narratives), namely the central section of the book of Isaiah, chapters 40-55, (and especially the so-called "servant" passages—see, e.g., Moo 1983). So I declare this text to be a significant intertext of Judges 13-16, indeed a subtext (if not a pretext) of my reading, though in the reading itself it is undeclared. Only when I have a better sense of how these intertexts relate shall I be able better to relate (Samson) text and context. Whatever happens to my reading, I do not believe that I can just make this subtext go away.

As will quickly become apparent, the relation between these intertexts is complex. In some cases the texts are analogous, in some cases they are contrastive, and in yet others the relation between them cannot simply be defined in those terms but partakes of them both. I offer no explicit commentary or cajoling. The selection and its placement in my paper is my sole device for nudging and luring my reader into seeing something of what I see. That way my reader has a greater freedom to see what I perhaps cannot see. That way, too, my reader may feel less constrained by any lurking christological frame (made explicit now that I include the typological pictures in my text). For it is my hope that Jewish and other (non-Christian) readers may find a reading of Samson and the servant as intertexts to have its own creative integrity within the borders of the Hebrew Bible itself, howbeit that these texts are, for the present, being retextualized by my own (Christian?) text.

A MAN OF ZORAH AND HIS WOMAN

Samson's is no ordinary birth (Judges 13). Samson, like Isaac and Jacob/Israel before him, is the gift of God to a childless woman. "Behold you are barren and have not given birth; but you shall conceive and give birth to a son," says the messenger/angel (13:3). Samson, like Israel, is chosen to be "separate" (*nazir*) to God. "For a nazirite [*nazir*] to God shall the boy be from the womb . . ." (13:5).

> So now hear, Jacob my servant, Israel whom I have chosen!
> Thus says YHWH who made you and shaped you
>   from the womb he will help you . . . (Isa 44:1)
> YHWH from the womb called me, from the belly of my mother
>   he made known my name . . . (Isa 49:1)

Samson has a mission from conception—he is to begin to deliver Israel from the hand of the Philistines (13:5).

Thus Samson's life-to-be takes on a distinctive shape from its beginning. The outward mark of his dedication to the divine purpose is the nazirite vow, made on his behalf by no less than the angel of God. Three instructions, oddly broken between the mother who is to carry him and Samson himself, recall the conditions of the vow in Numbers 6. Of her: (1) "Drink no wine or strong drink" and (2) "eat nothing unclean." Of him: (3) "No razor shall come upon his head." Our assumption and the mother's are likely to be similar: she is to maintain a state of ritual purity while carrying the baby who is to be ritually pure; he, designated a nazirite, is to maintain ritual cleanliness and observe all three conditions of abstinence/avoidance.

The messenger's intrusion into the mundane world of Manoah and his wife produces divergent and sometimes amusing responses.

The woman, unnamed, senses from the outset that she is in the presence of the divine (13:6): "A man of God came to me, and his countenance was like the countenance of the angel of God, most awesome." For her that is apparently enough. In tune with the divine and directly receptive to God's message, she is content to leave it at that. "I did not ask him where he was from," she adds, as though anticipating her husband's anxiety, "and he did not tell me his name."

Her man, by contrast (he *does* get a name, which means something like "security"!), is far from content, if not to say more than a little suspicious. Who exactly was this "man of God" who had come visiting his wife (in her husband's absence) and announcing, of all things, her pregnancy? And *if* there were to be a child, should they not have plans, a pedagogical program, a clear definition of the rules, of what bringing up a nazirite entailed? Yet on Manoah's pressing the issue with YHWH, "God listened to the voice of Manoah—and the angel came again to the *woman* as she sat in the field (and Manoah her husband was not with her!)" (13:8-9). Even when Manoah is finally brought into the scene his probing gets him nowhere. He asks, "What is to be the regimen [*mishpat*; meaning also 'judgment'] of the boy and his work?"[4] He gets in reply less than the visitor's original speech, with pointedly *nothing* said of Samson. Indeed, it is only after a mystery of great wonder as the angel disappears into the heaven that Manoah, his skepticism finally assuaged, recognizes the visitor's identity.

But now that he knows, he knows even more—"We shall surely die, for we have seen God." For Manoah knows the rules of holiness. He panics, as indeed those "rules" suggest he should. Yet a reader may decide that he has seen God but learned little. It is his wife who makes the obvious, commonsense, response. What matter the rules? she says. If YHWH had meant to kill us, would he have gone to all this trouble to announce all these things and accept our offering for good measure?

So "the woman bore a son, and called his name Samson; and the boy grew, and YHWH blessed him."

In the story's outset, then, we may see a contrast. There is Manoah, named and (ostensibly) in charge, who must be sure, must map out the future, must fit his experience to the rules of religious life. There is Manoah's woman, unnamed and dependent, blessed in her childlessness, who knows God when she meets him, and is satisfied to ask (or presume) no more. The man and the woman may be read as emblematic in a story about knowledge—about the knowledge of life by which we try to secure our future, about self-knowledge, and knowledge of the transcendent.[5]

Indeed, as many a reader has noticed, to read this text is itself an exercise in the vagaries of knowledge. At every turn we meet the unexpected. We read, for example, that "Samson shall begin to deliver Israel from the hand of the Philistines." We may think that we know what that means. We may look for a "devoted charismatic consciously co-operating with God" in the waging of an heroic war of independence. What we find is different. (For one thing, we have likely overlooked the word "begins"—*hll*; or does it mean "pollutes"!?)

A WOMAN AT TIMNAH
OF THE DAUGHTERS OF THE PHILISTINES

We meet Samson in action first in chapter 14 as a young man. Having gone down to Timnah one day, he sees one of the daughters of the Philistines, returns to his parents and urges them, "I have seen at Timnah one of the daughters of the Philistines; so now take her for me as my wife." His father—and mother—remonstrates with him: "Is there not a woman among the daughters of your kinsmen, or among all my people, that you are going to take a woman from the uncircumcised Philistines?" But to his father he is doubly insistent: "Take *her* for me; for she is right in my eyes" (14:1-3).

What are we to make of his curt urging? Is it simply a rash and thoughtless impetuosity? Does it indicate the intensity of his desire? Is it a reflex of YHWH's spirit (Vickery 1981:66)? Whatever else we may surmise, the immediate context is explicit only about divine responsibility. The young man's urging is above all the urgency of God seeking to stir up trouble.

> So the woman gave birth to a son and she called his name Samson; and the boy grew up and YHWH blessed him. But YHWH's spirit began [*hll*] to beat on him [*p'm*] in Mahanehdan, between Zorah and Eshtaol. So Samson went down to Timnah and he saw a woman at Timnah, one of the daughters of the Philistines . . . Now his father and mother did not know that this was from YHWH, that he was seeking a quarrel with the Philistines . . . So Samson went down with his father and mother to Timnah. (13:24-5, 14:4)

> *Behold my servant—I shall grasp him;*
>   *my chosen—my soul is pleased;*
> *I have put my spirit upon him;*
>   *judgment [mishpat] for the nations*
>   *he will bring forth. (Isa 42:1)*

That Samson desires the woman is obvious. Less clear, however, is the nature of that desire. Mieke Bal, seeking purely sexual motivation, infers it from a single clue: the narrator recounts that Samson *saw* the woman and then returned to his parents to urge them to arrange a marriage. "He had only seen the woman and she pleased him immediately" (1987:42). That seems a possible but very narrow reading to me. It mandates, unnecessarily, a strictly literal understanding of the verb "to see" (Dinah, for example, goes out to see—that is, visit—the women of Canaanite Shechem). And it avoids the meaning of "pleased." In fact Samson says, and the narrator confirms it, that the Timnite woman was "right [*yashar*] in his eyes" (14:3, 7). Sexual attraction alone would demand at least "beautiful," "lovely to look at" (*yaphah, yephat-mar'eh, yephat-to'ar*).[6] Bal's reading also avoids mentioning Samson's other pre-marital contact with the woman—so, too, Robert Alter, who finds him rushing impetuously into marriage (1981:61-62). In fact the narrator has him going back down to Timnah with his parents, spending time talking with the woman (presumably with her parents' consent), returning home for a further period of time before returning (*wayashob miyyamîm*) with his parents (father?) to take her in marriage, all according to decorum. In short, given that Samson's desire likely includes sexual desire, that need not be read as its sum. Nor, from this episode, can he be so simply dubbed an impetuous man.

I conclude that as far as Samson is concerned, he wishes to be married—not just have sex—and believes that he has found a woman who would be right for him. Whatever precisely that might mean it likely includes adult companionship as well as sex. What the woman thinks of the arrangement can only be guessed at, since she is given no voice, and possibly (in the story world's social context) no choice. Her positive interest in the marriage is, however, a reasonable reading. Would Samson, having spoken with her and found her hostile, have pressed on with a marriage so obviously opposed by his own parents?

What ensues? Samson kills a lion (corpses pollute, and are off-limits to a nazirite), the root of his troubles to come in connection with his Timnite bride. For it is the lion's carcass that provides a home for the bees and their honey. That bizarre combination offers him the idea of the riddle, which in turn leads to the break with his bride, the killing of the innocent men of Ashkelon, and the ensuing feud with the Philistines. All of this activity culminates in the slaughter of the Philistines with the jawbone at Ramath-Lehi (chaps. 14-15).

Why does he kill the lion? Because "the spirit of YHWH gripped him" (14:6, JPS TANAKH). This is the first we know of any special gift of strength. Here, then, is another crucial twist in the events leading to Samson's conflict with the Philistines, and it is a turn made by God.

> I have put my spirit upon him;
> judgment [mishpat] for the nations he will bring forth.
> His voice—it will not cry for help, it will not raise itself,
> it will not be heard outside.
> A crushed reed, he will not snap,
> and a flickering wick, he will not be snuffed out.
> Rely on it, he will bring forth judgment [mishpat].
> He will not flicker, he will not be crushed,
> until he has set judgment in the land,
> until the coastlands [i.e., Philistia, Phoenicia]
> await his law. (Isa 42:2-3)

So the young man sits at his wedding feast (the very word spells [strong] drinking, also off-limits to a nazirite), and, provided by "chance" and a sharp wit with the subject of a riddle,[7] sees an opportunity to make an excellent start to the business of providing for his bride. Whether we should judge him foolhardy rather than adventurous, rash rather than bold, is debateable. He was on to a winner and he knew it. The thirty companions were totally at a loss. On the other hand he quite underestimated the degree to which he would remain an outsider among the men of Timnah. He did not anticipate that the male company would suspend all the rules of civility and threaten his bride and her family with burning unless she extracted the secret. *That* he did not bargain for—although he certainly had misgivings about letting anyone, including his bride, know the riddle's answer. Are we to blame the bridegroom for telling his bride? (On the contrary we might be inclined to say that he trusted her not enough.) Seven days of his bride's weeping at her wedding feast was a long time to hold out! Hardly the behavior of an impulsive man.

For her part, faced with an intolerable dilemma the young woman chooses life and her own kin. For their part, the Philistine men not only secure their prize but they also block any merging or blurring of the boundaries between Philistine and Israelite—boundaries that Samson's move towards marriage threatens to obscure.[8]

Perhaps it could be said, then, that the difference between success and failure for Samson here lay beyond the wager, in the greed, violence, and chauvinism in the companion's hearts.

But even so, it could be retorted, did he have to accuse his wife of prostituting herself with the companions?

> And he said to them,
> "Unless you plowed with my heifer,
> you would not have discovered my riddle." (14:18)

Listen to me, coastlands!
   Attend, peoples far and wide!
YHWH from the womb called me,
   from the belly of my mother he made known my name.
He set my mouth like a sharp blade,
   in the shadow of his hand he hid me;
he made me a polished arrow,
   in his quiver he concealed me. (Isa 49:1-2)

Was that not a fatal impulsiveness? For his reply could have been taken by the woman and her father as nothing less than a crude accusation of wanton promiscuity. Nothing could have sounded more debasing and final to them. Hence, assuming that the social context of the story world is typically patriarchal, the father's action in giving his daughter to another man (ironically the "best man") could be construed as perfectly reasonable—no doubt he was delighted to find that Samson's companion would take the young woman.

From Samson's point of view, his own conclusion might also have seemed very reasonable. The companions answer Samson's riddle with one of their own. "What is sweeter than honey? What is stronger than a lion?" Taken as an answer the couplet provides the answers "honey" and "lion," the literal answers, of course, to Samson's riddle. The answer, however, to the couplet taken as a riddle, is, of course, "love" or "sex." The wedding comes into focus. Samson assumes that his Philistine bride must be the source of this discovery. And, not knowing of the threat to her life, he assumes that the love or sex at issue cannot be for him. The companions lure him into seeing his bride, the betrayal of the secret, the companions themselves and "love/sex" as linked in a seemingly obvious pattern of cause and effect. His wife has traded favors and secrets. Just like the Timnite's father, Samson reads a message that is reasonable but false. He knows less than he thinks. Deft with words, the man who took the time earlier to speak with the young woman whom he wished to marry now fails to speak with her and in an instant destroys his marriage with deft words. If then we see him here as impulsive his impulsiveness is highly nuanced by its context.

But there is more to the riddle's aftermath than this. From the interchange flows the killing of thirty innocent men of Ashkelon (and more nazirite prohibition breaking). Here surely we see wildly misdirected anger, bound to cause bitter resentment. Yet once again the narrator interposes divine intervention:

> And the spirit of YHWH gripped him, and he went down to Ashkelon and killed thirty men of the town . . . (14:19)
>
> YHWH *like a mighty man goes forth,*
>   *like a warrior he wakens his rage;*
> *He shouts, he roars aloud,*
>   *he bears mightily upon his enemies. (Isa 42:13)*

Plainly Samson leaves the feast in anger, and "in hot anger," we are told, "he went back to his father's home." Nevertheless, his subsequent slaughter of the innocent men of Ashkelon is, the narrator insists, initiated by the spirit of YHWH.

Now (at the beginning of chapter 15) comes an incident which is, I believe, very significant for any assessment of Samson. Despite all that has happened,

> After some time, at the wheat harvest season, Samson sought out his wife with a kid. He said, "Let me go [in]to my wife in the chamber." But her father would not allow him to go in. (15:1)
>
> *For like a wife abandoned and hurt at heart, YHWH has called you,*
> *A wife of youth when she is rejected, says your God.*
> *For a short moment I abandoned you,*
>   *but with great compassion I will gather you.*
> *In a tide of anger I hid my face for a moment from you,*

> But in lasting loyalty I have had compassion on you,
> says your redeemer, YHWH. (Isa 54:6-8)

Despite what he has seen as the Timnites' double betrayal, he seeks reconciliation. He goes, gift in hand ("bringing a kid as a gift," JPS TANAKH), to start afresh. He goes as the one seeking to make amends, though he believes himself the injured party. Where YHWH desires a quarrel, Samson desires a wife.

His discovery that his visit is in vain, that he has lost his bride for good, is made all the worse by the father's bumbling attempt to play down his daughter's attractions and offer the younger daughter instead. To Samson, the marriage was not just a marriage of convenience, nor the Timnite's daughter just a beautiful face. The woman was one who was "right in his eyes." To Samson the father's speech smacks of inexcusable casualness. It produces a furious response: "This time I shall be innocent regarding the Philistines, when I do them evil" (15:3).

> Behold, I will make you into a sharp threshing sledge,
> new and full of teeth.
> You shall thresh the mountains to powder,
> and the hills you shall make like chaff;
> You shall winnow them and the wind [ruah] shall bear them away,
> the whirlwind shall scatter them. (Isa 41:15-16)

He proceeds to destroy the Philistines' grain and orchards by fire (ironically echoing the companions' threat), using the stratagem of tying a torch between the foxes' tails—a stratagem in deadly earnest, not a practical joke. The words "this time" are interesting. Perhaps Samson recognizes that "last time" his attack on the Philistines had been inexcusable (though, again ironically, he does not know that he was then the agent of YHWH). "This time" he feels his retaliation is justified. And at least his action is more commensurate with the injury—the Philistines have taken away his woman, who would bear his seed, so he will take away the fruit of the Philistines' fields.

Nevertheless, despite the provocation, his action may well be judged indiscriminate and excessive. The "Philistines" did not take away his woman. Her father and the companion(s) did. And Samson is unwilling to recognize the father's quandary. His sense of injustice and his anger have trapped him.

My back I gave to those who smote,
  my cheeks to those who pulled out hair. (Isa 50:6)

But then his action pales somewhat besides the flames of the burning Timnites, father and daughter(s), set ablaze by the outraged Philistines. These, for their part, see this action as the execution of justice, since they retaliate against the true instigators (as they see it) of the crop burning. (As Crenshaw has observed [1978], the narrator does not caricature the Philistines.) For Samson, however, the burning is clearly a travesty of justice (*mishpat?*)—and it is the murder of his woman, sometime wife.

Behold, all of you are kindlers of fire, bearers of firebrands.
Walk by the light of your fire,
  and by the firebrands you have set ablaze.
From my hand you shall have this—
  for pain you shall lie down. (Isa 50:11)

And so more revenge follows. But note that Samson, at least, desires an end to it:

"If this is how you do things, I vow revenge on you. And then I shall quit [*hdl*]." So he struck them hip and thigh—a great slaughter—and went down to live in a cave of the Etam Rock. (15:7-8)

He was spurned and quit [hdl] the company of men,[9]
  he was a man who suffered,
  who was acquainted with weakness. (Isa 53:3)

Like fire, however, retaliation has a habit of spreading endlessly, and so indeed it proves. The Philistines, seeking Samson in order "to do to him what he did to us," overrun Lehi in Judah. Frustrated, and wishing to avoid unnecessary trouble (like the Hebrews in Egypt), the men of Judah descend upon Samson.

"Surely you know that the Philistines are our masters? So why have you done this to us?" He said to them, "As they did to me, so I did to them." (15:11)

My back I gave to those who struck,
  my cheeks to those who pulled out hair. (Isa 50:6)

And they said to him, "We have come down to bind you and give you into the hands of the Philistines." (15:12)

Like one who must hide his face from us,
  he was despised, we did not value him. (Isa 53:3)

Samson accommodates his neighbors by giving himself up. But "Swear to me that you will not attack me yourselves," he demands, perhaps fearing that otherwise he would have to attack them, his own people. Then at Lehi, like the lion roaring against him (14:5), "the Philistines came shouting to meet him."

> YHWH like a mighty man goes forth . . .
> He shouts, he roars aloud,
>   he bears mightily upon his enemies. (Isa 42:13)

To do what, we are never told, for once more the spirit of YHWH intervenes and more slaughter transpires.

The scene ends with Samson praying to YHWH from his desperate thirst and YHWH granting him life-giving water on top of the gift of strength which Samson acknowledges:[10]

> "You Yourself have granted this great victory through [by the hand of] your servant" (15:18, JPS TANAKH).

> Who has roused a victor from the East,
> Summoned him to His service?
> Has delivered up nations to him,
> And trodden sovereigns down?
> Has rendered their swords like dust,
> Their bows like wind-blown straw? . . .
> He pursues them, he goes on unscathed;
> No shackle is placed on his feet.
> Who has wrought and achieved this? . . .
> I, the LORD . . . (Isa 41:2-4, JPS TANAKH)

Certainly Samson's prayer is no meek and mild prayer. Its form as a (rhetorical?) question contains just a hint of pressure, like many other biblical prayers—you, YHWH, have given this victory, "so now shall I die of thirst, and fall into the hands of the uncircumcised?" But it shows unmistakably that Samson believes he has a working relationship with God.

Unmistakably, too, the divinity confirms Samson's belief:

> So God split open the hollow at Lehi, and from it there came out water; and he drank and his spirit [Samson's? God's?] returned and he lived. (15:19)

> The poor and the needy seek water, and there is none;
>   their tongue is parched with thirst.
> I, YHWH, will answer them, Israel's God will not abandon them.

> *I will open upon the bare hills streams, midst the valleys fountains;*
> *I will make the wilderness a pool of water,*
>   *the dry land springs of water . . .*
> *that they may see and know, consider and comprehend,*
> *that the hand of YHWH has done this . . . (Isa 41:17-20)*
> *For I give water in the wilderness, streams in the desert,*
> *so my chosen people can drink, the people I formed for myself.*
> *My praise they will declare. (Isa 43:20)*
> *They did not thirst as he led them through the waste places;*
> *water from a rock he made flow for them;*
> *he split open a rock and out gushed water. (Isa 48:21)*

A plateau in Samson's career is now reached: "And he judged Israel in the days of the Philistines for twenty years" (15:20). This bald remark coopts Samson, the man whose birth was hedged with nazirite vows, into a line of "judges" or "saviors" raised up by YHWH, from Othniel to Jephthah. At the same time it caps an account of his constant disregard for the nazirite requirements for ritual purity. Of course, those disregarding actions we have seen to be constitutive of Samson's life—as determined by the divinity. YHWH gave Samson to the barren Danite woman, to bring the deliverance of Israel from the hands of the Philistines (13:5). YHWH propelled Samson into the arms of the Timnite woman "for he was seeking a quarrel with the Philistines" (14:4); it was YHWH's spirit that came mightily upon him so that he went down to Ashkelon and slew thirty men of the town, YHWH who enabled the slaughter at Lehi (with the freshly pilfered—doubly polluting—jawbone) to take place.

Yet it was not just YHWH who instigated (paradoxically) the vow-breaking. Samson on his own account disregarded the nazirite conventions from the outset. If his tearing of the lion was God-prompted, his eating of the carcass-polluted honey was his own chosen action. Why? And why was he silent before his parents about the lion and the honey? Was he perhaps determined to resist his naziritehood, determined to resist his "separateness"? He had already challenged it by demanding a Philistine wife in the first place. So then does he deliberately contaminate himself and his mother?

> *My lord YHWH opened my ear,*
> *and I, I did not rebel, did not turn backwards. (Isa 50:5)*

Here, then, is my reading. The man who looks for marriage, who seeks a companion, who desires to make love (and needs to love and be loved?), who ignores national boundaries (unless it suits him), is also the "consecrated" one who seeks to shed the constricting conditions of that ritual "consecration." The nazirite vow was not of his making, and as a human being, Samson chooses to be "ordinary," not "separate" or "dedicated." (That he knows he has been designated "separate" is an assumption confirmed finally in 16:17—"for I have been a nazirite to God from my mother's womb.")

> YHWH *from the womb called me,*
> *from the belly of my mother he made known my name . . .*
> *And he said to me,*
> *"You are my servant, Israel, by whom I will get glory."*
> *But I said,*
> *"I have labored in vain,*
> *I have spent my strength for empty nothingness;*
> *yet surely my judgment [mishpat] lies with* YHWH,
> *my recompense with my God." (Isa 49:1, 3-4)*

Perhaps he wondered whether his vow-breaking had come home to roost in the form of a devastated marriage plan. But then equally he must have reflected that his miraculous strength had not left him despite all. Moreover the culmination of vow-breaking in the slaughter at Lehi (chap. 15) brings home the point. It is not just that his strength does not leave him as he journeys along this road littered with ignored or broken "vows," but that YHWH confirms, positively, unambiguously, that his strength is divinely given. At Lehi, praying among the (unclean) corpses, he is revived by the water of God.

"So he judged Israel in the days of the Philistines for twenty years" (15:20). The sentence is enigmatic. Is this "judging" a period in the middle of a story of beginnings and ends? Or is it coterminous with the events of our story? Does the narrator signal a period of freedom from Philistine rule, or does Samson judge Israel in some other way which we must yet search out?

> *Behold my servant—I shall grasp him;*
> *my chosen—my soul is pleased;*
> *I have put my spirit upon him;*
> *judgment [mishpat] for the nations he will bring forth.*

> *His voice—it will not cry for help, it will not raise itself,*
> *it will not be heard outside.*
> *A crushed reed, he will not snap,*
> *and a flickering wick, he will not be snuffed out.*
> *Rely on it, he will bring forth judgment [mishpat].*
> *He will not flicker, he will not be crushed,*
> *until he has set judgment in the land,*
> *until the coastlands [i.e., Philistia, Phoenicia]*
> *await his law. (Isa 42:1-3)*

AT GAZA, A WOMAN, A PROSTITUTE

Abutting the announcement of judgeship is the brief account of Samson going to Gaza, seeing there a woman, a prostitute, going in(to) her, and in due course escaping with the city's gates on his shoulders. The episode deserves more attention than I can give it here. Why he was in Gaza we are not explicitly told. On the face of it he goes for his sexual pleasure, yet he leaves with the city gates. A more sophisticated reader might find in the episode clues to the sexual dimensions of the story as a whole, for it is a story riddled (if I may) with sexual overtones—and a prostitute, strongman (who leaves early), and despoiled city gates (cities are feminine), have all the makings of sexual dimensions.[11] A more mundane reader might see here a man with remarkable sexual desire (he went *where* to find a prostitute!?) but also a man in control of his situation—against the expectation of the men of Gaza that he would stay all night, he waits only till midnight before leaving. Or then again, he might have had much desire and little staying power.

Other questions arise. Who told the men of Gaza that Samson was visiting so that they lay in wait for him? Are we to fill this gap by rough analogy from the Timnite and Delilah episodes? Is the prostitute the betrayer? But then the question would be, Why? Samson was right about the Timnite's betrayal, but totally wrong about what that betrayal signified. Or might our analogy be the spies in the house of Rahab at Jericho (Joshua 2)? Is the prostitute in league with him?

If the episode recalls the Rahab story, the reminiscence might point up a contrast between, on the one hand, the two spies from the victorious army of Israel, agents of a successful leader, and, on the other, the lone figure, spurned by his people and acting upon his own initiative to an unspecified end. The contrast is a measure of the large difference between the two "deliverers" (that is, Yehoshua' and the man who is "to begin to deliver [*lehoshia'*]")—the one supported at the center of a homogeneous and autonomous Israel, the other isolated on the periphery of a diverse and subject people. Yet by taking the gates and so rendering the city vulnerable (which is what the medieval typologists saw), Samson also demonstrates the small difference between himself and Joshua. The great general, commissioned to take the land, has a suspiciously ambiguous record when it comes to Gaza and the inhabitants of the plain (cf. Josh 10:40-42; 11:21-23; 13:1-7; Judg 1:18-19; and see Hawk 1991). Nor is the tribe of Judah, to whom Gaza has been allotted, any more obviously successful. The narrator's attempt to talk up the Judean capture of Gaza evaporates before residual stories of resistance, independence, and, by Samson's time, ascendancy. Samson's removal of the gates to Hebron—high in the central hill country, where Abraham first purchased land, the heartland of the nation and of Judah—conjures the picture of some very uncomfortable Judeans contemplating those gates, brought by the man they tried to dispossess, from the city they were meant to possess but which instead possessed them. Gaza cuts Joshua and Judah down to size. Gaza makes Samson look good.

The Gaza episode may also be seen as metaphorically central to the theological story. By pulling up the gateposts Samson renders YHWH's enemies defenseless. (And the metaphor will be repeated at the story's close when he collapses the pillars of Dagon's temple.) Whether or not this is his intention—a matter the narrator leaves strictly moot—he has once again become party to YHWH's purpose for him, to seek a quarrel with the Philistines.

> *Thus says YHWH to his anointed,*
>   *to Cyrus, whom I have seized by the right hand,*
> *to tread down nations before him, to ungird the loins of kings;*
> *to open doors before him and not let gates be closed:*
> *"I will go before you and level the puffed up,*
> *I will shatter doors of bronze and cut apart bars of iron . . .*
> *that you may know that it is I, YHWH, who call you by your name,*
>   *the God of Israel. (Isa 45:1-2)*

But let me now press on to the final episode.

A WOMAN IN THE VALLEY OF SOREK

> And it happened after this that he loved a woman in the valley of Sorek. Her name was Delilah. (16:4)

Delilah's nationality is not specified and the location of Sorek leaves the matter unresolved. In chapter 14 the narrator makes it plain that the Timnite woman was a Philistine and, as has been often observed, this dimension of kinship is one that helps confound the relationship. Now it is as though the slate has been wiped clean and that Samson is back starting again, but this time without any obvious complications darkening the relationship from its inception.

The earlier woman, of the daughters of the Philistines at Timnah, was "right in [Samson's] eyes." His tenderness towards her, desire perhaps, was demonstrated in his reconciling, gift-bringing, return. Yet the word "love" was not used. It is reserved for Delilah, the woman, of whatever nationality she is.

Thus the opening sentence of the new episode is both simple and striking—striking because it conveys a new, not just a repeat, experience. He loves a woman. For an instant we glimpse the possibility of a relationship sustained, of fulfillment, marriage, stability. It is no more than a glimpse. Within a few verses Delilah is bought, with pieces of silver, without protest. Is this greed? Economic necessity (here is a remarkable woman, apparently living independently)? Or simply a version of the Timnite's dilemma—when the lords of the Philistines come to Delilah, has she any more chance of denying powerful men than the other woman? Whatever the case, there is no sign that Delilah loves Samson. Rapidly we learn that Samson's is unrequited love, and that he is thus in a classic state of vulnerability. However the story moves now, it must be downwards for Samson. To survive he must renounce his love; to renounce his love is to put himself back to the very beginning again, seeking a woman, a relationship, a marriage.

> And Delilah said to Samson, "Please tell me, what gives you your great strength? How can you be bound, to abuse [rape] you?" And Samson said to her . . . (16:6)

Three times Delilah tests his answer, to no avail. Whether he is aware of her intended betrayal, of the waiting Philistines, the narrator does not clarify. We have some exegetical choices. Samson may well imagine, *want* to imagine, that she is playing a game of love, perhaps an erotic game of reversal, with her strength and his weakness as ingredients. Or he may suspect at the beginning, or in the middle, or at the end, that she is playing for other more deadly stakes. In that case, why, at some point, does he not protest? A simple answer would take in earnest the one thing we do know about his relationship to Delilah—that he loves the woman. Thus: trapped by his love, unwilling to break with his loved one, he plays out the game with a kind of optimistic fatalism, always looking, as only a lover can, for the signal that all is well after all, for the sign of love returned.

The moment of consummated love never arrives.

> And it happened that she pressed him with her words day after day, and pushed him until his soul was wearied to death and he confided everything to her . . . (16:16)

The Timnite comes to mind: "[The Timnite] wept about him for the seven days of their feast; and on the seventh day he told her, because she pressed him . . ." (14:17). The narrator's words suggest a crucial moment of life and death: Samson tells of the nazirite vow for he is "wearied to death."

> And he confided everything to her, saying to her, "A razor has not come near my head; for I have been a nazirite to God from my mother's womb. If I am shaved, my strength will leave me, and I shall be weak and become like any other human." (16:17)

Does Samson *really* believe that his strength will leave him if his hair is cut? A reasonable answer would be "probably not." Reflect for a moment. At some point earlier in his life he must have decided that there was a likely connection between his extraordinary strength and his divine designation as nazirite (which we assume he learned about from one or other of his parents). On the other hand, events had not borne out the likelihood. He had in fact been given every reason to believe that his persisting strength was both God-given and unaffected by any infringement of the nazirite rules. *However*, while he may have broken all the other rules, with impunity, he had not yet broken the one specifically enjoined on him by the angel. He had not cut his hair. I suggest, therefore, that he reluctantly offers an explanation which he considers just possibly might be the truth, but which deep down he doubts.

He is in a dilemma, watching the "game" going out of control. His tie to his loved one seems close to snapping. "How can you say you love me," he hears Delilah finally accusing him, in an ominous echo of the Timnite woman's words: "You only hate me, you do not love me." Weak with love, he cannot walk away to safety. As she has sought to bind him he seeks to bind her, by giving her what she wants, an answer. It is an answer that he wishes to be true—to grant her desire—and not true—to safeguard himself. It is an answer that he thinks could be true but feels is probably false. Somewhere deep down he trusts that, as before, YHWH will continue to guarantee him strength.

They play out the game. Delilah makes him sleep on (or between, LXX) her knees—she plays mother or mother/lover. His hair is cut. She calls out the cue.

> And he awoke from his sleep, thinking, "I will go out like the other times and shake myself free" ["exert myself," cf. Targum]. He, however, did not know that YHWH had left him. (16:20)

Samson's trust deceives him. His strength leaves him. YHWH leaves him.

> So the Philistines seized him and gouged out his eyes, and brought him down to Gaza, and shackled him with bronze; and he was made to grind in the prison mill. (16:21)

> *He was oppressed, and he was abused [raped];*
> *but he did not open his mouth.*
> *Like a sheep led to the slaughter,*
>   *like a ewe before her shearers is dumb,*
> *he did not open his mouth.*
> *After detention and judgment [mishpat] he was taken away,*
>   *and who protested his fate? (Isa 53:7-8)*

His prayer for strength—in practice for death—reveals someone still able to call to God, hoping at least to be heard. The hint of duress which tinged his prayer at Lehi is absent. His request to YHWH counts on little. He asks what least he can ask: "My lord

YHWH, remember me, please, and seize [strengthen] me, please, only this one time, God." But it ends with a flash of humor—"so I may take revenge upon the Philistines for one of my two eyes." That comment conveys to me a rising tone. Blind, degraded, and in chains, Samson has not yet abandoned all self-esteem. On the contrary, in a joke of deathly earnest, he can set the value of but one of his eyes against all the lords of the Philistines, all his tormentors. The Timnite woman was right in his eyes. His search for companionship began with her. At the end, defeated in his search, he is still willing to affirm those eyes and what they saw to be right. Not all readers will enjoy his appeal for vengeance. Still, his God-granted suicide is not a sign of psychological or spiritual collapse but a final affirmation of his personal worth and what he tried to find, despite God.

> *Come down and sit in the dust,*
> *young woman, daughter of Babylon . . .*
> *Take millstones and grind meal;*
> *take off your veil, strip off your skirt,*
> *bare your thighs, cross streams;*
> *your genitals shall be bared, your private parts seen.*
> *I will take revenge . . . (Isa 47:2-3)*

The story climaxes at the great festival of Dagon. The narrator reiterates the Philistines' claim to their god's supremacy.

> Now the lords of the Philistines gathered to offer a great sacrifice to Dagon their god, and to rejoice. They said, "Our god has given into our hand Samson our enemy." And the people saw him and praised their god, for they said, "Our god has given into our hand our enemy, who has laid waste our land, multiplied our slain." (16:23-24)

The reader knows that they are wrong. It was YHWH who gave Samson into their hands.

> *Who gave up Jacob for spoil, and Israel to plunderers?*
> *Was it not YHWH against whom we have sinned,*
> *in whose ways they were not willing to walk,*
> *and whose law they did not obey? (Isa 42:24)*
> *All of us went astray like sheep;*
> *every one turned to their own way;*
> *and YHWH made fall on him [pg']*
> *the guilt [punishment] of us all. (Isa 53:6)*

By deserting Samson at the cutting of his hair, YHWH deceives the Philistines into thinking that Samson's strength is merely a magical-mechanical thing, open to human manipulation. Even the reader may be kept wondering on this score by the narrator's mischievous remark about the regrowth of the hair (16:22). But what we do recognize in the story world is that YHWH is in control. And for the worshipers of Dagon the ensuing scene of death and destruction is a debacle of the greatest magnitude. The words of praise for their god must indeed have died coldly on the lips of his devotees.

> The makers of idols, all of them are nothing,
> and what they delight in does not prosper;
> their witnesses—these do not see, nor do they know,
>   so that they shall be put to shame . . .
> Let them all assemble, let them take up their stand;
> they shall be afraid,
>   they shall be put to shame together. (Isa 44:9-11)
>
> Evil is coming upon you,
> Which you will not know how to charm away;
> Disaster is falling upon you
> Which you will not be able to appease;
> Coming upon you suddenly
> Is ruin of which you know nothing. (Isa 47:11, JPS TANAKH)

Thus the narrator claims the power of YHWH, the irrelevance of Dagon. The victory is YHWH's, even if only through the suffering and death of his servant.

> He was given his grave with the wicked, his tomb with evildoers;
> because he did no violence, and there was no lie on his lips.
> It was YHWH who pleased to crush him, who made him weak.
> If his life is an offering for the guilt of others
>   he will see his offspring [seed], he will have a long life,
> and YHWH's pleasure will prosper by his hand. (Isa 53:9-10)

> So the dead whom he [Samson? YHWH?] slew in his death
> were more than he slew in his life (16:30)

Undoubtedly more, since the dead include this time a god! To bring low the god of the Philistines is perhaps Samson's real contribution to YHWH's purpose. His achievement is, ironically, not a (heroic) physical blow, but a theological one!

Spawning Samson's story is the story of the people and their god: "And yet again the Israelites did evil in the eyes of YHWH and YHWH gave them into the hand of the Philistines for forty years" (13:1). YHWH defeats his own people, giving them into the power of their enemies. YHWH, if he chooses, can turn such defeat into victory. The burning question for the god, however, is whether his people *recognize* that he controls their destiny.

But recognized by whom? By the reader? Clearly. By the Israelites of the story world? Of them, no mention. The irony is that if Israel recognized this manifestation of YHWH we are not told so. The silence is ominous. On the contrary the only one who calls upon YHWH is Samson.

> So they came down, his father and all his father's house and they lifted him up and brought him up to bury him between Zorah and Eshtaol in the grave of Manoah his father. He it was who judged Israel, twenty years. (16:31)

The story's beginning breaks the pattern hitherto in the book: Israel does not even cry to YHWH for deliverance from oppression. Here at the end it is Samson who lifts up that cry for help, but alone and, on the face of it, for himself. What has happened to YHWH's "lofty purpose" for Samson?

> Hear, you who are deaf,
>   and look up, you who are blind, and see!
> Who is blind if not my servant,
>   or so deaf as my messenger I send?
> Who is so blind as the dedicated one [meshullam, cf. RSV]
> [or "the one who makes good/performs/pays (a vow)"],
>   or so blind as the servant of YHWH? (Isa 42:18-19)

But is Samson's thwarted life then of no value?

SERVICE OR SERVITUDE?

So where has this exploration of Samson's character led me? Not, I think, to a "reckless and irresponsible practical joker," motivated by mere "whims and impulses"—unless they be impulses of YHWH. Not to a clear-cut "negative example" of sheer ineptitude. "Here," says Gray, "is no charismatic quickened and directed by the spirit of God to a sober end"—yet that description would seem to be not wholly inappropriate to what I have read in Samson's story.

Samson, so often the negative example who warns (men) of the dangers of dalliance with "foreign women," seems on my reading somewhat less crass. Quite apart from the question of whether all the women are non-Israelite, what have been the nature of these attachments? First, he makes a (God-prompted) commitment to marry a young woman—a relationship which he tries to retrieve, despite terrible misunderstanding, by an attempt at reconciliation that is hard to match (for a man) in the larger story of Genesis-Kings. Second, he makes a visit to a prostitute during the gap in his personal life after the destruction of his first relationship. Third, he entertains love, unreturned, for a woman.

Why are critics so ready to judge Samson's search for a woman's companionship as culpable? Is it that the goal of personal relationship is not deemed worthy of a "judge," a hero, a national deliverer, a wager of wars—a man? Samson is, after all, no great military commander, no single-minded or systematic dispenser of death, destroyer of cities, ravager of the land. He is, for example, no Joshua, no Gideon. If theirs is a "lofty purpose" he certainly does not share it. He is, indeed, a dealer in death, but largely at the dictate of YHWH while he himself searches for domesticity, attempts vainly to nurture personal connection. His desire to "quit" (15:7), to shed his divinely appointed name of Nazir, Separate, to let his life simply grow in a "world of home" (Vickery's phrase, 1981:69), all is frustrated, but not, I have argued, simply by his own recklessness or folly.

To be sure, his accusation against his Timnite bride is hasty and deeply wounding. But the companions have him far more tightly ensnared than he can possibly realize. Certainly, his retaliation against the Philistines is, even when not urged by YHWH, usually indiscriminate. Yet this tendency to identify his adversary generically is crucial to YHWH's purpose! So, then, if he is defeated in his search for an ordinary life of his own by God allied with the evil in the hearts of other people, in what sense is he to be judged?

We have seen how the greed, power (and powerlessness) of others throws him off course. We have also seen how God sets the lines of that alternative course from beginning to end. At the moment of final betrayal God in the form of strength leaves him. At the season of death God in the form of strength reappears.

Samson's god resists scrutiny. The character slides in and out of the narrative. Sometimes strategically absent, sometimes provocatively present, usually unannounced. He is there to urge, impel and imperil, there to define present and future, there to be addressed, there to be trusted. But as Samson perhaps learns, trust in this god is a moot matter. It will not secure life. It may bring life or death, pleasure or pain. The servant of YHWH has only the choice of accepting "devotion" or "dedication" or attempting to rebel. Even acceptance may be no real option, as Saul comes to know in his utter loneliness.

Two people in this story seem to know YHWH. There is Samson. At his end he calls for help and because of this, even in his death he executes God's purpose, whether knowingly or not. And there is Samson's mother, the wife of Manoah. In a curious way, as Alter has noticed (1981:101), the wife of Manoah glimpses the heart of YHWH's pleasure for Samson right there at the beginning of the story. The angel had told her: "For the boy shall be a nazirite to God from the womb; and he shall begin to deliver Israel from the hand of the Philistines" (13:5). She reports this speech to her husband differently, however. "For the boy shall be a nazirite to God from the womb *to the day of his death*" (13:7). Somehow Samson's beginning of deliverance from the Philistines and Samson's death will coalesce. And *she* seems to know what no one else in Israel knows—that he will be *nazir*, dedicated to God the whole of his life, from the day of his birth to his death.

Samson's experience of the divine differs from that of his mother. She is a bearer of life, he of death. Ironically, her expression of trust in the goodwill of the god who announces the gift of a son and accepts her sacrifice turns out, in Samson's case, to be misplaced. Protective Manoah was not, after all, so far off the mark when he asked what would be the judgment (*mishpat*) of the young man and his work. In the event YHWH could dictate Samson's sacrifice of his personal life in service against the Philistines and still deal him death for all that.

But now, thus says YHWH,
   who created you, Jacob, who formed you, Israel:
"Fear not, for I have redeemed you;
   I have called you by your name, you belong to me . . .
When you walk through fire you shall not be scorched,
   and flame shall not burn you . . .
Because you are precious in my eyes,
   and honored, and I love you,
I give a human being in return for you,
   other peoples in return for your life." (Isa 43:1, 4)

For YHWH, a rather convenient arrangement.
Or, as Isaiah might have put it, "Here am I, send Samson."

NOTES

[1] An earliest version—"Dedicated Samson"—was presented in 1981 at St. Anne's College, Oxford, and in 1982 at the Society of Biblical Literature Annual Meeting (Rhetorical Criticism Section), New York. Revised, it became intertextual—"Samson, Suffering, and Servant"—for the Atlanta Biblical Studies Forum in 1989. I have since further modified and reframed it. My special thanks to Peter Ackroyd, Jim Crenshaw and John Vickery for motivating its beginning, and to Tim Beal and Danna Fewell for encouraging its (present) end.

As always, my work partakes of a network of influences, coincidences and connections (mostly unacknowledged here). I urge exploration of that network, which includes: Crenshaw 1978; Exum 1980, 1981, 1983, 1992; Exum and Whedbee 1985; Fewell 1992; Polzin 1980; Greenstein 1981b; Vickery 1981; Bal 1987, 1988; Webb 1987; Matthews 1989; Camp and Fontaine 1990; Alter 1990; Niditch 1990.

[2] Among recent exceptions: Eslinger 1985 and 1989; Humphreys 1985; Miscall 1986; Exum 1992; and cf. Crenshaw 1984.

[3] The so-called "poor person's Bible" found in medieval manuscript and renaissance printed versions represents a tradition of Christian typological interpretation. The subject of the central frame is usually Christ, prefigured in the Old Testmanent side frames. Thus Samson carries off Gaza's gates as Christ breaks down death's doors, while Jonah, like Christ, is delivered up from its jaws. Texts top left and right summarize the Old Testament stories below. At the margins prophets speak to the central subject: David (Ps 77:65), Jacob (Gen 49:9), Hosea (6:2) and Zephaniah (3:8). The illustration on p. 251 is from a mid-fifteenth century "block book," each page a single block. For a recent reprint, see Labriola and Smeltz (1990).

[4] Lillian Klein (1988:123-24) nicely observes the ambiguity of *mishpat* here, so that the question can be variously asked as: What will be the boy's manner of life? How will he be judged? What can he be expected to do? How will his work be judged?

[5] A fuller version of this reading appears in Gunn and Fewell (1993:chap. 3). Other discussions that converge significantly are those of Exum (1980), Polzin (1980), and Alter (1983).

This formulation, I recognize, is ideologically double edged. It values the woman's way of knowing over the man's in a patriarchal story world. It also lends itself to perpetuating a stereotype: male/intellectual/skeptical/independent and female/intuitive/trusting/dependent.

[6] Not that these terms necessarily, let alone only, connote sexual attractiveness. But where context suggests that to be a likely and significant dimension of "looks" these terms regularly appear. Cf. *yaphah*: 2 Sam 13:1 (Tamar), 1 Kgs 1:3 (Abishag), and Songs 4:1,7,10

or 7:2[1],7[6] (the female lover); *yephat-mar'eh:* Gen 12:11 (Sarai) and 29:17 (Rachel); *yephat-to'ar:* Gen 29:17 (Rachel), Deut 21:11 (the female captive), and Esth 2:7 (Esther). The same emphatically cannot be said for *yashar*, a word commonly and regularly used of what is agreeable in the sense of right, upright, and proper. As for the term "in his eyes," its metaphoric uses—of thought, feeling, judgment—are ubiquitous. Bal, whose ideological strictures on others are keen and often devastating, could usefully problematize her own perception here where she uncritically adopts the stereotype: when a man sees a woman and is pleased he invariably is reading only a sexual code.

7 I cannot here enter into the important question of whether or not the riddle was inherently answerable (and so "fair")—suffice to say, I am persuaded that it is, though barely. The question is well discussed by Crenshaw (1978) and others, including recently and most helpfully Camp and Fontaine (1990) who also provide pertinent bibliography. Crenshaw's book and the article by Camp and Fontaine are important resources generally for exploring further the richly dimensioned account of the riddle and its riddling answer.

8 In this respect see how Samson's reply to his bride—"Look, I have told neither my father nor my mother, so why should I tell you?" —places her either at or below parity with them. Despite his boundary crossing he still conceives of himself as owing significant allegiance to his own "father's house." Perhaps he does not sufficiently reckon on the same bonds tying the Philistines (cf. Bal 1987:43-44).

9 David Clines (1976) translates, "Spurned and withdrawing from human society." My translations below are indebted at several points to Clines's translation of Isaiah 53. His book offers invaluable help for anyone wrestling with this difficult text, at whatever level of linguistic and interpretational construal.

10 Some commentators find in this episode only a self-centered Samson, interested only in his own triumph: "With the jawbone of an ass have *I* slain a thousand men." That is not such an obvious reading. "I have slain" translates simply an inflected finite verb. By contrast, his prayer stresses the divine agency of victory with a personal pronoun: "*You* ['attâ] gave this great victory . . ."

11 Camp and Fontaine (1990) explore some of these resonances in chap. 14. Bal (1987) offers a richly textured psychoanalytic reading of the whole story that draws its main strength from its account of the Delilah story in chap. 16. For her, the kernel of Samson's portrait is that he is insecure in his sexuality. Among valuable potential overlaps with the present paper are her explorations of the individual/personal and social/public tension, identity and boundary issues, initiative and passivity (including the initiation of speech), the sexual-symbolic order (particularly in the Samson and Delilah relationship), and the identification of God within the gender structures of the story (does God represent the "masculine" aspect of Samson's personality?).

BIBLIOGRAPHY

INDEXES

CONTRIBUTORS

BIBLIOGRAPHY

Aberbach, Moses and Leivy Smolar. 1967. "Aaron, Jeroboam, and the Golden Calves." *JBL* 86:129-40.

Abrams, M. H. 1971. *A Glossary of Literary Terms*. 3rd edn. New York: Holt, Rinehart and Winston.

———. 1981. *A Glossary of Literary Terms*. 4th edn. New York: Holt, Rinehart and Winston.

Ackerman, James S. 1990. "Knowing Good and Evil: A Literary Analysis of the Court History in 2 Samuel 9-20 and 1 Kings 1-2." *JBL* 109:41-60.

Alter, Robert. 1981. *The Art of Biblical Narrative*. New York: Basic.

———. 1983. "How Convention Helps Us Read: The Annunciation Type-Scene in the Bible." *Prooftexts* 3:115-30.

———. 1985. *The Art of Biblical Poetry*. New York: Basic.

———. 1990. "Samson Without Folklore." In *Text and Tradition*. S. Niditch, ed.

Althusser, Louis. 1971. *Lenin and Philosophy*. B. Brewster, trans. London: Monthly Review.

Anderson, Francis I. and David Noel Freedman. 1980. *Hosea*. AB. Garden City: Doubleday.

Aurelius, Erik. 1988. *Der Fürbitter Israels: Eine Studie zum Mosebild im Alten Testament*. Stockholm: Almqvist & Wiksell.

Babcock, Barbara. 1984. "Arrange Me Into Disorder: Fragments and Reflections on Ritual Clowning." In *Rite, Drama-Festival, Spectacle*. J. J. MacAloon, ed. Philadelphia: Institute for the Study of Human Issues.

Bailey, Randall C. 1990. *David in Love and War: The Pursuit of Power in 2 Samuel 10-12*. Sheffield: JSOT.

Bakhtin, Mikhail. 1984a (1968). *Rabelais and His World*. H. Iswolsky, trans. Bloomington: Indiana Univ.

———. 1984b (1973). *Problems of Dostoevsky's Poetics*. C. Emerson, ed. and trans. Minneapolis: Univ. of Minnesota.

Bal, Mieke. 1987. *Lethal Love: Feminist Literary Readings of Biblical Love Stories*. Bloomington: Indiana Univ.

———. 1988a. *Murder and Difference: Gender, Genre, and Scholarship on Sisera's Death*. M. Grumpert, trans. Bloomington & Indianapolis: Indiana Univ.

———. 1988b. *Death and Dissymmetry: The Politics of Coherence in the Book of Judges*. Chicago: Univ. of Chicago.

Barth, Karl. 1961. *Church Dogmatics IV:3:1*. Edinburgh: T&T Clark.

Barthes, Roland. 1977. "The Death of the Author." In *Image, Music, Text*. S. Heath, trans. New York: Hill & Wang. Pp. 142-8.
———. 1981. "Theory of the Text." In *Untying the Text: A Post-Structuralist Reader*. R. Young, ed. Boston: Routledge & Kegan Paul.
Beal, Timothy K. and David M. Gunn. 1993. "The Book of Judges." In *A Dictionary of Biblical Interpretation*. J. H. Hayes, ed. Nashville: Abingdon.
Beardslee, William A. "Ethics and Hermeneutics." In *Text and Logos: The Humanistic Interpretation of the New Testament*. T. Jennings, ed. Atlanta: Scholars.
Begg, Christopher T. 1986. "The Significance of Jehoiachin's Release: A New Proposal." *JSOT*:49-56.
Ben-Porat, Ziva. 1976. "The Poetics of Literary Allusion." *PTL: A Journal for Descriptive Poetics and Theory of Literature* 1:105-28.
Berlin, Adele. 1982. "On the Bible as Literature." *Prooftexts* 2:323-327.
———. 1989. "Lexical Cohesion and Biblical Interpretation." *Hebrew Studies* 30:29-40.
Blank, Sheldon H. 1977. *Prophetic Thought: Essays and Addresses*. Cincinnati: Hebrew Union College.
Bloom, Harold. 1973. *The Anxiety of Influence: A Theory of Poetry*. New York: Oxford Univ.
———. 1975. *A Map of Misreading*. New York: Oxford Univ.
———. 1976. "Poetic Crossing: Rhetoric and Psychology." *The Georgia Review* 30:495-526.
———. 1982. *The Breaking of the Vessels*. The Wellek Library Lectures. Chicago: Univ. of Chicago.
———. 1984. "'Before Moses Was, I Am': The Original and Belated Testaments." In *Notebooks in Cultural Analysis: An Annual Review* 1:3-14.
———. 1990. *The Book of J*. New York: Grove Weidenfeld.
Boling, Robert G. *Judges*. AB 6a. Garden City: Doubleday.
Booth, Wayne C. 1961. *The Rhetoric of Fiction*. Chicago: Univ. of Chicago.
———. 1974. *A Rhetoric of Irony*. Chicago and London: Univ. of Chicago.
Bottigheimer, Ruth B. 1987. *Grimms' Bad Girls and Bold Boys: The Moral and Social Vision of the Tales*. New Haven: Yale Univ.
Brenner, Atalya. 1989. "Job the Pious? The Characterization of Job in the Narrative Framework of the Book." *JSOT* 43:37-52.
Brueggemann, Walter. 1977. "A Neglected Sapiential Word Pair." *ZAW* 89:234-58.
———. 1985. *David's Truth in Israel's Imagination and Memory*. Philadelphia: Fortress.
———. 1990. *First and Second Samuel*. IBC. Louisville: John Knox.

BIBLIOGRAPHY

Buss, Martin. 1969. *The Prophetic Word of Hosea*. BZAW. Berlin: Alfred Topelmann.
Butler, Trent C. 1983. *Joshua*. WBC. Waco: Word.
Calvino, Italo. 1986. *The Uses of Literature*. New York: Harcourt Brace Jovanovich.
Camp, Claudia V. 1981. "The Wise Women of 2 Samuel: A Role Model for Women in Early Israel." *CBQ* 43:14-29.
Camp, Claudia V. and Carol Fontaine. 1990. "The Words of the Wise and their Riddles." In *Text and Tradition*. S. Niditch, ed.
Carroll, Robert P. 1977. "The Aniconic God and the Cult of Images." *ST* 31:51-64.
Catlett, Michael. 1988. *Reversals in Hosea: A Literary Analysis*. Emory University Dissertation.
Clines, David J. A. 1990. *What Does Eve Do to Help? and Other Readerly Questions to the Old Testament*. Sheffield: Sheffield.
———. 1976. *I, He, We, and They: A Literary Approach to Isaiah 53*. JSOTSup 1. Sheffield: JSOT.
Cogan, Mordechai and Hayim Tadmor. 1988. *II Kings*. AB 11. Garden City: Doubleday.
Crenshaw, James L. 1978. *Samson: A Secret Betrayed, a Vow Ignored*. Atlanta: John Knox.
———. 1984. *A Whirlpool of Torment: Israelite Traditions of God as an Oppressive Presence*. Philadelphia: Fortress.
Cross, Frank Moore. 1973. *Canaanite Myth and Hebrew Epic*. Cambridge, MA: Harvard Univ.
Culler, Jonathan. 1976. "Presupposition and Intertextuality." *MLN* 91:1380-96.
———. 1981. *The Pursuit of Signs*. Ithaca: Cornell Univ.
Culley, Robert. 1976. *Studies in the Structure of Hebrew Narrative*. SBL Semeia Studies. Missoula and Philadelphia: Scholars and Fortress.
Damrosch, David. 1987. *The Narrative Covenant: Transformations of Genre in the Growth of Biblical Literature*. San Franciso: Harper & Row.
de Man, Paul. 1979. *Allegories of Reading: Figural Language in Rousseau, Nietzsche, Rilke, and Proust*. New Haven: Yale Univ.
de Vaux, Roland. 1971. *The Bible and the Ancient Near East*. Garden City: Doubleday.
De Vries, Simon J. 1985. *1 Kings*. WBC 12. Waco: Word.
Debus, Jörg. 1967. *Die Sünde Jerobeams: Studien zur Darstellung Jerobeams und der Geschichte des Nordreichs in der deuteronomistische Geschichtsschreibung*. Göttingen: Vandenhoeck und Ruprecht.
Delitzsch, Franz. 1853. *Commentar zur Genesis*. Leipzig: B. Tauchnitz.
Derrida, Jacques. 1979. "Living On: Border Lines." In *Deconstruction and Criticism*. H. Bloom et al, eds. New York: Seabury.
———. 1981 (Fr. 1972). *Dissemination*. B. Johnson, trans. Chicago: Univ. of Chicago.

Des Pres, Terrence. 1976. *The Survivor: An Anatomy of Life in the Death Camps*. New York: Washington Square.
Draisma, Sipke, ed. 1989. *Intertextuality in Biblical Writings: Essays in Honor of Bas van Iersel*. Kampen: J. H. Hok.
Driver, Samuel R. 1890. *Notes on the Hebrew Text of the Books of Samuel*. Oxford: Clarendon.
———. 1902. *Deuteronomy*. ICC. 3rd edn. Edinburgh: T&T Clark.
Eagleton, Terry. 1983. *Literary Theory: An Introduction*. Minneapolis: Univ. of Minnesota.
Eco, Umberto. 1983. *Postscript to the Name of the Rose*. San Francisco: HBJ.
Edelman, Diana. 1991. *King Saul in the Historiography of Judah*. Sheffield: JSOT.
Eliot, T. S. 1964 (orig. 1919). "Tradition and the Individual Talent." In *Selected Essays, 1917-1932*. New York: Harcourt, Brace, Jovanovich. Pp. 3-11
Ellul, Jacques. 1972. *The Politics of God and the Politics of Man*. Grand Rapids: Eerdmans.
Eslinger, Lyle M. 1985. *Kingship of God in Crisis: A Close Reading of 1 Samuel 1-12*. Sheffield: Almond.
———. 1989. *Into the Hands of the Living God*. Sheffield: Almond.
———. 1992. "Inner-biblical Exegesis and Inner-biblical Allusion: The Question of Category." *VT* 42:47-58.
Exum, J. Cheryl. 1990. "Murder They Wrote: Ideology and the Manipulation of Female Presence in Biblical Narrative." In *The Pleasure of Her Text*. A. Bach, ed. Philadelphia: Trinity International.
———. 1980. "Promise and Fulfillment: Narrative Art in Judges 13." *JBL* 99:39-59.
———. 1981. "Aspects of Symmetry and Balance in the Samson Saga." *JSOT* 19:3-29.
———. 1983. "The Theological Dimension of the Samson Saga." *VT* 33:30-45.
———. 1992. *Tragedy and Biblical Narrative: Arrows of the Almighty*. Cambridge: Cambridge Univ.
Exum, J. Cheryl and J. William Whedbee. 1985. "Isaac, Samson, and Saul: Reflections on the Comic and Tragic Visions." In *Tragedy and Comedy in the Bible*. J. C. Exum, ed. SBL Semeia Studies 32. Decatur: Scholars. Pp. 5-40.
Fackenheim, Emil L. 1990. *The Jewish Bible after the Holocaust: A Rereading*. Bloomington: Indiana Univ.
Faur, José. 1978. "The Biblical Idea of Idolatry." *JQR* 69:1-15.
Fewell, Danna Nolan. 1991. *Circle of Sovereignty: Plotting Politics in the Book of Daniel*. Nashville: Abingdon.
———. 1990. "Feminist Hermeneutics." In *Mercer Dictionary of the Bible*. W. Watson, ed. Macon: Mercer Univ.
———. 1992. "Judges." In *The Women's Bible Commentary*. C. A.

Newsom and S. Ringe, eds. Louisville: Westminster/John Knox.
Fiorenza, Elisabeth Schüssler. 1988. "The Ethics of Interpretation: Decentering Biblical Scholarship." *JBL* 107:3-17.
Fishbane, Michael. 1979. *Text and Texture*. New York: Schocken.
———. 1985. *Biblical Interpretation in Ancient Israel*. Oxford: Clarendon.
———. 1989. *Garments of Torah: Essays in Biblical Hermeneutics*. Bloomington: Indiana Univ.
Fletcher, Angus. 1964. *Allegory: The Theory of a Symbolic Mode*. Ithaca: Cornell Univ.
———. 1981. *Narrative Art and Poetry in the Books of Samuel, Vol 1: King David (2 Sam 9-20; 1 Kgs 1-2)*. Assen, The Netherlands: Van Gorcum.
Fokkelman, J. P. 1987. "Genesis." In *The Literary Guide to the Bible*. R. Alter and F. Kermode, eds. Cambridge: Harvard Univ.
Fowl, Stephen E. 1990. "The Ethics of Interpretation, or What's Left After the Elimination of Meaning." In *The Bible in Three Dimensions*. D. J. A. Clines, et al, eds. Sheffield: JSOT.
Fox, Michael V. 1991. *Character and Ideology in the Book of Esther*. Columbia, SC: Univ. of South Carolina.
Freeman, James A. 1982. "Samson's Dry Bones: A Structural Reading of Judges 13-16." In *Literary Interpretations of Biblical Narratives II*. K. R. R. Gros Louis, with J. S. Ackerman, eds. Nashville: Abingdon. Pp. 145-60.
Freud, Sigmund. 1959. *Group Psychology and the Analysis of the Ego*. New York: Norton.
Friedman, Richard E. 1981."From Egypt to Egypt: Dtr1 and Dtr2." In *Traditions in Transformation*. B. Halpern and J. D. Levenson, eds. Winona Lake, IN: Eisenbrauns. Pp. 167-192.
Frye, Northrop. 1982. *The Great Code: The Bible and Literature*. New York: Harcourt Brace Jovanovich.
Gilbert, Sandra M. and Susan Gubar. 1984. *The Madwoman in The Attic: The Woman Writer and the Nineteenth-Century Literary Imagination*. New Haven: Yale Univ.
Ginzberg, Louis. 1968. *Legends of the Jews I*. Philadelphia: JPS.
———. 1969. *Legends of the Jews II*. Philadelphia: JPS.
Good, Edwin M. 1981. *Irony in the Old Testament*. 2nd edn. Sheffield: Almond.
Gordis, Robert. 1965. *The Book of God and Man: A Study of Job*. Chicago: Univ. of Chicago.
———. 1978. *The Book of Job*. New York: Jewish Theological Seminary.
Gottwald, Norman. 1959. *A Light to the Nations: An Introduction to the Old Testament*. New York: Harper.
Graff, Gerald. 1990. "Determinacy/Indeterminacy." In *Critical Terms for Literary Study*. F. Lentricchia and T. McLaughlin, eds. Chicago: Univ. of Chicago.
Gray, John. 1963. *I & II Kings*. OTL. Philadelphia: Westminster.

———. 1970. *I & II Kings*. OTL. 2nd rev. edn. Philadelphia: Westminster.
———. 1967. *Joshua, Judges and Ruth*. London: Nelson.
Greenstein, Edward L. 1981a. "Biblical Narratology." *Prooftexts* 1:201-208.
———. 1981b. "The Riddle of Samson." *Prooftexts* 1:237-60.
Gros Louis, Kenneth R. R. 1974. "The Book of Judges." In *Literary Interpretations of Biblical Narrative I*. K. R. R. Gros Louis, with J. S. Ackerman and T. S. Warshaw, eds. Nashville: Abingdon. Pp. 141-62.
Gunn, David M. 1976. "Traditional Composition in the 'Succession Narrative.'" *VT* 26:214-229.
———. 1980. *The Fate of King Saul*. Sheffield: JSOT.
———. 1982. "The 'Hardening of Pharoah's Heart': Plot, Character and Theology in Exodus 1-14." In *Art and Meaning: Rhetoric in Biblical Literature*. D. J. A. Clines, D. M. Gunn and A. J. Hauser, eds. Sheffield: JSOT. Pp. 72-96.
———. 1985. "The Anatomy of a Divine Comedy: On Reading the Bible as Comedy and Tragedy." In *Tragedy and Comedy in the Bible*. J. C. Exum, ed. Decatur: Scholars. Pp. 115-29.
———. 1987a. "New Directions in the Study of Hebrew Narrative." *JSOT* 39:65-75.
———. 1987b. "Joshua and Judges." In *The Literary Guide to the Bible*. R. Alter and F. Kermode, eds. Cambridge, MA: Harvard. Pp. 102-21.
———. 1988. "2 Samuel." In *Harper's Bible Commentary*. J. L. Mays, ed. San Francisco: Harper and Row.
———. 1989. "In Security: The David of Biblical Narrative." In *Signs and Wonders: Biblical Texts in Literary Focus*. J. C. Exum, ed. SBL Semeia Studies. Atlanta: Scholars.
Gunn, David M. and Danna Nolan Fewell. 1993. *Narrative in the Hebrew Bible*. Oxford: Oxford Univ.
Habel, Norman. 1985. *The Book of Job*. OTL. Philadelphia: Westminster.
Hagan, Harry. 1979. "Deception as Motif and Theme in 2 Sam 9-20; 1 Kgs 1-2." *Biblica* 60:301-326.
Hahn, Joachim. 1981. *Das "Goldene Kalb": Die Jahwe-Verehrung bei Stierbildern in der Geschichte Israels*. Frankfurt a. M., Bern: Peter Lang.
Halpern, Baruch. 1983. "Doctrine by Misadventure: Between the Israelite Source and the Biblical Historian." In *The Poet and the Historian: Essays in Literary and Historical Biblical Criticism*. R. Friedman, ed. Chico: Scholars. Pp. 41-74.
———. 1988. *The First Historians: The Hebrew Bible and History*. San Francisco: Harper & Row.
———. 1991. "Jerusalem and the Lineages in the Seventh Century BCE: Kinship and the Rise of Individual Moral Liability." In *Law and Ideology in Monarchic Israel*. B. Halpern and D. W. Hobson, eds. Sheffield: JSOT. Pp. 11-107.

Handelman, Susan. 1982. *The Slayers of Moses: The Emergence of Rabbinic Interpretation in Modern Literary Theory.* Albany: SUNY.

Hanson, Paul D. 1986. *The People Called: The Growth of Community in the Bible.* San Francisco: Harper & Row.

Hardy, Daniel and David Ford. 1985. *Praising and Knowing God.* Philadelphia: Westminster.

Hartman, Geoffrey and Sanford Budick, eds. 1986. *Midrash and Literature.* New Haven: Yale Univ.

Hartman, Geoffrey. 1975. "War in Heaven." In *The Fate of Reading.* Chicago: Univ. of Chicago.

Hawk, L. Daniel. 1991. *Every Promise Fulfilled.* LCBI. Louisville: Westminster/John Knox.

Hays, Richard B. 1989. *Echoes of Scripture in the Letters of Paul.* New Haven: Yale Univ.

Hebel, Udo J. 1989. *Intertextuality, Allusion, and Quotation: An International Bibliography of Critical Studies.* New York: Greenwood.

Hertzberg, Hans Wilhelm. 1964. *I & II Samuel: A Commentary.* J. S. Bowden, trans. OTL. Philadelphia: Westminster.

Herzfeld, M. 1987. "'As In Your Own House': Hospitality, Ethnography, and the Stereotype of Mediterranean Society." In *Honor and Shame and the Unity of the Mediterranean.* D. D. Gilmore, ed. Washington: American Anthropological Association. Pp. 75-89.

Hoffman, Yair. 1981. "The Relation between the Prologue and the Speech Cycles in Job." *VT* 31:160-70.

Hoffmann, Hans-Detlef. 1980. *Reform und Reformen: Untersuchungen zu einem Grundthema der deuteronomistischen Geschichtsschreibung.* Zürich: Theologischer.

Hoftijzer, J. 1970. "David and the Tekoite Woman." *VT* 20:419-444.

Hollander, John. 1981. *The Figure of Echo: A Mode of Allusion in Milton and After.* Berkeley: Univ. of California.

Hoy, David Couzens. 1986. "Must We Say What We Mean? The Grammatological Critique of Hermeneutics." In *Hermeneutics and Modern Philosophy.* B. R. Wachterhauser, ed. New York: SUNY. Pp. 397-415.

Humphreys, W. Lee. 1973. "A Life-Style for Diaspora: A Study of the Tales of Esther and Daniel." *JBL* 92:211-23.

———. 1985. *The Tragic Vision and the Hebrew Tradition.* Philadelphia: Fortress.

Hurvitz, Avi. 1974. "The Date of the Prose-Tale of Job Linguistically Reconsidered." *HTR* 67:17-34.

Hutcheon, Linda. 1986/7. "Postmodern Paratextuality and History." *Texte* 5/6:301-12.

Iser, Wolfgang. 1980. "The Reading Process: A Phenomenological Approach." In *Reader Response Criticism.* J. Tompkins, ed. Baltimore: Johns Hopkins Univ.

Jacobsen, Thorkild. 1987. "The Graven Image." In *Ancient Israelite Religion: Essays in Honor of Frank Moore Cross*. P. D. Miller, Jr., P. D. Hanson and S. D. McBride, eds. Philadelphia: Fortress. Pp. 15-32.
Jameson, Fredric. 1981. *The Political Unconscious: Narrative as a Socially Symbolic Act*. Ithaca: Cornell Univ.
Janzen, J. Gerald. 1985. *Job*. Atlanta: John Knox.
———. 1989. "The Root pr' in Judges V 2 and Deuteronomy XXXII 42." *VT* 39:393-406.
———. 1990. "The Character of the Calf and Its Cult in Exodus 32." *CBQ* 52:597-607.
Jeansonne, Sharon Pace. 1990. *The Women of Genesis: From Sarah to Potiphar's Wife*. Minneapolis: Fortress.
Jenks, Alan W. 1977. *The Elohist and North Israelite Traditions*. SBLMS 22. Missoula: Scholars.
Jones, G. H. 1984. *I and II Kings*. New Century Bible Commentary. Grand Rapids: Eerdmans.
Jüngling, H. W. 1981. *Richter 19--Ein Pladoyer für das Konigtum: Stilistische Analyse der Tendenzerzahlung Ri 19, 1-30a; 21, 25*. AnBib 84. Rome: Pontifical Biblical Institute.
Kaufmann, Yehezkel. 1972. *The Religion of Israel: From its Beginnings to the Babylonian Exile*. New York: Schocken.
Keil, C. F. and F. Delitzsch. 1864. *Biblischer Commentar über die Prophetischen Geschichtsbücher des Alten Testaments, zweiter bank: Die Bücher Samuels*. Leipzig: Dörffling und Franke.
———. 1971. *Commentary on the Old Testament in Ten Volumes, Vol. 1: The First Book of Moses (Genesis)*. Grand Rapids: Eerdmans.
Kennedy, A. R. S. 1901. "Calf, Golden Calf." In *A Dictionary of the Bible, Vol 1*. 4th ed. J. Hastings, ed. Edinburgh: Clark. Pp. 340-43.
Kermode, Frank. 1966. *The Sense of an Ending*. London: Oxford Univ.
Klein, Lillian R. 1988. *The Triumph of Irony in the Book of Judges*. Sheffield: Almond.
Koch, Klaus. 1969. *The Growth of the Biblical Tradition*. New York: Scribner.
Kolodny, Annette. 1985. "A Map for Rereading: Gender and the Interpretation of Literary Texts." In *The New Feminist Criticism: Essays on Women, Literature, and Theory*. E. Showalter, ed. New York: Pantheon. Pp. 46-62.
Kristeva, Julia. 1971. *Essays in Semiotics*. The Hague: Mouton.
———. 1980 (Fr. 1969). *Desire in Language: A Semiotic Approach to Literature and Art*. L. S. Roudiez, ed. T. Gora, A. Jardine, and L. S. Roudiez, trans. New York: Columbia Univ.
———. 1984 (Fr. 1974). *Revolution in Poetic Language*. M. Waller, trans. New York: Columbia Univ.
———. 1986a (Fr. 1969). "Semiotics: A Critical Science and/or a Critique of Science." In *The Kristeva Reader*. T. Moi, ed. New York:

Columbia Univ. Pp. 74-88.

———. 1986b (Fr. 1973). "The System of the Speaking Subject." In *The Kristeva Reader*. T. Moi, ed. New York: Columbia Univ. Pp. 24-33.

Kugel, James. 1981. "On the Bible and Literary Criticism." *Prooftexts* 1:217-36.

———. 1982. "On the Bible as Literature." *Prooftexts* 2:328-332.

Labriola, Albert C. and John W. Smeltz (trans. and comm.). 1990. *The Bible of the Poor [Biblia Pauperum]: A Facsimile of the British Library Blockbook C.9 D.2*. Pittsburgh: Duquesne Univ.

Lacan, Jacques. 1977. *The Four Fundamental Concepts of Psycho-Analysis*. London: Tavistock.

Laffey, Alice L. 1988. *Introduction to the Old Testament: A Feminist Approach*. Philadelphia: Fortress.

Langlamet, F. 1971. "Josué, II, et les traditions de l'Héxateuque." *Revue Biblique* 78:5-17, 161-83, 321-54.

Lasine, Stuart. 1984. "Guest and Host in Judges 19: Lot's Hospitality in an Inverted World." *JSOT* 29: 27-59.

———. 1992. "Levite Violence, Fratricide and Sacrifice in the Bible and Later Revolutionary Rhetoric." In *Curing Violence: Religion and the Thought of René Girard*. T. H. Smith and M. I. Wallace, eds. Sonoma, CA: Polbridge. Forthcoming.

Le Bon, Gustave. 1960. *The Crowd: A Study of the Popular Mind*. New York: Viking.

Levenson, Jon D. 1984. "The Last Four Verses in Kings." *JBL* 103:353-61.

Lindbeck, George A. 1984. *The Nature of Doctrine: Religion and Theology in a Postliberal Age*. Philadelphia: Westminster.

Long, Burke O. 1984. *1 Kings, with an Introduction to Historical Literature*. FOTL IX. Grand Rapids: Eerdmans.

———. 1991. *2 Kings*. FOTL X. Grand Rapids: Eerdmans.

Luzzatto, Samuel David. 1965 (Heb. orig. 1871). *Commentary to the Pentateuch*. Tel Aviv: Dvir.

MacLeish, Archibald. 1958. *J. B.* Boston: Houghton Mifflin.

Maline, Bruce J. 1985. "Hospitality." In *Harper's Bible Dictionary*. P. J. Achtemeier, ed. San Francisco: Harper & Row. Pp. 408-9.

Matthews, Victor H. 1989. "Freedom and Entrapment in the Samson Narrative: A Literary Analysis." *Perspectives in Religious Studies* 16:245-57.

———. 1991. "Hospitality and Hostility in Judges 4." *BTB* 21:13-21.

———. 1992. "Hospitality and Hostility in Genesis 19 and Judges 19." *BTB* 22:3-12.

Mauchline, John. 1971. *New Century Bible: 1 and 2 Samuel*. Greenwood, SC: Attic.

Mays, James Luther. 1969. *Hosea*. OTL. Philadelphia: Westminster.

Mazar, Amihai. 1982. "The 'Bull Site'—An Iron Age I Open Cult Place." *BASOR* 247:27-42.

McCarter, P. Kyle. 1984. *2 Samuel*. Garden City: Doubleday.
McCarthy, Dennis J. 1974. "The Wrath of Yahweh and the Structural Unity of the Deuteronomistic History." In *Essays in Old Testament Ethics*. J. L. Crenshaw and J. T. Willis, eds. New York: KTAV. Pp. 97-110.
———. 1971. "The Theology of Leadership in Joshua 1-9." *Biblica* 52:165-75.
Meyers, Carol. 1988. *Discovering Eve: Ancient Israelite Women in Context*. New York and Oxford: Oxford Univ.
Miller, J. Maxwell and Gene M. Tucker. 1974. *The Book of Joshua*. CBC. Cambridge: Cambridge Univ.
Miller, Owen. 1985. "Intertextual Identity." In *Identity of the Literary Text*. M. J. Valdes and O. Miller, eds. Toronto: Univ. of Toronto.
Miscall, Peter D. 1979. "Literary Unity in Old Testament Narrative." *Semeia* 15:27-44.
———. 1983. *The Workings of Old Testament Narrative*. Philadelphia: Fortress.
———. 1986. *1 Samuel: A Literary Reading*. Indiana Studies in Biblical Literature. Bloomington: Indiana Univ.
———. 1990. "Jacques Derrida in the Garden of Eden." *USQR* 44:1-9.
———. 1991. "Isaiah: The Labyrinth of Images." *Semeia* 54:35-56.
Mitchell, Stephen. 1987. *The Book of Job*. San Francisco: North Point.
Moberly, R. Walter L. 1982. *At the Mountain of God: Story and Theology in Exodus 32-34*. JSOTSup 22. Sheffield: JSOT.
Moo, Douglas J. 1983. *The Old Testament in the Gospel Passion Narratives*. Sheffield: Almond.
Moore, Rick D. 1983. "The Integrity of Job." *CBQ* 45:17-31.
Morgan, Thaïs E. 1985. "Is There an Intertext in This Text?: Literary and Interdisciplinary Approaches to Intertextuality." *American Journal of Semiotics* 3.4:1-40.
———. 1989. "The Space of Intertextuality." In *Intertextuality and Contemporary American Fiction*. P. O'Donnell and R. Con Davis, eds. Baltimore: Johns Hopkins.
Morgenstern, Julian. 1948. "The Chanukkah Festival and the Calendar of Ancient Israel (Continued)." *HUCA* 21:365-496.
Muecke, D. C. 1982. *Irony and the Ironic*. The Critical Idiom 13. London: Methuen.
Nelson, Richard Donald. 1987. *First and Second Kings*. IBC. Atlanta: John Knox.
Niditch, Susan. 1982. "The 'Sodomite' Theme in Judges 19-20: Family, Community, and Social Disintegration." *CBQ* 44:365-378.
———. 1987. *Underdogs and Tricksters: A Prelude to Biblical Folklore*. San Francisco: Harper and Row.
———. 1990. "Samson as Culture Hero, Trickster, and Bandit: The Empowerment of the Weak." *CBQ* 52:608-24.
Noth, Martin. 1960. *The History of Israel*. 2nd edn. New York: Harper.

Bibliography

———. 1981 (Germ. 1957). *The Deuteronomistic History.* JSOTSup 15. Sheffield: JSOT.
O'Day, Gail R. 1993. "Intertextuality." In *A Dictionary of Biblical Interpretation.* J. H. Hayes, ed. Nashville: Abingdon.
———. 1986. *Revelation in the Fourth Gospel: Narrative Mode and Theological Claim.* Philadelphia: Fortress.
Oden, Robert A., Jr. 1987. *The Bible Without Theology: The Theological Tradition and Alternatives to It.* San Francisco: Harper & Row.
Olyan, Saul M. 1984. "Hašalôm: Some Literary Considerations of 2 Kings 9." *CBQ* 46:652-68.
———. 1985. "2 Kings 9.31—Jehu as Zimri." *HTR* 78:203-7.
Parsons, Mikeal C. 1987. "Narrative Closure in the Canonical Gospels: A Prospectus." Unpublished paper.
Peckham, Brian. 1985. *The Composition of the Deuteronomistic History.* Harvard Semitic Monographs 35. Atlanta: Scholars.
Penchansky, David. 1990. *The Betrayal of God: Ideological Conflict in Job.* LCBI. Louisville: Westminster/John Knox.
Perlitt, Lothar. 1969. *Bundestheologie im Alten Testament.* Neukirchen-Vluyn: Neukirchener.
Plimpton, George. 1988. *Writers at Work #8.* New York: Penguin.
Plottel, Jeanine and Hanna Charney (eds.). 1978. *Intertextuality: New Perspectives in Criticism.* New York: New York Literary Forum.
Poland, Lynn. 1990. "The Bible and the Rhetorical Sublime." In *The Bible as Rhetoric: Studies in Biblical Persuasion and Credibility.* M. Warner, ed. London: Routledge. Pp. 29-50.
Polzin, Robert. 1975. "'The Ancestress of Israel in Danger' in Danger." *Semeia* 3:81-98.
———. 1980. *Moses and the Deuteronomist: A Literary Study of the Deuteronomistic History.* New York: Seabury.
Pope, Marvin. 1973. *Job.* AB. Garden City: Doubleday.
Preuss, Horst Dietrich. 1971. *Verspottung fremder Religionen im Alten Testament.* BWANT 92. Stuttgart: Kohlhammer.
Rabinowitz, Peter J. 1977. "Truth in Fiction: A Reexamination of Audiences." *CI* 4:121-41.
———. 1987. *Before Reading: Narrative Conventions and the Politics of Interpretation.* Ithaca: Cornell Univ.
Renza, Louis A. 1990. "Influence." In *Critical Terms for Literary Study.* F. Lentricchia and T. McLaughlin, eds. Chicago: Univ. of Chicago. Pp. 186-202.
Ricoeur, Paul. 1970. *Freud and Philosophy: An Essay on Interpretation.* D. Savage, trans. New Haven: Yale Univ.
———. 1975. "Biblical Hermeneutics." *Semeia* 4:27-148.
Ridout, G. P. 1971. *Prose Compositional Techniques in the Succession Narrative.* Berkeley: Graduate Theological Union.
Riffaterre, Michael. 1984. "Intertextual Representation: On Mimesis as Interpretive Discourse." *CI* 11:141-62.

———. 1985. "Transposing Presuppositions: on the Semiotics of Literary Translation." *Texte* 4:99-109.
Rimmon-Kenan, Shlomith. 1983. *Narrative Fiction: Contemporary Poetics*. New Accents. London: Methuen.
Robertson, David. 1973. "The Book of Job: A Literary Study." *Soundings* 56:446-69.
Rosenberg, Joel. 1984. "Biblical Narrative." In *Back to the Sources: Reading the Classic Jewish Texts*. B. W. Holtz, ed. New York: Summit. Pp. 31-82.
———. 1986. *King and Kin: Political Allegory in the Hebrew Bible*. Bloomington: Indiana Univ.
———. 1987. "1 and 2 Samuel." In *The Literary Guide to the Bible*. R. Alter and F. Kermode, eds. Cambridge, MA: Harvard Univ.
Rusinko, Elaine. 1979. "Intertextuality: The Soviet Approach to Subtext." *Dispositio* 4:213-35.
Sandmel, Samuel. 1961. "The Haggadah within Scripture." *JBL* 80:105-22.
Sarna, Nahum M. 1986. *Exploring Exodus: The Heritage of Biblical Israel*. New York: Schocken.
———. 1989. *Genesis*. Philadelphia: JPS.
Savran, George. 1987. "1 and 2 Kings." In *The Literary Guide to the Bible*. R. Alter and F. Kermode, eds. Cambridge, MA: Harvard Univ.
Scharbert, Josef. 1968. *Prolegomena eines Alttestamentlers zur Erbsündenlehre*. Freiberg, Basel, Wien: Herder.
Schwartz, Regina M. 1991. "The Histories of David." In *Not in Heaven: Coherence and Complexity in Biblical Narrative*. J. P. Rosenblatt and J. C. Sitterson, Jr., eds. Bloomington: Indiana Univ. Pp. 192-210.
Segal, Lore. 1987. "II Samuel." In *Congregation: Contemporary Writers Read the Jewish Bible*. D. Rosenberg, ed. Orlando: HBJ.
Seitz, Christopher. 1989. "Job: Full Structure, Movement, and Interpretation." *Interpretation* 43:5-17.
Simon, Uriel. 1967. "The Poor Man's Ewe Lamb: An Example of a Juridical Parable." *Biblica* 48:207-242.
Skinner, John. 1925. *Genesis*. ICC. New York: Scribners.
Smith, Barbara Herrnstein. 1968. *Poetic Closure: A Study of How Poems End*. Chicago: Univ. of Chicago.
Speiser, Ephraim A. 1964. *Genesis*. AB 1. Garden City: Doubleday.
Spiegel, Shalom. 1945. "Noah, Daniel, and Job: Touching on Canaanite Relics in the Legends of the Jews." In *Louis Ginzberg Jubilee Volume*. New York: American Academy for Jewish Research. Pp. 305-55.
Spivak, Gayatri Chakravorty. 1976. "Preface" to *Of Grammatology* by Jacques Derrida. Baltimore: John Hopkins Univ. Pp. ix-xxxvii.
Stager, Lawrence E. 1991. "When Canaanites and Philistines Ruled Ashkelon." *BAR* 17:24-43.

Stallybrass, Peter. 1985. "Drunk with the Cup of Liberty: Robin Hood, the Carnivalesque, and the Rhetoric of Violence in Early Modern England." *Semiotica* 54½:113-45.
Steinsaltz, Adin. 1984. *Biblical Images: Men and Women of the Book.* Y. Hanegbi and Y. Keshet, trans. New York: Basic.
Sternberg, Meir. 1985. *The Poetics of Biblical Narrative: Ideological Literature and the Drama of Reading.* Bloomington: Indiana Univ.
Talmon, Shemaryahu. 1958. "Divergences in Calendar-Reckoning in Ephraim and Judah." *VT* 8:48-74.
Tarlin, Jan. 1992. "Towards a 'Female' Reading of the Elijah Cycle: Ideology and Gender in the Reading of the Hebrew Bible." Presented at the 1992 SBL Annual Meeting (Reading, Rhetoric, and the Hebrew Bible Section).
Terrien, Samuel. 1954. "Job." In *Interpreter's Bible, III.* Nashville: Abingdon. Pp. 875-1198.
Thomas, Keith. 1976. *Rule and Misrule in the Schools of Early Modern England.* Reading: Reading Univ.
Todorov, Tsvetan. 1984. *Mikhail Bakhtin: The Dialogical Principle.* Minneapolis: Univ. of Minnesota.
Tolbert, Mary Ann. 1983. "Defining the Problem: The Bible and Feminist Hermeneutics." *Semeia* 28:113-126.
Torgovnick, Marianna. 1981. *Closure in the Novel.* Princeton: Princeton Univ.
Trible, Phyllis. 1978. *God and the Rhetoric of Sexuality.* Philadelphia: Fortress.
———. 1984. *Texts of Terror: Literary-Feminist Readings of Biblical Narratives.* Philadelphia: Fortress.
Tsevat, Matitiahu. 1966. "The Meaning of the Book of Job." *HUCA* 37:73-106.
Tucker, Gene M. 1972. "The Rahab Saga (Joshua 2): Some Form Critical and Traditio-Critical Observations." In *The Use of the Old Testament in the New and Other Essays.* J. M. Efird, ed. Durham: Duke Univ.
Uspensky, Boris. 1973. *A Poetics of Composition: The Structure of the Artistic Text and Typology of a Compositional Form.* V. Zavarin and S. Wittig, trans. Los Angeles: Univ. of California.
Vickery, John B. 1981. "In Strange Ways: The Story of Samson." In *Images of Man and God.* Sheffield: Almond. 58-73.
Vischer, Wilhelm. 1947. *Hiob, ein Zeuge Jesu Christi.* Zürich: Evangelischer.
von Rad, Gerhard. 1953. *Das erste Buch Mose.* Göttingen: Vandenhoeck & Ruprecht.
———. 1962 (Germ. 1957). *Old Testament Theology.* D. M. G. Stalker, trans. New York: Harper & Row.
———. 1967. "Hosea." In *The Message of the Prophets.* D. M. G. Stalker, trans. London: SCM.

———. 1972. *Genesis.* J. H. Marks, trans. Philadelphia: Westminster.
———. 1984 (Germ. 1966). "The Deuteronomic Theology of History in I and II Kings." In *The Problem of the Hexateuch and Other Essays.* E. W. T. Dicken, trans. London: SCM.
Wagner, Siegfried. 1964. "Die Kundschaftergeschichten im Alten Testament." *ZAW* 76:255-69.
Waldman, Nahum. 1986/87. "Two Biblical Parables: Irony and Self-Entrapment." *Dor le Dor* 15:11-18.
Webb, Barry G. 1987. *The Book of Judges: An Integrated Reading.* JSOTSup 46. Sheffield: JSOT.
Weems, Renita J. 1991. "Reading Her Way through the Struggle: African-American Women and the Bible." In *Stony the Road We Trod: African-American Biblical Interpretation.* C. H. Felder, ed. Minneapolis: Fortress.
———. 1989. "Gomer: Victim of Violence or Victim of Metaphor" *Semeia* 87-104.
Weinfeld, Moshe. 1970. "The Covenant of Grant in the Old Testament and in the Ancient Near East." *JAOS* 90:184-203.
———. 1972. *Deuteronomy and the Deuteronomic School.* Oxford: Clarendon.
———. 1985. "The Emergence of the Deuteronomic Movement: The Historical Antecedents." In *Das Deuteronomium: Entstehung, Gestalt und Botschaft.* N. Lohfink, ed. Leuven: University. Pp. 76-98.
Westermann, Claus. 1974. "The Role of Lament in the Theology of the Old Testament." *Interpretation* 28:20-38.
Whybray, R. N. 1968. *The Succession Narrative: A Study of 2 Samuel 9-20; 1 Kings 1 and 2.* SBT. Naperville, IL: Alec R. Allenson.
Wiesel, Elie. 1978. *A Jew Today.* New York: Vintage.
Wilden, Anthony. 1975. "Lacan and the Discourse of the Other." In J. Lacan, *The Language of the Self.* A. Wilden, ed. and trans. York: Delta.
Williams, James G. 1980. "The Beautiful and the Barren: Conventions in Biblical Type-Scenes." *JSOT* 17:107-19.
Wolff, Hans Walter. 1964. "Das Zitat im Prophetenspruch: Eine Studie zur prophetischen Verkündigungsweise." In *Gesammelte Studien zum Alten Testament.* München: Kaiser. Pp. 36-129.
———. 1974. *Hosea.* G. Stansell, trans. Philadelphia: Fortress.
———. 1982 (1975). "The Kerygma of the Deuteronomic Historical Work." In *The Vitality of Old Testament Traditions.* W. Brueggemann and H. W. Wolff, eds. Atlanta: John Knox.
Zakovitch, Yair. 1990. "Humor and Theology or the Successful Failure of Israelite Intelligence: A Literary Folkloristic Approach to Joshua 2." In *Text and Tradition.* S. Niditch, ed. Atlanta: Scholars.
Zeid, A. M. Abou. 1965. "Honour and Shame among the Bedouin of Egypt." In *Honour and Shame: The Values of Mediterranean*

Society. Peristiany, ed. London: Univ. of Chicago. Pp. 245-259.
Zenger, Erich. 1968. "Die deuteronomistische Interpretation der Rehabilitierung Jojachins." *Biblische Zeitschrift* 12:16-30.
Zuckerman, Bruce. 1991. *Job the Silent: A Study in Historical Counterpoint.* New York: Oxford Univ.

ABBREVIATIONS

AB	Anchor Bible
AnBib	Analecta biblica
BAR	*Biblical Archaeologist Reader*
BASOR	*Bulletin of the American Schools of Oriental Research*
BTB	*Biblical Theology Bulletin*
BWANT	Beiträge zur Wissenschaft vom Alten und Neuen Testament
BZAW	Beihefte zur *ZAW*
CBC	Cambridge Bible Commentary
CBQ	*Catholic Biblical Quarterly*
CI	*Critical Inquiry*
FOTL	Forms of Old Testament Literature
HTR	*Harvard Theological Review*
HUCA	*Hebrew Union College Annual*
IBC	Interpretation: A Biblical Commentary for Teaching and Preaching
ICC	International Critical Commentary
JBL	*Journal of Biblical Literature*
JQR	*Jewish Quarterly Review*
JSOT	*Journal for the Study of the Old Testament*
JSOTSup	JSOT—Supplement Series
LCBI	Literary Currents in Biblical Interpretation
MLN	*Modern Language Notes*
OTL	Old Testament Library
SBL	Society of Biblical Literature
SBLMS	SBL Monograph Series
SBT	Studies in Biblical Theology
ST	*Studia theologica*
USQR	*Union Seminary Quarterly Review*
VT	Vetus Testamentum
WBC	Word Biblical Commentary
ZAW	Zeitschrift für die alttestamentliche Wissenschaft

INDEXES

AUTHORS

Aberbach, M. 152
Abrams, M. H. 137, 187
Ackerman, J. S. 130-31
Ackroyd, P. 252
Alter, R. 115, 216, 232, 250, 252
Althusser, L. 37
Anderson, F. I. 201
Aurelus, E. 133
Babcock, B. 170
Bakhtin, M. 29-30, 157-71, 187
Bailey, R. C. 112
Bal, M. 29, 32-35, 112, 231-32, 252, 253
Barth, K. 209
Barthes, R. 22, 27-28, 38, 181-82, 187
Beal, T. K. 17-19, 22, 33, 227, 252
Beardslee, W. A. 99, 111
Begg, C. T. 173
Ben-Porat, Z. 21
Berlin, A. 57, 70
Blake, W. 224
Blank, S. H. 141
Bloom, H. 24, 44, 45-47, 56, 57, 88, 200
Boling, R. G. 151
Bottigheimer, R. 71
Booth, W. C. 138, 179
Boyarin, D. 200
Brenner, A. 221

Brueggemann, W. 104, 110, 112, 204-06, 221
Budick, S. 70
Buss, M. 194
Butler, T. C. 97
Calvino, I. 110
Camp, C. V. 129, 131, 252, 253
Carroll, R. P. 137, 150
Catlett, M. 197, 201
Clines, D. J. A. 72, 253
Cogan, M. 152
Crenshaw, J. L. 252, 253
Cross, F. M. 135, 150
Culler, J. 28, 37, 86
Culley, R. 57-58
Damrosch, D. 115, 131, 167
Davis, E. F. 18-19, 22
de Man, P. 44, 72
de Vaux, R. 136
De Vries, S. J. 134, 143
Delitzsch, F. 64, 129, 223
Derrida, J. 21, 22, 24, 27-28, 37, 44, 77
Des Pres, T. 16
Driver, S. R. 129, 151, 206
Eagleton, T. 31, 37
Eco, U. 112
Edelman, D. 152
Eliot, T. S. 24, 37, 86, 215
Ellul, J. 170
Eslinger, L. 22, 252
Exum, J. C. 112, 225-26, 252

Fackenheim, E. 108, 111
Faur, J. 150
Fewell, D. N. 16, 100, 252
Fiorenza, E. S. 99, 111
Fishbane, M. 22, 30, 69, 197, 214, 223, 224
Fletcher, A. 46, 48, 55-56
Fokkelman, J. P. 72, 116, 117, 129, 130, 131
Fontaine, C. 252, 253
Ford, D. 224
Fox, M. V. 17
Fowl, S. E. 99, 111
Freedman, D. N. 201
Freeman, J. A. 225
Freud, S. 44, 46, 61, 67-68, 151
Friedman, R. E. 173
Frye, N. 156
García-Treto, F. O. 17-20
Gilbert, S. M. 47
Ginzberg, L. 223
Girard, R. 151
Good, E. M. 73, 170
Gordis, R. 208, 220, 221, 224
Gottwald, N. 221
Graff, G. 112
Granowski, J. J. 18-19
Gray, J. 135, 170, 173, 225
Greenstein, E. L. 225, 227, 252
Gros Louis, K. R. R. 225
Gubar, S. 47
Gunn, D. M. 13, 18-20, 33, 100, 104, 111, 130, 131, 226, 227
Habel, N. 220
Hagan, H. 129
Hahn, J. 150, 151
Halpern, B. 70, 152
Handelman, S. 70

Hanson, P. 156
Hardy, D. 224
Hartman, G. 70, 71
Hawk, L. D. 18-20, 242
Hays, R. B. 21
Hebel, U. J. 21
Hertzberg, H. W. 108, 129
Hillers, D. R. 194
Hoffer, V. 222
Hoffman, Y. 221, 222
Hoffmann, H. D. 133, 143
Hoftijzer, J. 131
Hollander, J. 21, 46-47, 55-56
Hoy, D. C. 37
Humphreys, W. L. 15, 225, 252
Hurvitz, A. 221
Iser, W. 99
Jacobsen, T. 150
James, H. 175
Jameson, F. 28, 31, 37
Janzen, J. G. 134, 151, 220, 224
Jeansonne, S. P. 71
Jenks, A. W. 134, 135
Johnson, B. 21, 44
Kaufmann, Y. 150
Keil, C. F. 64, 129
Kennedy, A. R. S. 135
Kermode, F. 175, 186
Klein, L. 225, 252
Koch, K. 70
Kolodny, A. 47
Krause, D. 18-19, 23, 39, 113
Kristeva, J. 22, 28-31, 35, 37-39, 44, 60, 158, 181, 187, 200
Kugel, J. 70
Labriola, A. C. 252
Lacan, J. 59-60

Laffey, A. L. 112
Langlamet, F. 89, 96
Lasine, S. 18-19, 87, 151
Le Bon, G. 151
Linafelt, T. 18-19
Lindbeck, G. A. 23, 30
Long, B. O. 140, 170
Luzzatto, S. D. 223
MacLeish, A. 222
Maimodides 224
Maline, B. J. 71
Marx, K. 31, 36, 38
Matthews, V. H. 87-88, 252
Mauchline, J. 108
Mays, J. L. 39, 191, 192-94
Mazar, A. 150
McCarter, P. K. 108, 129
McCarthy, D. J. 97, 151
Meyers, C. 88
Miller, O. 182, 187
Milton, J. 24
Miscall, P. D. 18-20, 23, 24, 31, 56, 70-72, 100, 178, 188, 252
Mitchell, S. 221, 224
Moberly, R. W. L. 150
Moo, D. J. 228
Moore, R. D. 221, 222
Morgan, T. E. 23, 181, 182
Morgenstern, J. 133-34
Muecke, D. C. 112, 141, 200
Nelson, R. D. 136
Niditch, S. 69, 72, 87-88, 252
Nietzsche, F. 44
Noth, M. 136, 173-74
O'Day, G. R. 37, 201
Oden, R. A., Jr. 35
Olyan, S. 156, 170-71
Parker, S. 171
Parsons, M. C. 175
Penchansky, D. 18-19, 24, 110

Perlitt, L. 145, 150
Plimpton, G. 113
Poland, L. 70
Polzin, R. 70-71, 252
Pruess, H. D. 137
Rabelais 168
Rabinowitz, P. J. 19, 138
Rashkow, I. N. 18-20, 22
Renza, L. A. 23
Ricoeur, P. 38, 71, 224
Ridout, G. P. 129
Riffaterre, M. 73
Rimmon-Kenan, S. 175-76
Robertson, D. 224
Rosenberg, J. 58, 69, 112, 155, 223, 166-67
Sandmel, S. 68, 70
Sarna, N. 69, 134
Savran, G. 156, 170
Scharbert, J. 133
Schwartz, R. M. 155
Segal, L. 106, 111
Seitz, C. 221
Simon, U. 129, 131
Skinner, J. 64, 197
Smeltz, J. W. 252
Smith, B. H. 175-76
Smolar, L. 152
Sophocles 201
Speiser, E. A. 42-43, 45, 69, 72, 197, 211
Spiegel, S. 221
Spivak, G. C. 77
Stager, L. E. 150
Stallybrass, P. 158
Steinsaltz, A. 72
Sternberg, M. 109, 131, 156
Stevens, W. 186
Tadmor, H. 152
Talmon, S. 143
Tarlin, J. 38
Terrien, S. 221

Thomas, K. 158
Todorov, T. 169
Tolbert, M. A. 112
Torgovnick, M. 175-81
Trible, P. 56, 71, 80, 86-87, 197
Tsevat, M. 224
Tucker, G. M. 97
Uspensky, B. 113
Vickery, J. 231, 249, 252
Vischer, W. 224
von Rad, G. 173-74, 197, 202, 212, 223
Waldman, N. 129, 130
Webb, B. G. 252
Weems, R. J. 112, 202

Weinfeld, M. 140, 151, 152, 210, 212
Wellhausen, J. 129
Westermann, C. 222
Whedbee, J. W. 226, 252
Whybray, R. N. 129
Wiesel, E. 111, 113
Wilden, A. 71
Willey, P. K. 18-19
Williams, J. G. 57
Wolff, H. W. 39, 141, 174, 187, 191, 192-94, 199, 201
Zackovitch, Y. 96
Zeid, A. M. A. 88
Zuckerman, B. 221

BIBLICAL REFERENCES

GENESIS
—— 41-56
1:1-2:4a 42-43,
　　44-45, 47-56
1:1 52
1:9-10 54
1:20-28 201
1:26-29 54-55
1:30 201
1:31 53
1-3 48
2:22-29 90
2:25 53-54
3 53
3:7 50, 53-54
4:1-16 56
4:8 72
6:4 96
6:9 214
7:11 56
8:2 56
9:1-17 56
11 183
11:31 186
12 57-73
12:3 213
12:10-20 70
12:11 253
12:11-13 63-64
12:16 66
12:18 72
13:6 201
15:5 201
16:2 96
17:1 210, 223
18:25 111
18:27 218
19 78-88, 196, 201
19:1 95

19:1-3 89
19:1-29 89-97
19:4-11 90
19:5 91
19:11 92
19:13-14 90
19:14 92
19:15-22 90
19:16 95
19:17 93-94
19:18-20 94-95
19:18 91
19:29 95
19:37-38 97
20 57-73
20:1-18 70
20:5 63
20:13 67
21:1-5 72
22 222
22:3-4 222
22:12 222
22:21 222
24 78-88
24:51 72
25:27 211, 214, 223
26 57-58
26:1-17 70
26:8 164
26:24 201
27:1-28:9 223
27:41 72
27:46 211
28:1-2 201
28:6-9 211
28:10-22 212
28:14 201
29:17 253
30:3 96

32:23-33 212
32:29 204
33:18 212
34:4 53
34:7 97
34:13 212
34:25-26 72
35:4-5 213
35:11 213
35:30 213
38:8-9 96
39:7-12 97
40-41 178, 183,
　　184-86
40:8 185
41:41 185
47:7 213
49:9 252
49:25 192, 196-98,
　　201

EXODUS
—— 12-15, 185
3:14 47
13:21-22 52
14:19-24 52
14:21-22 55
15:1-8 97
15:5-12 55
15:15-16 97
15:17 52
19:9-16 52
22:16 97
24:15-18 52
32 134-35, 142,
　　144-46
32-34 145
32:1-6 144
32:4 135, 150

EXODUS [cont.]
32:12 218
32:21 133
32:25 151
32:25-29 145
32:26-31 133
32:34 150
33:9-10 52
34:5 52
34:15 95
34:16 91
35:21-29 139
40:34-38 52

LEVITICUS
10:1-3 150

NUMBERS
5:13 97
6 229
14:1-25 97
25 198
25:1-5 97

DEUTERONOMY
1-3 177
1:19-40 97
4:39 97
7:1-6 95
7:3-4 91
7:25-26 141
9:21 148
12:2-8 140, 142
13:6 145
13:7 148
13:14 145
16:15 140, 142
18:6 140, 142
21:11 253
22:2 71
22:13 96
22:23 97

27:15 141
28:30 97
29:1-3 142
31:16-18 91
32:21 207
33:9 145

JOSHUA
2 241
2:1 89
2:1-24 89-97
2:2-7 90
2:3 91
2:4-5 91
2:7 92
2:8-11 92
2:8-14 90
2:9-11 97
2:12-14 93
2:15-20 94
2:15-23 90
2:17-20 95
6:15-25 90
6:22-25 89-97
6:25 95, 97
10:40-42 242
11:21-23 242
13:1-7 242

JUDGES
—— 32-35
1:18-19 242
13-16 225-53
13:1 248
13:5 239, 250
13:5-6 229
13:7 250
13:8-9 230
13:24-25 231
14 243, 253
14-15 233
14:1-3 231

14:3 232
14:4 231, 239
14:5 238
14:6 233
14:17 244
14:18 234
14:19 235
15:1 235
15:3 236
15:7 249
15:7-8 237
15:11-12 237
15:18-19 238
15:20 239, 240
16 253
16:4 243
16:6 243
16:16 244
16:17 240, 244
16:20-21 245
16:22 247
16:23 166
16:23-24 246
16:28 226
16:30 247
16:31 248
17-21 140
19 62, 78-88
19-21 71

1 SAMUEL
1:15 130
2 105-06
8 109-10
8:11-17 109
9:16 225
9:17 144
11-15 198
12:24 96
15:21 202
15:24 144
16:1-13 170

1 SAMUEL [cont.]
16:21 96
18 101
19:5 131
20:7-9 130
24-26 112
25 71, 100
25:17 130
25:22 169
25:34 169
25:35 100
25:43-44 100
26:18 103
30:1-6 101
30:18 101

2 SAMUEL
1-4 103
3:1-15 102
3:2-5 129
3:17-39 117
3:28 131
5:12-13 102
6:16 164
6:20 169
7 155
9 178, 183-84, 188
9:7 183
9:11 184
9:13 184
11-12 71, 102
11-14 115, 126
11:1 104
11:11 126, 131
11:25-27 126
11:27 103
12 115-16
12:1-7a 105-06
12:1-15a 102-113
12:4 104
12:5-6 103
12:6 126

12:7 125
12:7-12 103-04
12:7b-15 106-08
12:11 97
12:12 107, 126
12:13 103, 104
12:14 126
12:21 126
12:27-28 105
13 72, 124-25, 129
13:1 252
13:3 117
13:12 128
13:12-13 117
13:20-21 126
13:34 120
13:38-39 120
13:39 130
14 115-31
14:3-22 127
14:17 125, 129
14:20 129
15:3-4 118
16:22-23 107
19:24-30 130
20:18-19 117
21-25 112
23:39 107

1 KINGS
1:1-4 178
1:3 252
5:18 140
8 155
8:12-13 169
8:56 140
9:4 72
11:26-12:27 150
12 133-52
12:18 143
12:21 143
12:24 143

12:26-27 139, 143-45
12:26-28 137
12:26-33 139-45, 146
12:28 135, 142, 143, 149, 150
12:30 133, 143
12:31-32 142
12:32 133
12:32-33 140
12:34 133
13:2 133, 145
13:2-3 142
14:7-16 142
14:9 142
14:10 169
14:15-16 133
14:16 142
14:17 150
14:23 148
15:27 150
16:11 169
18:27 171
21:10-13 207
21:21 169

2 KINGS
8:18 169
8:27 169
9-10 153-71
9:1-4 161
9:1-14 159-60
9:3 163
9:4 161
9:5 171
9:7 163
9:7-9 155, 169
9:7-10 161, 164
9:8 165
9:10 163
9:10-12 171

2 KINGS [cont.]
9:11 161, 162
9:12 163
9:13 162
9:15-26 160
9:16-28 171
9:18-19 163
9:20 162
9:22 164
9:23 163
9:27 154, 163
9:27-29 160
9:30 164
9:30-37 154, 160, 163
9:31 155
9:32 163
9:33 165
9:34 164
9:36-37 164-65
9:37 170
10:1-11 160
10:2-3 171
10:4-5 165
10:5 154
10:9 165
10:10-11 169
10:11 165
10:12 154
10:12-14 160
10:14 154
10:15 163
10:15-16 171
10:15-28 160
10:17 165
10:19 166
10:23 171
10:24 163
10:27 170
10:29 145
10:29-31 159-60
10:30 169

17 178
17:10 148
17:13-14 142
17:21 133, 145, 149
17:23 142
18 146
18:3 149
18:4 148
18:22 149, 152
18:28 149
18:29 148
18:30-32 148
18:32-33 149
18:34-35 152
18:36 149
21:3 148, 167
21:13 167, 169
22-23 146
23:14-15 148
23:20 145
24:8-9 179
24:12 179
24:15 179
25:26-27 186
25:27 177
25:27-30 19, 173-88
25:28 177-78, 185
25:29 184

2 CHRONICLES
28:2 152
28:19 151
29-31 148
32:11-12 149

NEHEMIAH
6:8 140

ESTHER
1 11
2:7 253
3 11

4:13-14 13
7:4 13
7:7 130
8:38 11
8:9-14 12
9:20-22 12
9:32 12

JOB
1:1 203, 204, 214, 221-23
1:5 207, 222
1:8 203
1:9 218
1:11 207
1:11-12 222
1:15 208
1:21 207
2:3 203
2:5 207, 222
2:9 203, 206, 207
2:10 206
2:12 222
3:8 216
4:6 203
8:20 203
9:20-22 203
13:4 219
14:14 221
21:23 203
25:5-6 221
27:2-6 222
27:5 203
28 203, 224
28:20-28 217
29-31 221
29:4 208
29:13 208
30:1-8 224
30:19 224
31:6 203
31:13 215

JOB [cont.]
31:15 216
31:20 208
31:6 221
32-37 203
37:7 216
37:13-15 216
38-41 216
38:8-9 216
38:26-27 217
39:19-25 217
40:8 217
40:11-14 216
40:15 216
41:26 216
42:3 207
42:5-6 215, 218
42:7 207
42:8 206, 208, 222
42:10 208
42:12 208
42:14-15 220

PSALMS
10:3 207
10:6-13 151
14:1 151, 207
22:10 201
27:12 195
35:25 151
74:18 207
74:19 195
74:22 207
77:65 252
78:72 72
83:11 171
85:7 195
101:2 72

PROVERBS
6:29 96
10:9 204
11:20 206
20:7 210
28:10 210
28:18 204
29:10 206
29:18 151
30:18-19 217

ECCLESIASTES
12:12 17

SONG OF SONGS
4:1 252
4:7 252
4:10 252
5:1 72
5:2 72
7:2(1) 253
7:7(6) 253

ISAIAH
——— 41-56
1 49
1:10 53
1:15 53
1:16-17 53
1:19 53
1:26 53
1:29 50, 53
2:2-4 49
3:12 72
4 52
4:1 51
4:2-6 52
4:4 50
4:6 49
5:19 141
6:11 193-94, 200
7:2 50
8:5-8 51
9:1 49
9:15 72
10:8-11 152
10:17 49
10:22 51
11:4 50
11:12 50
11:15 50
14:3 151
15:6 54
17:13 56
24:7 56
24:10 50
24:23 50
24-26 50
25:8 51
26:9 56
26:21 56
27:8 56
27:11 56
28:1-22 51
28:6 50
28:15 141, 148
29:24 56
30:1 56, 141, 148
31:3 56
32:2 49, 56
33:9 50
34 49-50, 53
34:4 50
34:11 50
35 51
37:1-24 51
37:35 56
38:16 50
40-55 228
40:7 50
40:7-8 54
40:8 52
40:13 56
40:17 50
40:23 50
40:24 56
41 51

ISAIAH [cont.]
41:2-4 238
41:15-16 236
41:17-20 238-39
41:29 50
42:1 50, 231
42:1-3 240-41
42:2-3 233
42:6 49
42:7 49
42:13 235, 238
42:15 54
42:18-19 248
42:24 246
43 51
43:1 251
43:4 251
43:18 48
43:20 239
44:1 229
44:1-4 54
44:3 56
44:9 50
44:9-11 247
44:19-20 141
44:27 54
45:1-2 242
45:18-19 50
47:2-3 246
47:3 51
47:8-10 151
47:11 247
47:14 49
48:21 239
49:1 229, 240
49:1-2 234
49:2 49
49:3-4 240
49:6 49
49:8 71
50:5 239
50:6 237

51:7 51
51:9-11 51-52
53 253
53:3 237
53:6 246
53:7-8 245
53:9-10 247
54:1 71
54:4 50, 51
54:6 56
54:6-8 235-36
56:3 54
57:13 50
57:15 56
57:16 50
59:19 56
59:21 50
60-62 49
60:1-2 49
60:19-61:11 56
62:4 71
64:5 56
65:17 48
66:2 50
66:22 48

JEREMIAH
7:18 151
8:2 171
8:6 218
9:3-5 215
9:21 171
16:4 171
25:7 151
25:33 171
32:29 151

EZEKIEL
23:44 96
33:28 71
39:17 171

DANIEL
—— 15-16
5-6 16

HOSEA
1:2 201
1:9 201
2:1 201
2:5 195
2:9 195
2:12(14) 195
2:20 201
4:3 201
4:10 194
4:11 72
4:15 198
5:6 194
6:2 252
7:2 151
7:8-11 148
8:4 148
8:4-6 136, 141
8:7 194
9:9 192
9:10-13 192
9:10-17 192-94, 198-201
9:11-13 193-94
9:12 194
9:14 191-202
9:15 193, 202
9:15-16 194
9:17 194, 198, 199
10:5 136
11:1-7 196
11:8 195-96, 201
12 197, 201, 215
12:11 198
13:2 136, 142
13:6(14:1) 201
13:10 195
13:11 196

HOSEA [cont.]
14:9 199-200

AMOS
7:2 193-94, 200
7:3 218
7:5 193-94, 200

ZEPHANIAH
3:8 252

MATTHEW
5:45 219

JOHN
8:56-58 47

1 JOHN
3:2 224

JAMES
5:11 223

CONTRIBUTORS

DANNA NOLAN FEWELL teaches at Perkins School of Theology, Southern Methodist University, in Dallas, Texas.

TIMOTHY K. BEAL is a doctoral student in Hebrew Bible at Emory University in Atlanta, Georgia.

PETER D. MISCALL teaches at St. Thomas Seminary in Denver, Colorado.

ILONA N. RASHKOW teaches at the State University of New York at Stony Brook in Stony Brook, New York.

DAVID PENCHANSKY teaches at the University of St. Thomas in St. Paul, Minnesota.

L. DANIEL HAWK teaches at the Centenary College of Louisiana in Shreveport, Louisiana.

TOD LINAFELT is a doctoral student in Hebrew Bible at Emory University in Atlanta, Georgia.

PATRICIA K. WILLEY is a doctoral candidate in Old Testament studies and homiletics at Emory University in Atlanta, Georgia.

STUART LASINE teaches at the Wichita State University in Wichita, Kansas.

FRANCISCO O. GARCÍA-TRETO teaches at Trinity University in San Antonio, Texas.

JAN JAYNES GRANOWSKI is a doctoral candidate in Hebrew Bible at Baylor University in Waco, Texas.

DEBORAH KRAUSE teaches at Eden Theological Seminary in St. Louis, Missouri.

ELLEN F. DAVIS teaches at Yale Divinity School, Yale University, in New Haven, Connecticut.

DAVID M. GUNN teaches at Columbia Theological Seminary in Decatur, Georgia.

www.ingramcontent.com/pod-product-compliance
Lightning Source LLC
Chambersburg PA
CBHW031237290426
44109CB00012B/326